Abstaining with the Saints

No and Low Alcoholic Beverages for Sober Souls

Michael P. Foley

Regnery History

Regnery History books may be purchased in bulk at special discounts for sales promotion, corporate gifts, fund-raising, or educational purposes. Special editions can also be created to specifications. For details, contact the Special Sales Department, Regnery History, 307 West 36th Street, 11th Floor, New York, NY 10018 or info@skyhorsepublishing.com.

Regnery History is an imprint of Skyhorse Publishing, Inc.®, a Delaware corporation.

Visit our website at www.regnery.com.
Please follow our publisher Tony Lyons on Instagram @tonylyonsisuncertain.

10 9 8 7 6 5 4 3 2 1

Library of Congress Cataloging-in-Publication Data is available on file.

Cover design by Kai Texel
The painting on the front cover, *Saint John the Baptist*, is an oil on canvas painting by Titian, from c. 1540. It is part of the collection of the Gallerie dell'Accademia in Venice. The added mocktail is courtesy of Getty Images.

Print ISBN: 978-1-5107-8374-4
Ebook ISBN: 978-1-5107-8502-1

Printed in China

Contents

DEDICATION

This book is dedicated to the memory of Michael Bordlee, Mario Cortez, and Peter Fivel, and to all others who have suffered on account of alcohol abuse.

INTRODUCTION

After the publication of *Drinking with the Saints* (2015), *Drinking with Saint Nick* (2018), and *Drinking with Your Patron Saints* (2020), a friend whose son had recently taken the Pledge suggested that I write a book for those who are abstaining from alcohol. It was not the first time that someone had recommended a sequel, although usually, the recommendation was in jest. When the first book came out, one friend asked if the sequel would be *Hangovers with the Saints* while another (a Southerner) asked if it would be *Cussin' with the Saints*.

But this request was different. It was made out of love for a son and was applicable to a growing number of sober-curious souls. And her request came at just the right time. During the lockdowns of Covidtide in 2020, alcoholic consumption increased 20 to 30 percent and alcohol-related deaths went up 25 percent. Several of the nonalcoholic spirits now on the market were invented in response to the binging that took place during the pandemic. And thanks to these new concoctions, we are currently witnessing an unprecedented growth in mature alternatives to hard liquor, some of which cleverly mimic our favorite cocktails, others of which include mood-enhancing ingredients such as kava, ashwagandha, and lion's mane mushrooms. We've come a long way from having to choose between a Shirley Temple and a Roy Rogers.

And a "mocktail book" is not just for teetotalers or folks recovering from COVID-era cabin fever. The effects of alcohol on health are being scrutinized as never before, and although we still maintain that a moderate consumption of alcohol is both ethical and healthy, it is also the case that excessive drinking can disrupt sleep, weaken the immune system, and make things like cancer, heart disease, and liver disease more likely. And even the most dedicated of drinkers knows that a plenitude of reasons exists to warrant a dry night (or fortnight): taking certain medications, pregnancy, illness, a Lenten resolution, a sober October or a dry January, the periodic need to rejuvenate your liver, or simply a desire to get up earlier in the morning and with more energy. At the very least, every host should be prepared to serve nonalcoholic beverages to a guest who, for whatever reason, is abstaining.

And so we are pleased to present *Abstaining with the Saints: No and Low Alcoholic Beverages for Sober Souls*. Like its predecessors in the With the Saints series, *Abstaining* offers drink suggestions for the feast days of the

Church year. Like its predecessors, it offers more than recipes for mixed drinks (we also include nonalcoholic beers and wines). And like its predecessors, it is written in order to encourage merriment, fellowship, and gratitude to God for the blessings of friends, family, and the fruits of the earth, except now, you can invite the kids to your evening happy hour—if you want, that is (grin).

Abstaining differs from other manuals of its kind in three respects. First, we are more comprehensive. In addition to the latest breakthroughs in nonalcoholic wines, beers, and spirits (the latter being a relatively new and promising category), we include a venerable, international panoply of alcohol-free potations, such as the Gunner from Singapore and the Atole from Mexico. Different cultures have been producing different delicious booze-free beverages for centuries, and this book tracks them down for you.

Second, a minority of our entries include trace amounts of alcohol, thanks to bitters, kombucha, and residual alcohol in some beers and spirits (usually less than 0.5% ABV). Popular bitters like Angostura may be as high as 89 proof, but two dashes of the stuff lack the power to intoxicate. (We used a breathalyzer to test a drink with ten dashes of Angostura bitters—five times the normal amount—and found that it failed to affect our blood alcohol content.) In Trinidad, where Angostura was invented, locals young and old use it as a topping on a wide variety of foods, including ice cream. (That said, there are several nonalcoholic bitters currently available on the market, and so you can always use one of these products instead.) Similarly, *Abstaining* contains a few recipes with kombucha, a beverage made with sweetened black or green tea. Homemade kombucha usually contains 0.5-1.5% alcohol while bottled kombucha marked as nonalcoholic must contain less than 0.5% (most cough syrups, by contrast, are more than 20%). In the United States, one does not have to be the legal drinking age to purchase or consume bitters or kombucha. But please take heed: if you are pregnant or a recovering alcoholic, you may wish to avoid these offerings. Many rehab centers and counselors, for example, advise against even the smallest amounts of alcohol for fear that it will put one on a slippery slope or awaken bad habits. Please consult your therapist or sponsor about what is best for you.

And speaking of warnings, although we do not include anything that has THC or CBD (the active ingredients in marijuana), several beverages contain mood-enhancing agents like adaptogens and nootropics (see Appendix III, Glossary of Terms). *Caveat potor*: Let the drinker beware. Such drinks may not be suitable, for example, for drinkers under the age of twenty-one. Check out our list of mood-enhancing beverages in Appendix I (Soberish Septuagesima) to be on the safe side.

Third, we are especially pleased to include a practical program for going "soberish," that is, rebooting one's appetites to regain control of one's life and one's relationship to the Drink without necessarily going dry for life. For as with so many of God's creatures, alcohol may be a great handmaid, but she is a cruel mistress. Our Soberish Septuagesima program, which is designed for current drinkers who wish to go sober or "soberish" (that is, moderate), is included as Appendix I.

HOW TO USE THIS BOOK

Abstaining with the Saints gives specific suggestions for specific feast days, but do not be beholden to our pairings. If the Spirit moves you to enjoy one beverage more than another, feel free to have it whenever you want. The saints are not jealous.

One advantage to drinking or serving no- and low-alcoholic beverages is that you are not limited by local supply; for unlike many beers, wines, and liquors, the ingredients can easily be purchased online. The disadvantage, however (at least at the time of this writing) is that not all local retailers have caught up to demand. Because online shopping obviously requires time for your shipment to arrive, *be sure to plan ahead*. Also, be prepared for sticker shock: nonalcoholic spirits can be pricier than a single-malt scotch, but that is because the same amount of craft, time, and ingredients that go into an alcoholic spirit go into their nonalcoholic equivalent. It is not the C_2H_6O in a bottle of Lagavulin Islay that makes it expensive; it is everything else.

Several of the recipes use jargon from the world of mixology or botanica. Turn to our helpful Glossary of Terms in Appendix III when there is a word you do not recognize.

Abstaining with the Saints can also be part of a wet night. Dr. Peter Butt, an expert on alcohol consumption, recommends alternating between an alcoholic drink and a nonalcoholic one as a way of slowing your alcohol intake and making you feel full: the practice is called "zebra striping." A mocktail or two is also a superior alternative to black coffee as the denouement to an intoxicating evening. Thanks to this book, you can make the parting glass refreshing, recuperating, and rehydrating rather than one step closer to a DUI.

As with our other books, *Abstaining* follows the traditional Roman calendar in use before Vatican II. If you see two dates for an entry, the first date in boldface is for the 1962 calendar and the second date in italics is for the 1970/2002 calendar; if you see only one date, it usually means that the feast falls on the same date in both calendars, at least implicitly. For cross-referencing, please consult Appendix II.

To your health and holiness, and may we all be left high and dry!

—Michael and Alexandra Foley
May 4, 2025
(Traditional) Feast of Saint Monica, patron saint of alcoholics

PART I

THE FEASTS OF THE SAINTS
(THE SANCTORAL CYCLE)

CHAPTER ONE

January

SAINTS

FOR JANUARY 1 THROUGH JANUARY 6,
SEE PART II: THE LITURGICAL SEASONS (THE TEMPORAL CYCLE)

OUR LADY OF PROMPT SUCCOR, JANUARY 8

As every son and daughter of New Orleans knows right well, the patroness of their city, of the Archdiocese of New Orleans, and of the state of Louisiana is Our Lady of Prompt Succor ("quick help"). It was devotion to Our Lady under this title that obtained victory for the USA during the Battle of New Orleans on January 8, 1815. The night before the battle, the Ursuline nuns, who had introduced this devotion to the city, prayed that if God saved New Orleans from the British, they would have a Mass of Thanksgiving celebrated every year. Their prayers were answered. Although the battle lasted roughly thirty minutes, it claimed over 2,000 British casualties and only a few dozen American. General Andrew Jackson, though a Protestant, personally thanked the Ursuline nuns for their intercession. And a Mass of Thanksgiving continues to be said every year on January 8 in the Ursuline convent.

In honor of Our Lady's speedy aid, we present a nonalcoholic drink invented for the NOLA wedding of our friends Kevin and DeAnn Stuart: the Almost Prompt Succor Punch. Consider the play on words as a reminder of how the British must have felt after the Battle of New Orleans.

Almost Prompt Succor Punch

Makes 8 drinks

2 cups sugar
2 cups water
2 cups lemon juice
2 cups lime juice
8 thin slices lemon and lime

In a saucepan, mix sugar and water and bring to a boil, stirring until the mixture is clear. Remove from heat and let cool. Add to a punch bowl or pitcher filled with ice, along with all the other ingredients, and stir well.

SAINT AGATHO, JANUARY 10

Pope Agatho (577–681)—or if you want to translate his name from Greek, Pope Good—was a Sicilian monk well-versed in Latin and Greek when he was elevated to the throne of Peter in 678. That same year, St. Wilfrid of York appealed to him for being unjustly deposed from his bishopric, and Agatho ruled in his favor. But Agatho was also worried about the condition of the Church in Britain, and so he sent envoys to the English to teach them chant and to report back. This good pope also helped define the doctrine that because Jesus Christ has two natures (human and divine), He also has two wills. St. Agatho succumbed to a plague in 681.

Saint Wilfrid of York owes Agatho a solid, and so let him provide the drinks tonight. Wilfred's Non-Alcoholic Aperitif is outstanding, with hints of rosemary and bitter orange (the flavors of St. Agatho's native Sicily). Another compelling option on St. Agatho's Day is **Curious Elixir**'s delicious No. 4, **Sicilian Blood Orange Spritz**.

Spritz by Wilfred's

Makes 1 drink

1½ oz. Wilfred's Non-Alcoholic Aperitif
3 oz. tonic water
1 orange slice, garnish

Pour liquid ingredients into a large wine glass with ice and stir. Garnish with orange slice.

SAINT SATYRUS, JANUARY 12

We do not know much about St. Satyrus except that he was probably born in Arabia and that he was martyred for performing a rather peculiar miracle. Satyrus was in the Greek region of Achaia when he passed by an idol. No doubt miffed by the sight of this false god, he breathed upon it and made the sign of the cross over it. The idol immediately fell to the ground, and Satyrus was subsequently beheaded.

When Our Lord breathed upon others, He worked miracles and gave His Apostles the power to forgive sins, and so we are confident that the breath of His faithful disciple Satyrus had in it more holiness than halitosis. The image of someone's breath making a stone statue crumble to the ground might sound like it belongs in a mouthwash commercial, but in this case it was the saint's odor of sanctity that caused the idol to faint.

To celebrate St. Satyrus' fragrant soul, try Sentia's GABA Gold on the rocks, but smell it in the bottle first. It has an amazing bouquet.

Satyrus' Breath

Makes 1 drink

1½ oz. Sentia GABA Gold
1 orange slice, garnish

Pour GABA Gold into an old-fashioned glass with ice. Garnish with orange slice.

SAINT HILARY, JANUARY 14 (JANUARY 13)

Hilary of Poitiers (300–368) is a Confessor and Doctor of the Church. A powerful opponent of the Arian heresy, he labored tirelessly to promote the orthodox teaching on Jesus Christ as true God and true man and was persecuted for it. A convert from neo-Platonic philosophy, he was chosen to be Bishop of Poitiers in France even though he was married with a daughter (Saint Abra).

Hilary's name means "cheerful" in Latin, and Three Spirit makes a dark herbal elixir called Social that promises precisely such a mood. Social can be used in several different mixed drinks. We include two here: one for a group on a cold winter's night and one for individual servings, whatever the weather.

Mulled Social Cider

Makes 7 drinks

30 oz. apple cider
12 oz. Three Spirit Social
3 lemon wheels
3 orange wheels
1 stick cinnamon, broken
5 cloves
1 star anise
1 black cardamon pod, cut open
5 allspice berries, crushed
7 orange wheels, garnish
7 cinnamon sticks, garnish

Pour all ingredients (except garnishes) into a pot or crockpot. Heat gently and stir slowly until the liquid comes to a low simmer. Pour into Irish coffee glasses or wine glasses and garnish with orange wheels and cinnamon sticks.

Light & Stormy

Makes 1 drink

2 oz. Three Spirit Social
3–4 oz. ginger beer
1 lime wheel, garnish

Pour Social into a highball with ice, top with ginger beer, and stir. Garnish with lime wheel.

LAST CALL

In Catalan, Spain, there is a toast invoking Saint Hilary used throughout the year. Unfortunately, it is vulgar: "Saint Hilary, Saint Hilary, whoever does not empty his glass is an S.O.B." (and that's a nice translation: the Catalan Spanish is even rougher). We were not able to find any explanation as to why the saintly Bishop of Poitiers was brought into this particular judgment about imperfect drinkers, but perhaps we can clean up the sentiment by replacing "S.O.B." with "monkey's uncle" or "Arian heretic."

FRANCISCAN PROTOMARTYRS, JANUARY 16

Three priests (Berardo, Pietro, Ottone) and two lay brothers (Adiuto and Accursio) are called the Protomartyrs of the Franciscan Order because they were the first members of that order to give their lives for Christ. Following an ardent wish of St. Francis of Assisi to see all Muslims converted to the Catholic Faith, the friars first preached in Seville, Spain, which was then under Muslim rule. The king was not amused and had them exiled to the Kingdom of Morocco. There they boldly preached the Gospel and denounced Islam, leading the locals to wonder if they were insane. They were exiled more than once but kept returning. Finally, they were imprisoned and, after refusing to apostatize, beheaded by the frustrated Moorish king with his own scimitar. When their bodies were returned to Europe and solemnly processed through Portugal on their way to Assisi, a young man was so moved that he left the Canons Regular of St. Augustine of which he had been a part and joined the Franciscans. His name? The great Saint Anthony of Padua.

A marocchino is an Italian espresso drink so named because it resembles the color of Moroccan leather; it is especially delicious during the doldrums of January. Whip one up to honor these Italian friars whose blood watered the sands of Morocco.

Marocchino

Makes 1 drink

2 tsp. chocolate spread or Nutella
1 shot espresso
1/3 cup milk
cocoa or cacao powder

Spread the chocolate spread or Nutella along the inner surface of an Irish coffee glass or clear small glass. Add espresso. Heat the milk and froth it with a milk frother; pour the milk over the espresso. Using a fine mesh sieve, dust the top with cocoa or cacao powder.

LAST CALL

See if you can figure out the meaning of this line from Bing Crosby and Bob Hope in the 1942 movie *Road to Morocco*: "Like Webster's Dictionary, we're Morocco-bound."

SAINT ANTONY THE ABBOT,

JANUARY 17

Antony is the founder of Western monasticism. At the age of twenty, he walked into church just as the Gospel was being proclaimed: "If thou wilt be perfect, go sell what thou hast" (Matthew 19:21). Interpreting the verse to refer to himself then and there, he relinquished his possessions and took up the ascetical life. Initially, he stayed near his village, residing in a tomb outside of town, where he was assaulted by the devil in the form of terrifying beasts. Later, he withdrew into the Egyptian desert, where for twenty years he did not set sight on another human being. Eventually, however, a group of disciples gathered around him, and so he agreed to become their spiritual director. He instructed this community of monks for five years and then withdrew again, spending the last forty-five years of his life as a hermit and dying at the age of 105.

In his old age, Antony struggled with the proud thought that he was the first hermit. Our Lord then led him further into the desert, where he met St. Paul the First Hermit. Paul had been living on half a loaf of bread that a raven carried to him each day, but when Antony visited, the raven dropped a full loaf. When Paul died, Antony dug his grave with the help of two lions.

For this great monk of the desert, we present an original mocktail called the Desert Au Pair—you can think of the "pair" as the friendship of Antony and Paul. And if you want the mocktail to enhance your mood, add one ounce of **Ketohol Raw Concentrate** by **Hard Ketones**, the motto for which is "Real buzz, no booze." The concentrate comes in two-ounce bottles, but because it is extremely bitter, we prefer a one-ounce dose. (For more on Ketohol, see January 20).

JANUARY

The Desert Au Pair

Makes 1 drink

1 oz. desert pear syrup
½ oz. fresh lemon juice
4–6 oz. sparkling water

Pour syrup and lemon juice into a shaker with ice and shake 40 times. Strain into a cocktail glass and top with sparkling water.

LAST CALL

Since it is a universal custom to toast to someone's longevity, on this day toast to your guests and wish them the long life of St. Antony—and his solitude, only if they want it.

SAINT SEBASTIAN, JANUARY 20

At your next cocktail party, you can pose to your guests the following question: Which saint was martyred twice? The answer is today's reason for festivity. St. Sebastian (d. 288) was a soldier in the Roman army who exhorted imprisoned Christians to stand firm in their faith despite torture and death and who was responsible for a number of conversions. He was appointed by both Emperors Diocletian and Maximian to be captain of the Praetorian Guard, neither of them knowing that he was a Christian. When Diocletian discovered the truth, he ordered Sebastian to be bound to a tree and killed with arrows. The saint was shot so many times that his biographers say he looked like an urchin. Yet when a saintly widow came to bury his body, she discovered that he was alive and nursed him back to health. Undeterred, Sebastian found Diocletian and upbraided him. When the stunned Emperor recovered from his shock, he again ordered Sebastian to be executed, this time by being beaten to death with clubs. A tough saint through and through, St. Sebastian is the patron of athletes, soldiers, and archers.

The current king of the no- or low-alcoholic beer market is the Athletic Brewing Company. They produce a variety of brews, but the two that best tie into Saint Sebastian's patronage of athletes are a lager called **Cerveza Atlética** and **Athletic Lite.**

Other options are **Ketone Aids** and **Hard Ketones,** which promise "clean energy for athletic performance, mental clarity, metabolic health, and deep sleep." Ketohol converts to ketones, a longevity molecule your body naturally produces after fasting or a keto diet. You can choose between several canned carbonated drinks or small bottles that can be added to your favorite mocktail. The products do indeed provide a healthy boost, but all of the products except their **Ketohol Raw Concentrate** contain stevia, which we do not care for. Perhaps as a soldier-athlete, Sebastian would simply tell us to suck it up.

OUR LADY OF ALTAGRACIA, JANUARY 21

The spiritual protectress of the people of the Dominican Republic is the Blessed Virgin Mary under the title of Our Lady of Altagracia ("High Grace"). According to the legend, a father asked his daughter what he could get her when he went to the city for supplies, and she told him that she wanted an image of Our Lady of Altagracia, which she had seen in a dream. The father looked everywhere, even asking the archbishop, but no one had ever heard of this devotion. Staying at an inn on his way home, the father was sharing his woes when an old man approached him and gave him a parchment with the image of Our Lady of Altagracia on it. When the father went to thank the old man the next morning, he was gone. The father gave the image to his daughter, who joyfully showed it to those present. The group was under an orange tree, and the date was January 21.

The Dominican Republic. A dream. Oranges. A sweet ending. A traditional Dominican beverage that captures some of these details is a Morir Soñando, which means, "to die dreaming."

Morir Soñando

Makes 6 drinks

4 cups evaporated milk, chilled
¾ cup sugar
1 tbsp. clear vanilla extract, optional
2 cups ice cubes
2½ cups fresh orange juice, without pulp
6 orange wheels, garnish

Put milk, ice, sugar, and vanilla in a pitcher and stir. Slowly pour in orange juice while stirring vigorously. Serve in highball glasses with ice and garnish with orange wheels.

SAINT RAYMOND OF PEÑAFORT, JANUARY 23 (JANUARY 7)

Raymond of Peñafort (1175–1275) was a Spaniard and a relative of the King of Aragon. A famous professor of law at the University of Bologna, he entered the Dominican order at the age of forty-seven. Raymond was also instrumental in founding, along with King James I of Aragon and St. Peter Nolasco, the Order of Our Lady of Ransom, a.k.a the Mercedarians. The brave members of this order took a fourth vow to die for Jesus Christ if necessary and to offer

themselves as slaves in order to emancipate a Christian enslaved by the Muslim Moors.

Speaking of the Moors, St. Raymond's most famous miracle took place while he and King James were on the island of Majorca trying to convert the Moors who were living there. James, however, had brought his mistress with him (not exactly a great move in terms of evangelical witness), and Raymond insisted that either she go or he go. James was not about to dismiss his concubine, but he did not want Raymond to leave either, so he forbade any captain from giving him passage. Undeterred, Raymond went down to the shore, tied one end of his cappa (the large black Dominican cloak) to his staff, and threw the other end on the water. Hopping on the cappa and making the sign of the cross, he then sailed the 160 miles to Barcelona in an impressive six hours. Dozens of sailors saw him and cheered him on, and a crowd of amazed spectators saw him land. After that, the king dumped his mistress.

Hiyo produces nonalcoholic seltzers (blackberry lemon, peach mango, strawberry guava, and watermelon lime) made from organic adaptogens, natural nootropics, and functional botanicals. Hiyo claims that their drinks provide a stress-relieving, mood-boosting lift they like to call "the float"—an apt term for our floating Raymond, the unofficial patron saint of windsurfers. Throw a Hiyo party tonight and see how close you get to Barcelona.

> **LAST CALL**
>
> **Combine the name of the manufacturer, the signature cry from the Lone Ranger, and St. Raymond's miracle into a toast: "Hiyo, cappa, away!"**

Yoro also makes two products that fit the theme of our evening. Their Surf Pineapple Ginger can is formulated with Rhodiola root extract and B12 to restore energy midday while boosting clarity and mood, while their Surge Guava Passionfruit (sic) is made with Panax Ginseng and Guarana to energize you without giving you the jitters (caffeine- and sugar-free).

CONVERSION OF SAINT PAUL, JANUARY 25

Paul (ca. 5–67) shares his principal feast day on June 29–30 with the other Prince of the Apostles, St. Peter. Today's feast focuses on Paul's dramatic conversion around A.D. 35, when he went from being a persecutor of Christianity to one of its greatest promoters. Saul of Tarsus was a

well-educated Pharisee on his way to Damascus to round up Christians and return them to Jerusalem as prisoners when a light from heaven suddenly shone around him and a voice spoke to him saying, "Saul, Saul, why persecutest thou Me?" (Acts 9:4). Afterwards, Saul discovered that he was blind and did not eat or drink for three days.

"Buzzkill" might be an apt way to describe Saul's experience after going from a hyped-up zealot to the "least of the Apostles." **Buzzkill Wines Sauvignon Blanc** from California comes in a can and delivers everything that a Sauvignon Blanc lover might want from a glass, with notes of tropical fruit like pineapple and mango, juicy peaches, and green herbs. Another option is from Seedlip, which has a cocktail named after Saul's destination.

Damascus

Makes 1 drink

- 2 oz. Seedlip Spice 94
- 1¼ oz. cold coffee
- 2 tsp. cherry cordial
- 1 Toschi Amarena cherry, garnish

Pour all liquid ingredients into a mixing glass with ice and stir 40 times. Strain into a wine glass or cocktail glass and garnish with cherry.

Note: To make cherry cordial, take the syrup from a high-quality jar of cherries such as Toschi Amarena cherries.

SAINT JOHN CHRYSOSTOM, JANUARY 27 (SEPTEMBER 13)

John Chrysostom (347–407) was a Patriarch of Constantinople. He was so powerful a preacher that he was given the posthumous epithet *Chrysostom*, meaning "golden mouthed;" and he was so unbending in the face of the Church's enemies that he was once called "the man without knees." In the Eastern churches, Chrysostom is considered one of the Three Holy Hierarchs, the other two being St. Basil the Great and St. Gregory of Nazianzus.

There is a plethora of golden drinks with which to toast today's Golden-Mouth (he almost sounds like a Bond villain, doesn't he?). Here are a few:

De Soi's **Golden Hour** comes in a can and bursts with sunny citrus notes of lemon and bergamot, perfectly balanced by earthy hops, rosemary, and bay leaf. With a blend of adaptogens like reishi mushroom, lion's mane, and L-theanine, this refreshing spritz promotes relaxation and mental clarity in every sip.

Sentia's **GABA Gold** has an amazing citrusy nose with a spicy ginger finish. Enjoy it neat or on the rocks.

Athletic Brewing Company's **Upside Dawn** is a golden nonalcoholic ale that will not disappoint.

Golden Hour Highball

Makes 1 drink

- 2 oz. The Pathfinder Hemp & Root Spirit
- ½ oz. fresh lemon juice
- 4 oz. dry ginger beer
- lemon wedge, garnish

Pour liquid ingredients into an old-fashioned glass with ice and stir gently. Garnish with lemon wedge.

SAINT FRANCIS DE SALES, JANUARY 29 (JANUARY 24)

Francis (1567–1622) was born into the noble Savoyard or Sales family and received a topnotch education in theology and law. His family's great plans for him were dashed when he broke off an arranged marriage to become a priest. He was appointed Bishop of Geneva over an area that had become overwhelmingly Calvinist, but through his hard work and patience he won back seventy thousand souls to Catholicism. Together with St. Jane de Chantal, he founded the Order of the Visitation. Of his many great writings,

his *Introduction to the Devout Life* stands out for making the devout life accessible not only to the clergy but to the laity in all walks of life.

St. Francis was also an expert on the human heart who not only understood humanity in all its spiritual and psychological complexity but who wrote in a way that touches the reader's heart and gives it the courage to improve. The heart is an apt symbol for St. Francis in other ways as well: his work on the heart of Mary as the perfect model for loving God inspired St. John Eudes' devotion to the Sacred Hearts of Jesus and Mary, and St. Francis' own heart was kept as a relic in Lyon, France, after he had passed away in that city.

De Soi's Très Rosé strikes us as a fitting tribute to this heart-warming saint. Crisp and refreshing, Très Rosé is created with adaptogens, such as lion's mane and reishi mushrooms that support a mood-boosting buzz without the booze.

SAINT JOHN BOSCO, JANUARY 31

"Don Bosco" (1815–1888) was the founder of the Salesian Order who worked tirelessly with underprivileged youth such as street children and juvenile delinquents. The kind-hearted saint often used magic tricks to attract their attention and then teach them about God or take them to Mass. St. John Bosco also pioneered a pedagogy of love rather than punishment later known as the Salesian Preventive System. In 1946 Pope Pius XII declared Don Bosco a patron of Catholic editors for his authorship of highly popular religious books and for replacing suspect passages in non-Catholic books with acceptable Catholic statements.

One fun way to honor Don Bosco's work with children through magic tricks is with a Magic Cotton Candy Daiquiri Mocktail. Supermarkets occasionally sell cotton candy and you can make your own or order online, but your best bet is to find a good candy store—and pick up an extra treat for yourself while you're there.

JANUARY

Magic Cotton Candy Daiquiri Mocktail

Makes 1 drink

- 2 oz. nonalcoholic light rum (like Lyre's White Cane Spirit or Caleño Light & Zesty)
- 1 oz. fresh lime juice
- 1 oz. simple syrup
- cotton candy
- 1 lime wheel, garnish

Place a big fluff of cotton candy in a cocktail glass. Pour rum and lime juice into a shaker with ice and shake 40 times. Strain into the cocktail glass, which "magically" dissolves the cotton candy. Garnish with a lime wheel.

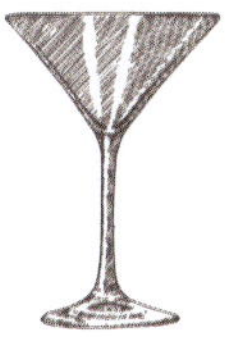

Your second option for the feast day of this native son of Turin, Italy is Turin's favorite coffee drink. Bicerin (bee-cher-een) has three temperatures and three layers: coffee, cocoa, and frothed milk. Here's how to make it:

Bicerin

Makes 1 drink

- 2 oz. heavy whipping cream
- 2¾ oz. milk
- 2 oz. dark chocolate (60–70%), chopped
- 1 tsp. dark cocoa powder
- 2 oz. espresso

Make hot chocolate by pouring cream and ¾ oz. milk into a small saucepan over low heat and adding the chocolate and cocoa. Whisk until a relatively thick, homogenous mixture has formed. Remove from the heat and keep covered.

Froth the remainder of the milk with a milk frother until it is as thick as possible.

Pour the espresso into a large wine glass or an Irish Coffee glass. Next, pour hot chocolate over a Black and Tan spoon into the glass (to layer the drink). Top with frothed milk.

Note: Do not stir the drink, but enjoy the flavors of each layer.

LAST CALL

May the prayers and example of St. John Bosco fill our hearts with a magical wonder and love for God and keep our kids out of juvie.

CHAPTER TWO

February

SAINTS

PURIFICATION OF THE BLESSED VIRGIN MARY, FEBRUARY 2

Forty days after giving birth to Our Lord and in keeping with the Mosaic Law, Our Lady presented Jesus in the Temple and was ritually purified (Luke 2:22–32). Subsequently, the Latin Church keeps the Feast of the Purification of the Blessed Virgin Mary on February 2, forty days after Christmas. The feast is also nicknamed "Candlemas" (Mass of the Candles) because it was the occasion for great candlelight processions to chase away the darkness of winter and to celebrate Jesus Christ who, as the prophet Simeon puts it on this day, is a "Light for the revelation of the Gentiles." Candles would be blessed on this day and used in the home throughout the year.

In Bolivia, today is known as the feast of Our Lady of Copacabana, so named after a town therein. Admit it. When you learned of this Marian title, you immediately heard in your mind Barry Manilow's 1978 hit, "Copacabana." If you are ignorant of the finer points of American pop culture history, find the song online and try not to groove to it. We dare you.

Everleaf Mountain nonalcoholic aperitif is an aromatic blend of sustainably sourced botanical distillates and extracts carefully chosen to capture mountain flavors. That profile maps well with Bolivia, which includes the Eastern Andes Mountain Range. And strawberry is a symbol of the Blessed Virgin Mary because like Mary's fruitful virginity, the plant both flowers and fruits at the same time. Time for a Shaken Strawberry Daiquiri:

Shaken Strawberry Daiquiri

Makes 1 drink

2 oz. Everleaf Mountain
1 oz. fresh lime juice
1 oz. strawberry syrup
strawberries, for garnish

Pour liquid ingredients into a shaker with ice and shake 40 times. Strain into a champagne coupe glass or cocktail glass and garnish with strawberries.

Note: To make strawberry syrup, pour half a cup water and half a cup sugar into a saucepan over medium-high heat and stir until the sugar dissolves. Then mix in 1 cup diced strawberries and bring the liquid to a boil for 10 minutes. Reduce heat to medium-low and let simmer until all the strawberries are mushy and becoming more of a sauce. Strain liquid into a sterilized jar.

LAST CALL

After listening to "Copacabana," make the following toast: "To Our Lady of Copacabana: with her guidance, may music and passion be always in fashion."

SAINT AGATHA, FEBRUARY 5

Agatha (d. ca. 251) is one of the saints who has the honor of being mentioned in the Canon of the Mass (known as Eucharistic Prayer I in the ordinary form of the Roman rite). A beautiful native of Sicily, she consecrated her life to God and refused to apostatize, even when a lustful governor had her breasts cut off (hence her depiction in Christian art holding a tray with two breasts on them). Happily, she was miraculously cured that night by a mysterious visitor to her cell who identified himself as an apostle of Christ.

Agatha eventually died from other wounds inflicted by her tormentors and quickly became a powerful intercessor in Heaven, curing St. Lucy's mother of an ailment. Today she is the patron saint of breast cancer patients, wet nurses, torture victims, and even bakers, as some folks in the Middle Ages thought that her tray was holding loaves of bread!

In *Drinking with the Saints*, we impishly recommend a Prohibition-era cocktail called Twin Peaks. Thanks to a new garnish, our Twin Mounds Mocktail is in even poorer taste (socially, that is: its flavor profile is great).

Twin Mounds (a.k.a Zambra)

Makes 1 drink

2 oz. Feragaia
2 tsp. balsamic vinegar
grapefruit soda
2 red currants, garnish
2 lychees from a can, garnish

Pour Feragaia and vinegar into an old-fashioned glass with ice, top with grapefruit soda, and stir. For garnish, spear 2 lychees with a cocktail sword and place a red currant on each.

LAST CALL

An appropriate toast would be, "To St. Agatha: may we have her faith, her fortitude, and her prayers." An inappropriate toast would be, "To St. Agatha: like the tray she holds, may she always be supportive and uplifting."

SAINT APOLLONIA, FEBRUARY 7

Apollonia (d. 249) was an early virgin-martyr from Alexandria whose teeth were pulled out in an attempt to make her apostatize. She is frequently depicted in art with her teeth or a pair of pincers and is understandably associated with dentistry and toothaches.

The **Casamara Club's Superclasico** is a canned bittersweet, Italian-style aperitivo made with real ingredients, including top-quality Demerara cane sugar. We're not saying that Demerara cane sugar causes cavities; on the contrary, it reminds us that we have a sweet tooth and that we should be grateful that we have any teeth at all (before modern dentistry, our ancestors were not so lucky).

Apollonia's Superclassico

Makes 1 drink

1 can Casamara Club Superclassico
1 orange slice, garnish

Pour a can of Superclassico into an old-fashioned glass with ice and garnish with orange slice.

LAST CALL

A toast: "To St. Apollonia: may she help us get to the Pearly Gates with pearly whites and keep us from the place where there is wailing and gnashing of teeth."

SAINT SCHOLASTICA, FEBRUARY 10

Scholastica (480–542) was the sister of St. Benedict, the founder of Western monasticism (March 21). After her brother founded his order on Monte Cassino, Scholastica founded a community of nuns about five miles away. Benedict and Scholastica used to meet at a house not far from the monastery gate once a year to discuss spiritual matters. At their last meeting, Scholastica, having a premonition of her death, begged Benedict to stay the night and talk. Benedict refused to spend a night outside the cloister and declined. Scholastica then prayed to God, and immediately a violent storm broke out that prevented his departure, the rain pouring down from heaven like the tears running down her face. When Benedict chastised her, she merely replied, "I asked a favor of you, and you said no. I asked a favor of God, and He said yes." Brother and sister then spent the entire night speaking of heavenly things. Gregory the Great praises Scholastica's prayer, for although St. Benedict was thinking in terms of justice, she was motivated by charity, and since "God is charity" (1 John 4:8), "she rightly did more who loved more." Three days later, Benedict had a vision of a white dove ascending to Heaven, and he knew that his sister had passed to her eternal reward.

A Dark and Stormy or a Light and Stormy cocktail is a fitting way to pay tribute to our illustrious saint, and so is a Paloma, which means "dove" in Spanish. **Little Saints** makes a canned Paloma.

Dark and Stormy

Makes 1 drink

¾ oz. GABA Black
1 dash fresh lime juice
ginger beer

Pour GABA Black into an old-fashioned glass with ice and add a dash of lime juice. Top with ginger beer.

Livener Paloma

Makes 1 drink

2 oz. Three Spirits Livener
3–4 oz. grapefruit soda
1 grapefruit wheel, garnish
sea salt or Tajín seasoning

Rim a highball glass by rubbing the edge with grapefruit wheel and dipping it in sea salt or Tajín. Add Livener and fill with ice. Top with grapefruit soda, stir, and garnish with grapefruit wheel.

Cut Above Paloma

Makes 1 drink

2 oz. Cut Above Agave Blanco
$1\frac{1}{2}$ oz. fresh pink grapefruit juice
$\frac{1}{4}$ oz. agave nectar
soda water
salt
1 grapefruit slice, garnish

Rim a highball glass by rubbing the edge with grapefruit and dipping it in salt. Add ice. Pour Cut Above Agave Blanco, grapefruit juice, and agave nectar into the glass, top with soda water, and stir. Garnish with grapefruit slice.

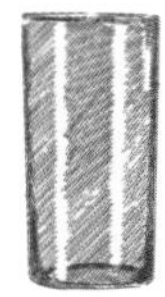

Everleaf Paloma

Makes 1 drink

$1\frac{1}{2}$ oz. Everleaf Marine or Everleaf Mountain
pink grapefruit soda
any citrus wheel for garnish

Pour Everleaf into a highball glass with ice and top with soda. Stir gently. Garnish with grapefruit, lime, or bergamot wheel, or any other citrus.

Feragaia Paloma

Makes 1 drink

2 oz. Feragaia
1 oz. pink grapefruit juice
1 pinch salt
grapefruit soda
1 grapefruit wheel, garnish

Pour Feragaia, juice, and salt into a highball glass with ice and top with soda. Stir gently. Garnish with grapefruit.

Seedlip Paloma

Makes 1 drink

2 oz. Seedlip Notas de Agave
1 oz. fresh grapefruit juice
½ oz. fresh lime juice
½ oz. simple syrup
3 oz. sparkling water
1 grapefruit peel

Pour Seedlip, grapefruit juice, lime juice, and simple syrup into a shaker with ice and shake 40 times. Strain into a highball glass with ice and top with sparkling water. Stir and garnish with grapefruit peel.

Lyre's Paloma

Makes 1 drink

2 oz. Lyre's Agave Blanco Spirit
½ oz. fresh lime juice
¼ oz. agave syrup
3 oz. bottle pink grapefruit or blood orange soda
black salt
1 grapefruit wheel, garnish

Rim a highball glass by rubbing the edge with grapefruit wheel and dipping it in black salt. Add ice. Pour in all liquid ingredients and stir. Garnish with grapefruit wheel.

Little Saints' Nostra Paloma

Makes 1 drink

2 oz. St. Ember
½ oz. fresh grapefruit juice
½ oz. Monin Triple Sec syrup
½ oz. fresh lime juice
hibiscus salt
1 lime wedge, garnish

Rim a highball glass by rubbing the edge with lime and dipping it in hibiscus salt. Add ice. Pour in all liquid ingredients and stir. Garnish with lime wedge.

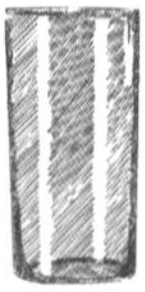

Spiritless Paloma

Makes 1 drink

2 oz. Spiritless Jalisco 55
4 oz. grapefruit soda
¼ oz. fresh lime juice
1 grapefruit peel, garnish

Pour Jalisco 55 and lime juice into a highball glass with ice. Top with soda and stir gently. Garnish with grapefruit peel.

LAST CALL

At the beginning of your drinking party, say "To St. Scholastica, and the primacy of charity!" As the night goes on, pick one man and one woman from your group to play Sts. Benedict and Scholastica and have them break into dance while singing, "Good morning, good morning! We've talked the whole night through!"

OUR LADY OF LOURDES, FEBRUARY 11

Beginning on February 11, 1858, and ending on July 16 of the same year, the Blessed Virgin Mary appeared eighteen times to a young girl named Bernadette Soubirous in the small village of Lourdes, France. Our Lady, dressed in white with a blue sash and golden roses on her feet, announced that she was the "Immaculate Conception," a phrase unknown to the illiterate Bernadette even though the dogma of the Immaculate Conception had recently been defined by Pope Pius IX in 1854. The Blessed Virgin instructed Bernadette to dig in the grotto where she appeared; when she did so, a spring of water gushed forth that to this day has miraculously cured myriads.

A "dirty soda" is a Mormon invention designed to circumvent their prohibition on alcohol, but it aptly describes our saint's hands as she dug into the grotto.

St. Bernadette's Dirty Hands Soda

Makes 1 drink

1 can Dr Pepper (or your favorite cola)
2 tbsp. coconut creamer
1 lime, squeezed (approx. 1 oz.)

Pour cola, creamer, and lime juice into a highball with ice and stir.

SAINT VALENTINE (AND SAINT ANTONINUS), FEBRUARY 14

Valentine was a priest in Rome who was martyred on this day in A.D. 270. There are several theories regarding his patronage of young lovers. According to one, he administered Holy Communion and last rites to Christian prisoners before becoming imprisoned himself. As a prisoner, he wrote a letter to the jailer's daughter, signing it "your Valentine." Another version has it that the saintly priest played matchmaker for the jailer's daughter. But the most likely reason is historical happenstance. Valentine's martyrdom falls on the day before the Roman Lupercalia, when young people would choose courtship partners for a year or even propose marriage. It was only natural that once the old gods were dethroned, the Christian faith should baptize some of these harmless customs.

Curious Elixirs' Curious No. 2 is described as "a chance encounter between a spicy Margarita and a Dark & Stormy." Its ingredients include damiana, which was used by the Mayans as an aphrodisiac. Please don't tell us if it works.

Valentine Surprise

Makes 2 drinks

1 bottle Curious No. 2, chilled
salt
2 lime wedges, garnish

Rim 2 old-fashioned glasses by rubbing the edges with lime wedge and dipping in salt. Pour Curious No. 2 into the glasses with ice and garnish with lime wedges.

We don't recommend Valentine's Day for a first date, but for established couples it is nice to treat Valentine's Day like it's a first date. De Soi has a First Date mocktail made with their Purple Lune, a relaxing aperitif with notes of blackberry nectar, vanilla oak, and rose petals.

First Date

Makes 1 drink

2 oz. De Soi's Purple Lune
½ oz. mint simple syrup
2 cucumber slices
1 mint sprig, garnish
1 cucumber slice, garnish

Muddle 2 cucumber slices in an old-fashioned glass. Add ice, Purple Lune, and mint syrup and stir. Garnish with a sprig of mint and cucumber slice.

Note: To make mint simple syrup, put half a cup water, half a cup sugar, and half a cup mint leaves in a saucepan and heat over medium heat, stirring occasionally, until the sugar dissolves. Let cool. Strain into a sterilized glass jar.

And since it doesn't feel like Valentine's Day unless chocolate is involved, we recommend for your after-dinner drink a can of **St. Agrestis' Phony Cacao Negroni**, which is made from Brazilian cacao beans and has "indulgent, rich aromas of chocolate." Simply pour into an old-fashioned glass with ice and garnish with an orange twist.

Saint Valentine does not need any help interceding for lovers, but today also happens to be the feast day of Saint Antoninus of Sorrento (d. 625). After the monastery of Monte Cassino was destroyed by the Lombards, Antoninus moved to the city of Sorrento and served there as both bishop and the abbot of San Agrippino. Sorrentini (the townsfolk of Sorrento) love Antoninus, as he is said to have saved a child from a whale that swallowed him and to have saved the town from a Moorish invasion. His relics continue to work miracles, "most chiefly in the delivery of them that are vexed by evil spirits."

Well, we know that at least some evil spirits won't be vexing users of this book. Let us toast to the patron of Sorrento with this tasty spritz.

Spicy Sorrento Spritz

Makes 1 drink

- 1 bottle De Soi Spritz Italiano
- 2 oz. pineapple juice
- 2 oz. ginger beer
- 2 oz. pomegranate juice
- Tajín seasoning
- 1 lime wedge, garnish

Rim a glass (highball or old-fashioned) by rubbing the edge with lime wedge and dipping it in Tajín. Add ice. Pour in all ingredients except wedge and stir gently. Garnish with lime wedge.

SAINT SIMEON, FEBRUARY 18

Simeon (d. 66 or 67) succeeded St. James the Less as Bishop of Jerusalem after the latter was martyred. Simeon, who is mentioned in the New Testament three times and was a cousin of Jesus Christ, guided the local Church under difficult circumstances: He was warned in a dream of the impending destruction of Jerusalem by the Romans, and relocated his flock to a small city called Pella on the other side of the river Jordan. He was probably crucified in the year 110, at the astonishing age of 120.

We're going with Curious Elixirs again. Their No. 5, Smoked Cherry Chocolate Old Fashioned, both speaks to Simeon's age and the conflagration in Jerusalem that he avoided.

Simeon's Old-Fashioned

Makes 2 drinks

1 bottle Curious No. 5, chilled
2 orange wheels, garnish

Pour No. 5 into 2 old-fashioned glasses with ice and garnish with orange wheels.

SAINT PAULA THE BEARDED, FEBRUARY 20

The story of this saint, declares the esteemed hagiographer Rev. Alban Butler, "would not deserve notice, but that it is sometimes represented in Spanish art." And "it is impossible to say," he concludes, "what foundation of truth there is in this curious story."

The story that has Fr. Butler flummoxed is that of St. Paula. Born near Avila, Spain to poor parents, Paula was very beautiful. As a result, a young nobleman became obsessed with her and started stalking her. The creep followed her to an oratory in the forest where she often prayed. Knowing that his intentions were evil and that there was no one around to help, Paula embraced the crucifix and begged Jesus to save her. "At once," the legend states, "a beard sprouted on her chin, and moustaches on her lip." (Moustach*es*? How many moustaches can the same face have?) The youth barged in and, not recognizing Paula, asked her if she had seen a young damsel pass by. Good Christian that she was, Paula did not lie but simply said that no one had entered the chapel except herself. The stalker was satisfied and took off.

None of the drinks in this book will put hair on your chest or chin, but Everleaf has a Picante cocktail that echoes some of the details of this legend. "Picante" is the Spanish word for "spicy," but it can also mean "itchy," which is how Paula's new beard must have felt to her. And the cocktail is made with Everleaf Forest, a bittersweet blend of sustainably sourced botanical distillates and extracts carefully chosen to capture the flavors of the forest, like the one Paula was in.

FEBRUARY

Picante Cocktail

Makes 1 drink

- $1\frac{1}{2}$ oz. Everleaf Forest
- $\frac{1}{2}$ oz. fresh lime juice
- $\frac{1}{4}$ oz. agave nectar
- 2 fresh chili peppers, divided
- 2–3 coriander leaves
- 1 lime wheel, garnish

Muddle a small piece of chili in a shaker. Clap the coriander (slap it on your wrist) and drop it in. Add Everleaf Forest, lime juice, agave nectar, and ice, and shake 40 times. Strain into an old-fashioned glass with ice. Cut off the top end of the second chili pepper and place, stem upwards, on the drink to garnish. Garnish with lime wheel as well.

LAST CALL

A toast: "Through the intercession of St. Paula, may all the women in our lives be safe from all cads and goons, preferably without recourse to facial hair."

SAINT MARGARET OF CORTONA, FEBRUARY 22

Margaret of Cortona (1247–1297) wasted her youth as the mistress of a man who promised to marry her but never did, even though she bore him an illegitimate son. One day Margaret noticed the man's dog acting as if it wanted her to follow it; she did, and the dog led her to a woodpile under which she found the body of her murdered lover. Margaret immediately repented of her past, abandoned her gay dress and pretty jewelry, and joined the Third Order of the Friar Minors (the Franciscans). She became renowned for her holiness, generosity to the poor, mystical visions of Christ, and ability to see into the hearts and consciences of others. Even to this day her body remains incorrupt and is known to emit a fragrance like sweet perfume.

What providence that St. Margaret's feast day happens to be National Margarita Day! And there are many nonalcoholic products bearing her name. **Curious Elixir No. 2 Spicy Pineapple Ginger Margarita** is a sparkling beverage infused with damiana to help you unwind (some believe that damiana is also an aphrodisiac, which oddly fits in with St. Margaret's torrid past). **Lyre's** also sells four-pack cans of Margarita made with their Agave Blanco; or you can use their Agave Blanco to make your own (see below). **Three Spirit** and **Free Spirits** also have tequila substitutes that work well in a margarita, as does **Everleaf Marine.** Finally, **Cut Above** has a Spicy Mezcal Margarita, the spice reminding us of St. Margaret's spicy history.

The Virgin Margarita

Makes 5 drinks

5 cups limeade
½ cup fresh orange juice
¼ cup fresh lime juice
¼ tsp. coarse sea salt
2 cups Topo Chico sparkling water
5 lime wedges, garnish
coarse sea salt, garnish

Rim 5 margarita or old-fashioned glasses by rubbing the edge with lime and dipping in salt. Pour limeade, orange juice, lime juice, and salt into a pitcher or punch bowl and stir until salt dissolves. Add sparkling water and ice and stir again. Pour into glasses and garnish with lime wedges.

Lyre's Classic Margarita

Makes 1 drink

1½ oz. Lyre's Agave Blanco Spirit
1 oz. fresh lime juice
½ oz. Lyre's Orange Sec
¼ oz. simple syrup
1 dash orange bitters, optional
1 lime wedge, garnish
salt

Rim a margarita or old-fashioned glass by rubbing the edge with lime and dipping it in salt. Pour liquid ingredients into a shaker with ice and shake 40 times. Strain into the margarita glass and garnish with lime wedge.

Livener Margarita

Makes 1 drink

2 oz. Three Spirit Livener
1 oz. fresh lime juice
1 lime wedge, garnish
salt or Tajín seasoning

Rim a margarita or old-fashioned glass by rubbing the edge with lime and dipping it in salt or Tajín. Pour liquid ingredients into a shaker with ice and shake 40 times. Strain into the margarita glass and garnish with lime wedge.

Tommy's Margarita

Makes 1 drink

2 oz. Free Spirits' The Spirit of Tequila
1 oz. fresh lime juice
½ oz. agave syrup
1 lime slice, garnish
kosher salt

Rim a margarita or old-fashioned glass by rubbing the edge with lime and dipping it in salt. Pour liquid ingredients into a shaker with ice and shake 40 times. Strain into the margarita glass and garnish with lime.

Everleaf Marine Margarita

Makes 1 drink

2 oz. Everleaf Marine
¼ oz. fresh lime juice
¼ oz. agave syrup
1 lime wedge, garnish
salt

Rim a margarita or old-fashioned glass by rubbing the edge with lime and dipping it in salt. Pour liquid ingredients into a shaker with ice and shake 40 times. Strain into the margarita glass and garnish with lime.

Spicy Mezcal Margarita

Makes 1 drink

2 oz. Cut Above Mezcal
1 oz. fresh lime juice
¾ oz. agave nectar
1 jalapeño slice, garnish
1 lime wedge, garnish

Pour all liquid ingredients into a shaker with ice and shake 40 times. Do not strain but pour everything directly into an empty margarita or old-fashioned glass. Garnish with lime and jalapeño.

SAINT MATTHIAS, FEBRUARY 24 (FEBRUARY 25 IN A LEAP YEAR) (MAY 14)

Judas Iscariot's betrayal of our Lord created a vacancy among the Apostles that needed to be filled, and so at an assembly called by Peter, Matthias (d. ca. 80) was chosen by lots to be his successor. (There must be some consolation when taking such an august position in knowing that you can't do much worse than your predecessor). Matthias had been a disciple of Jesus during His public ministry, and he was also a witness of His Resurrection. We don't know exactly where Matthias journeyed to spread the Gospel; one tradition claims that he was stoned and beheaded in Jerusalem, another that he was stoned by the "barbarians and meat-eaters" of "Ethiopia," which oddly enough, is supposed to be code for Georgia.

St. Matthias is a patron saint of alcoholics because of a single line that Clement of Alexandria attributes to him: "We must combat our flesh, set no value upon it, and concede to it nothing that can flatter it." Alcohol does indeed flatter the flesh, but doesn't my favorite dessert do so as well? No matter the logic: Matthias is an obvious patron of this book.

Just as Matthias is a substitute Apostle, Cut Above makes several substitute spirits. We chose two "crush" recipes as an homage to the manner in which St. Matthias was martyred.

Watermelon Crush

Makes 1 drink

- 1½ oz. Cut Above Gin
- 1½ oz. fresh watermelon juice
- ½ oz. basil simple syrup
- ½ oz. fresh lime juice
- 1 lime wheel, garnish

Pour all liquid ingredients into a shaker with ice and shake 40 times. Strain into an old-fashioned glass with ice and garnish with lime wheel.

Note: To make basil simple syrup, put equal parts water and sugar and one bunch of basil in a pan over low heat, stirring occasionally. When the sugar has completely melted, remove from heat, strain, and let cool.

Cantaloupe Crush

Makes 1 drink

3 oz. fresh cantaloupe juice
2 oz. Cut Above Mezcal
¾ oz. fresh lime juice
½ oz. of simple syrup
5 basil leaves
Topo Chico mineral water
1 candied melon or basil leaves, garnish

Combine syrup, lime juice, and basil leaves into a shaker and muddle. Add cantaloupe juice, mezcal, and ice and shake 40 times. Strain into an old-fashioned glass with ice and top with Topo Chico. Garnish with basil leaves or candied melon.

BLESSED SEBASTIAN OF APARICIO, FEBRUARY 25

One of the most interesting beatified men you have never heard of is Sebastian de Aparicio y del Pardo, O.F.M. (1502–1600). A Spanish peasant who emigrated to Puebla, Mexico in 1533, Sebastian was an outstanding entrepreneur who cultivated indigenous maize and European wheat as well as raised cattle, one of the first to do so in Mexico. Because he obtained permission to ride out into the bush and round up wild cattle, he is considered the first cowboy or *charro*. Recognizing the need for good infrastructure to facilitate trade, Sebastian spent ten years building a 466-mile road from Mexico City to Zacatecas that is still in use today. Given his business acumen and work ethic, it is not surprising that Sebastian became a wealthy man. Yet he lived ascetically, gave away his money generously, shared his faith with the native population, and taught them how to use horses, oxen, and wheeled vehicles, all of which were new to them. Feeling pressure to marry, he wed at the age of sixty to a young woman with no dowry (and thus no hope of finding a husband); they had a "white marriage," living as brother and sister. His bride died the next year, and Sebastian married a second time with the same arrangement and outlived her too. (Is celibacy good for men's health and bad for women's?) Finally, at the age of seventy-two, Sebastian became a lay Franciscan brother, begging alms for his community until his death

at the age of ninety-seven. He performed over three hundred miracles during his life, and his body remains incorrupt to this day (see photo).

To honor the world's first cowboy, let us turn to one of America's most famous cowboys. Roy Rogers (1911–1998), the "King of the Cowboys," was a singer, actor, and television host who appeared in over one hundred films, often with his wife, Dale Evans, his Golden Palomino, Trigger, and his German Shepherd, Bullet. One of the earliest mocktails is attributed to him, the Roy Rogers. Or, you can honor this holy rancher with **Ranch Water** on the feast day of Venerable Matt Talbot (see June 19).

Roy Rogers

Makes 1 drink

- ½–1 oz. grenadine, to taste
- 6 oz. cola
- 1 Toschi Amarena cherry, garnish

Pour the grenadine into a highball filled with ice. Top with cola. Stir well. Add cherry for garnish.

LAST CALL

A toast: "May Bl. Sebastian of Aparicio, the world's first and holiest cowboy, keep us safe on the road and tall in the saddle."

SAINT ROMANUS, FEBRUARY 28 (FEBRUARY 29 IN A LEAP YEAR)

Romanus or Romain of Condat (390–463) became a hermit in the Jura Mountains of France when his younger brother St. Lupicinus and other disciples joined him. He ended up founding several monasteries throughout France and Switzerland and is famous for healing two lepers by embracing them. Today, Saint-Romain is an appellation for red and white wines produced around the village of Saint-Romain in the region of Burgundy.

The French have a saying for this feast day:

Ciel clair à la Saint Romain
C'est beaucoup de bien et de bon vin.

Which loosely means:

If on St. Romain's the sun doth shine,
Then you'll have much fine, good wine.

Rain or shine, it is time to give nonalcoholic wines a shot. The white wines of Saint Romanus' region of Burgundy are principally made from Chardonnay grapes. **Thomson & Scott**'s first nonalcoholic still white wine, **Noughty Blanc**, fits the bill, for it is made from 98% Chardonnay and 2% Chenin Blanc grapes. Red Burgundies, on the other hand, use Pinot Noir grapes, and so does **Wölffer Estate's Spring** in a **Bottle Rosé**, a blend of Pinot Noir, Pinot Meunier, Saint Laurent, and Dornfelder grapes.

CHAPTER THREE

March

SAINTS

SAINT DAVID, MARCH 1

David (ca. 500–589) had a good start in life, being the son of King Sant of South Wales and Saint Non. Ordained a priest and consecrated Bishop of Menevia, he participated in two Church synods against the heresy of Pelagianism and became known as a great teacher and preacher. Today David is the patron saint of Wales.

Among his many accomplishments, St. David founded a monastery at Menevia in southwest Wales that had a reputation for "extreme asceticism;" despite a long day of study and manual labor, neither David nor his monks drank any wine or beer, and they ate only bread, herbs, and vegetables. Catholic folk logic being what it is, however, St. David's Day became the national holiday of Wales and an occasion for much merriment, fueled in part by the Drink.

LAST CALL

The Welsh toast to someone's health is *Iechyd da* (YAH-key DAH)!

Tonight, we can return to the original spirit of St. David's monastery with a spirit-free night. Dirwest in the Welsh Vale of Glamorgan makes a Yma o Hyd IPA nonalcoholic beer and a nonalcoholic botanical spirit called Gwirod, but for the time being, they only ship within the United Kingdom. We'll have to punt and use a leek, the symbol of both St. David and Wales, as a garnish for something else. Shakespeare mentions the custom of wearing a leek in one's hat "upon Saint Tavy's Day"; we can have our cocktail glasses wear one instead. Inspired by the classic negroni, the Agrodolce is, like St. David's diet, herb forward.

Ghia's [Welshified] Agrodolce

Makes 1 drink

- 2½ oz. Ghia Apéritif
- ¼ oz. date syrup
- 3 sprigs thyme
- 3 dashes orange bitters
- 1 sprinkle orange zest, garnish
- 1 leek leaf, garnish

Pour Ghia, date syrup, thyme, and orange bitters into a shaker with ice and shake 40 times. Strain into an old-fashioned glass with a large ice cube. Garnish with a dusting of orange zest and leek leaf.

SAINT CUNIGUNDE, MARCH 3

Cunigunde of Luxembourg (c. 975–1033) was Empress of the Holy Roman Empire thanks to her marriage to the Holy Roman Emperor Henry II. Cunigunde and Henry had a "white marriage," living as brother and sister, but otherwise their partnership was intimate. Cunigunde was a true *consors regni* ("partner in the rule"), advising her husband on important matters concerning Church and state. But she was also the object of envy. When wicked people accused the Empress of having committed a shameful sin, she chose to remain silent and Henry, sadly, believed them. Cunigunde then asked to be tried by fire, according to the customs of the time, and walked barefoot on red-hot metal for some time without being burned. Her husband and all the people then recognized her innocence.

After Henry died, Cunigunde stayed on as regent until a new Emperor was elected. By now, the saint was poor because of all the donations she had made. Cunigunde entered a Benedictine convent that she herself had founded and spent the last fifteen years of her life as a humble nun, always asking to take on the most menial job.

LAST CALL

A toast: "To St. Cunigunde: through her intercession, may we stay out of the hot seat."

It is providential that March 3 is National Mulled Wine Day, for mulled wine used to be heated with a hot poker rod, not unlike those pieces of metal that St. Cunigunde walked on. Here's a good recipe with nonalcoholic ingredients:

MARCH

Glogg

Makes 6 drinks

- 1 bottle nonalcoholic red wine like the No & Low Cabernet Sauvignon or Misty Cliffs red blend.
- 6 oz. Lyre's American Malt or nonalcoholic dark spirit alternative
- 3 tbsp. brown sugar
- 4 star anise pods, plus more for garnishes
- 3 cinnamon sticks, plus more for garnishes
- 6 whole cloves
- 2 whole oranges, peels, and juice, plus more slices for garnishes

Put all ingredients into a saucepan and set to medium heat. Let simmer on low for 20 minutes, remove from heat, and let cool until ready to serve. Strain into Irish coffee glasses or coffee mugs. Garnish each with an orange slice, cinnamon stick, and star anise.

SAINT THOMAS AQUINAS, MARCH 7 (JANUARY 28)

Thomas (1225–1274) was born of a noble family who had him educated by the Benedictines at Monte Cassino from the age of five and who expected him to enter that prestigious and influential monastery when he came of age. Thomas shocked them, however, when he became a Dominican, an order of (gulp) mendicants—beggars and itinerant preachers. They locked him in a tower of the family castle in an attempt to break his will, and his brothers even put a loose woman in his room, whom Thomas promptly chased out with a firebrand. Eventually he escaped with the help of his sisters, and Thomas Aquinas went on to be a Dominican priest, a professor at the University of Paris, a Doctor of the Church, the patron saint of Catholic schools and Catholic students, and arguably the greatest theologian of all time.

As St. Thomas Aquinas explains in his masterpiece the *Summa Theologiae*, in order to gain the wisdom that is sufficient for salvation, for most people it is necessary to abstain only from the immoderate use of wine. But for certain persons, Aquinas states, "it is requisite . . . that they abstain altogether" (II-II.149.3). Whichever category you fall into, tonight enjoy some nonalcoholic wine in honor of the Angelic Doctor. When we think of Thomistic thought, we think of something meaty and substantive, and so our thoughts turn to a hearty red wine. Two outstanding candidates are **Sovi Red Blend** and **Ariel Cabernet Sauvignon**, both alcohol-removed. The former comes in a can, but don't let that turn you off. Like St. Thomas himself (who is said to have been on the chubby side), good things sometimes come in unexpected packages.

FORTY HOLY MARTYRS, MARCH 10

The Forty Holy Martyrs (d. 320) were Roman soldiers of the famed Twelfth Legion condemned to die for the Faith by being exposed to the cold on a frozen pond near Sebaste, Armenia (present-day Sivas, Turkey). A warm bath was built nearby and promised to anyone who apostatized. In the course of the freezing night, one of the forty succumbed and renounced his faith, fleeing to the bath but dying soon after. Later, one of the guards, moved by the faithful men's constancy and seeing a supernatural light over them, professed himself a Christian, stripped down naked, and joined them, thereby restoring the holy number of forty.

Little Saints' Spice on Ice captures the mood of this story, as the spice can symbolize either the warm bath of temptation or the fire of charity that burned in the hearts of the martyrs.

Spice on Ice

Makes 1 drink

Tajín seasoning

2 oz. Little Saints' St. Ember

1 lime wedge, garnish

Rim an old-fashioned glass by rubbing the edge with lime and dipping it in Tajín. Add a single ice cube and pour St. Ember over it. Garnish with lime wedge.

POPE SAINT GREGORY THE GREAT, MARCH 12 (SEPTEMBER 3)

The son of a Roman senator and a Christian saint (Celia), Pope St. Gregory the Great is known for many things. He was the first monk ever to become Pope. After his election, he coined the title the "Servant of the Servants of God" for himself and his successors. He organized and contributed to the sacred music of the Church which now bears his name, Gregorian chant. And last but not least, he codified the Roman liturgy, which is why the traditional Latin Mass, when it is not called the extraordinary form of the Roman rite, is sometimes referred to as the Gregorian Rite.

There is an old yarn about St. Gregory and cherries. On St. Mark's Day (April 25), the ascetical Pontiff was overwhelmed by a hankering for cherries and commanded his servants to find some—a tall order given that the cherry trees along the hills of Trastevere were only just in bloom. One disconsolate gardener was searching the area when St. Mark appeared to him and granted his petition by blessing a tree and making it heavy with fruit. When the cherries were brought to Pope Gregory, the story goes, the Servant of the Servants of God "wolfed down a bellyful." Ever since then, it is customary for the Pope to enjoy a bowl of cherries on St. Mark's Day.

You can channel this charming legend with any number of cherry-flavored drinks. **HOPWTR** has a **Black Cherry** in 16-oz. tallboy cans made with mood-enhancing ingredients such as ashwagandha and L-theanine. And Curious Elixir's Curious No. 5, which has a delightful smoked cherry chocolate flavor, is an immunity booster thanks to the elderberry, ginger, chicory, and cayenne. Finally, Seedlip and Monday would also like to contribute.

Gregory's Curious No. 5

Makes 2 drinks

1 bottle Curious No. 5, chilled
2 orange peels, garnish
2 Toschi Amarena cherries, garnish
1 rosemary sprig, optional garnish
1 purple sage, optional garnish

Pour Curious No. 5 into 2 old-fashioned glasses with ice. Garnish with orange peels and cherries and, if you wish, rosemary and purple sage. (The purple sage can symbolize the season of Lent during which St. Gregory's feast day traditionally occurs.)

Seedlip's Cherry Blossom

Makes 1 drink

2 oz. Spice 94
2 tsp. cherry syrup
1 oz. cold brew jasmine tea
1 jasmine flower, garnish

Pour liquid ingredients into a terracotta glass or old-fashioned glass with ice and stir 40 times. Garnish with jasmine flower.

Monday's Cherry Blossom

Makes 1 drink

2 oz. Monday Mezcal
½ oz. fresh lime juice
¼ oz. fresh orange juice
¼ oz. fresh grapefruit
¼ oz. agave syrup
1 tsp. cherry juice
2 dashes orange bitters
lime zest, garnish

Combine all liquid ingredients in a cocktail shaker with ice. Shake until cold. Strain into a salt-rimmed short glass over fresh ice. Top with fresh lime zest.

Spiritless' Cherry Bourbon Crush

Makes 2 drinks

1 cup frozen cherries
1 cup fresh lemon juice
1 cup ice
4 oz. Kentucky 74
¾ cup grenadine
½ can Ollipop Cherry Vanilla
2 mint sprigs, garnish

Blend all ingredients except mint in a blender until smooth. Strain into 2 old-fashioned glasses and garnish with mint.

LAST CALL

Find a copy of St. Gregory's *Dialogues* and read some of its fabulous and immensely entertaining stories about the saints.

SAINT PATRICK, MARCH 17

Patrick, the Apostle of Ireland (387–460), first came to the Emerald Isle under less than auspicious circumstances: he was brought as a slave, having been abducted from his family at the age of sixteen by Irish pirates. For six years he labored as a shepherd, viewing the time as an opportunity to be converted to Christ and to pray. He escaped, but after being ordained, he answered a mystical call to return to his former home of captivity, this time as a shepherd of men. He encountered resistance from local chieftains and the Druids, was beaten, robbed, and enchained, but he persevered. Before his death, Patrick had baptized thousands, ordained numerous priests, and helped several noble women enter the religious life. And his feast day, as we all know, has taken on a life of its own, having grown from local pious gratitude for Ireland's conversion to Irish-American-Pride-Day to a worldwide excuse to drink beer, wear green, and decorate the walls with leprechauns and shamrocks. The holiday has even been celebrated on more than one occasion by astronauts in outer space.

For nonalcoholic beer, **Sober Carpenter** makes a nice **Irish Red Ale Craft Beer**, and the **Athletic Brewing Company** has a limited released **Irish Red** as well as an **Emerald Cliffs** Irish-style stout. **Guinness** has **Guinness 0**, a nonalcoholic draught made with the same ingredients and in the same way as their famous stout, only that the alcohol is removed through a cold filtration process that protects the brew from thermal stress and preserves its taste and character. **Hoplark** makes a **0.0 Stout Style** patterned after a classic stout, **Bravus Brewing** has a **Barrel-Aged Bourbon Stout**, **Grüvi** has a **Mocha Nitro Stout**, and **Barrel Brothers** makes a **Dark Sarcasm Porter**.

MARCH

Grafton Street Irish Coffee

Makes 1 drink

- 2½ oz. Free Spirits' Spirit of Bourbon
- 2 oz. cold brew coffee
- ¾ oz. brown sugar simple syrup (1:1)
- 4 dashes All The Bitter Chocolate Mole Bitters
- whipped cream, sweet
- cacao chips or grated nutmeg, garnish

Pour the Spirit of Bourbon, coffee, simple syrup, and bitters in a shaker with 1 large ice cube and shake 40 times. Strain into a footed pilsner glass or large latte glass. Top with whipped cream and garnish with cacao chips or nutmeg.

Lyre's Irish Cream

Makes 4 drinks

- 6¾ oz. Lyre's American Malt
- 4¼ oz. light (low-fat) condensed milk
- 4¼ oz. heavy cream
- 1 oz. espresso
- ½ tsp. vanilla extract
- 1 tsp. chocolate syrup
- 4 pinches cinnamon and grated nutmeg, garnish

Pour all ingredients (except cinnamon and nutmeg) into a blender and mix on low speed. Pour into 4 old-fashioned glasses with ice and garnish each with a pinch of cinnamon and nutmeg.

LAST CALL

To toast the Apostle of Ireland, a simple Irish Gaelic *Sláinte*! (pronounced SLAHN-chuh), meaning "To your health," will suffice. Or how about the following:

Saint Patrick was a gentleman,
Who, through strategy and stealth,
Drove all the snakes from Ireland:
Here's a bumper to his health.
But not a bumper with booze,
Lest we lose ourselves, and then
Forget the good Saint Patrick,
And see the snakes again.

SAINT JOSEPH, MARCH 19

The foster-father of our Lord and the most chaste spouse of the Blessed Virgin Mary is not just a patron saint but a *universal* patron. Consider the following: 1) Joseph is the Head of the Holy Family; 2) the Holy Family is the Church *in ovo*; 3) therefore, Joseph extends to the entire Church the same tremendous love and protection that he showered on his earthly family. "Some saints are privileged to extend to us their patronage with particular efficacy in certain needs but not in others," St. Thomas Aquinas is said to have written. "But our holy patron St. Joseph has the power to assist us in all cases, in every necessity, in every undertaking." Numerous other saints agree (like St. Teresa of Ávila), turning to Joseph in times of need and never walking away disappointed.

One people that turns often to St. Joseph is Italy: the richly-endowed "Saint Joseph tables" (*tavola di San Giuseppe*) are a great Italian tradition on his feast day, and so is the Italian-American custom of wearing red, even though Joseph was not a martyr (the speculation is that red is one of the colors of the Italian flag and that Italian-Americans were tired of the Irish and all their green from two days ago!). **Casamara Club** makes several delicious **Italian-style sodas.** Or, have an orange and tonic:

Lyre's Italian Orange and Tonic

Makes 1 drink

2 oz. Lyre's Italian Orange
4 oz. premium bottled tonic water
1 orange slice, garnish

Pour Lyre's and tonic water into a highball glass with ice and stir gently. Garnish with orange.

LAST CALL

There is a pious custom of placing a written petition under a statue of St. Joseph, although for the Little Sisters of the Poor, notes are not enough: they place the very object they need in front of his statue: "a potato, a lump of coal, even a can of beer." Throw a St. Joseph's party with his statue in a prominent place. Let your guests come with their petitions in whatever form, and then make the following toast. "Heeding the words of Genesis, 'Go to Joseph,' let us go to our universal patron with confidence: and may he save us from this world's Herods, pilot us through this world's Egypts, and equip us with what we need to make it to our heavenly destination."

SAINT BENEDICT, MARCH 21 (JULY 11)

Benedict of Nursia (480–543 or 547) was born in the Umbrian region of Italy. The son of a noble family, he was receiving a liberal arts education in Rome when he decided to dedicate his life entirely to Christ and become a hermit, which he did by living alone in a cave for three years. Others heard of Benedict's holiness and asked him to become their abbot, but when he rebuked them for their wicked lives, they tried to murder him by putting poison in his drink. St. Benedict, however, foiled their plot by making the sign of the cross over the cup, which then broke. Having had enough of those fellows, Benedict went on to found thirteen monasteries, including the great Abbey of Monte Cassino.

To help his fledgling monasteries, Benedict wrote his masterpiece *The Rule of St. Benedict*, a simple yet comprehensive set of instructions on how to be a good monk. Chapter 40, On the Quantity of Drink, is famous for allowing each monk half a pint of wine per day so long as he is not late for meals. But he also states that this is a concession to his stubborn monks and that "to whom God granteth the endurance of abstinence, let them know that they will have their special reward."

Let us seek our special reward tonight with a nod to the mimosa flower, a symbol of St. Benedict:

Lyre's Festive Mimosa

Makes 1 drink

- 1 oz. Lyre's Apéritif Rosso
- 1 oz. Lyre's Dry London Spirit
- 1½ oz. fresh orange juice
- 2 oz. alcohol free sparkling wine
- 1 tsp. premium vanilla syrup (not vanilla extract)
- 1 orange slice

Pour all ingredients (including orange slice) into a large wine glass with ice and stir 40 times.

FEAST OF THE ANNUNCIATION OF THE BLESSED VIRGIN MARY, MARCH 25

The true Feast of the Incarnation, when the Word first became flesh and dwelt among us, is not Christmas but today. The moment that the Blessed Virgin Mary, a fifteen- or sixteen-year-old girl at the time, said "Yes" to St. Gabriel's message inviting her to be the Mother of God, she conceived of the Holy Spirit and Jesus Christ, the Son of God, took flesh or became incarnate in her womb.

Adding an extra layer of meaning to this feast is an old legend that Adam was created and fell on March 25, while another legend credits this date with being both the first day of Creation and the date of the Crucifixion.

The Annunciation is one of the oldest and greatest Marian feasts that we have. In the Middle Ages up to modern times, "Lady Day" (as it was known in England) was a holy day on which no servile work would be done.

And how about something with strawberry? In medieval art the strawberry is a symbol of, among other things, Mary's fruitful virginity because the plant both flowers and fruits at the same time. Our Strawberry Fiat Forever honors Mary's Yes (*Fiat*—Let it be done unto me according to Thy word), a Yes that lasts forever, thanks be to God.

Strawberry Fiat Forever

Makes 1 drink

1 oz. strawberry puree
1 oz. fresh lime juice
4 oz. ginger beer
2 oz. sparkling water
1 strawberry slice, garnish

Build all liquid ingredients in a highball and stir 40 times. Fill with ice and garnish with a strawberry slice.

LAST CALL

Raise your glass and toast to the Blessed Virgin Mary, whose *fiat* brought into the world the Son of God. You may wish to begin your soirée with a recitation of the Angelus. Or you can simplify things by just saying the verse, "The Word was made flesh" with the reply, "And dwelt among us." If the feast day occurs in Eastertide, throw in lots of Alleluias.

Lady Day was also a time to celebrate the coming of the spring and new life. A saying from Austria that could be converted into a toast is: "Saint Gabriel to Mary flies/ This is the end of snow and ice."

POPE SAINT SIXTUS III, MARCH 28

Sixtus (d. 440) lived in tumultuous times. He corresponded with St. Augustine of Hippo in an effort to quell Pelagianism, the "I can get to Heaven by my own bootstraps" heresy that still tempts us today. He also sought to reconcile a rift between the (orthodox) Cyril of Alexandria and the not-so-orthodox John of Antioch over Nestorianism, the heresy that Jesus Christ had both a human and divine person (wrong: He had a human and a divine *nature* but was one Divine Person). Finally, Sixtus worked hard to build up Christian Rome: he is responsible for the beautiful Santa Sabina Basilica on the Aventine Hill and St. Mary Major Basilica on the Esquiline Hill. To honor today's saint, turn to drinks regarding the Basilica of St. Mary Major (see August 5).

SAINT RENOVATUS, MARCH 31

Renovatus (ca. 633) was the abbot of the monastery at Cauliana in Lusitania (present-day Portugal and Spain). Other than being described as "a very stately, handsome man with a sweet expression of countenance," one of the only other details we have of him is his treatment of one of his monks, who sounds like Friar Tuck on crack. The tale is worth repeating verbatim from Butler's *Lives of the Saints*:

"Renovatus was much troubled in his abbey by the conduct of one of his monks, whose love of eating and drinking was a governing passion. The fellow would steal what he was not given, and he became a scandal to the community. Renovatus exhorted him, and reproached him, in vain. Then he ordered him to be whipped; but the whipping proved as inefficacious as the admonitions.

"The abbot then gave him leave to depart if he liked, or, if he stayed in the monastery, to take anything he found most succulent and dainty in the house. The monk went into the kitchen, opened the cupboards, and helped himself to everything he fancied, then descended to the cellars and carried off some flasks of wine under his arm, out of the abbey gates; and finding a pleasant shady nook among some bushes, picnicked on what he had brought, and ate and drank till he could contain no more, when he lay down and fell asleep. The dogs carried off the rest of his food, and the cellarer, who little liked the abstraction of the bottles of best wine, and had dogged his steps, when he heard him snoring, stole up to the half-consumed meal and recovered what was left of the precious wine. Towards evenfall the monk came home, tumbled into bed, was left undisturbed to sleep through matins and lauds, and rose when it pleased him, took another turn through the larder and cellar, helped himself to the best of everything, and spent another jovial day of eating, drinking, and sleeping, with no churchgoing to interrupt its calm delight.

"So he lived for some days, and the daily surfeiting began to tell on his constitution. One morning, as he went forth with some wine bottles under his arm, and a fat capon in his hood, he heard the schoolboys reciting an antiphon they had been learning, "Consider the terrible judgment of the Lord, and the dread sentence at the trial; consider the dread avenging severity of His judgment; consider the years of thine age, and now at last change thy ways for the better, or even one day before thy death correct thy life." The monk feeling fever in his blood, and hearing the solemn appeal, was conscience-struck, and sending for the abbot, he confessed his sinful life with heartfelt contrition, and falling ill with fever, died a few days after."

Well, if that isn't a reason to embrace *Abstaining with the Saints*, we don't know what is. Tonight, avoid dying of a gluttony-induced fever with something from Three Spirit's Livener XS Picante. Renovatus' name means "revived," and this spicy concoction does just that.

Livener XS Picante

Makes 1 drink

2 oz. Three Spirit Livener XS
1 oz. fresh lime juice
½ oz. agave syrup
4 basil leaves
1 slice jalapeño or chili pepper, garnish

Pour all liquid ingredients into a shaker with ice, clap 3 basil leaves (slap on your wrist) to release the aroma, and put into the shaker. Shake hard 40 times. Strain into an old-fashioned glass, making sure you strain all the foam out of the shaker. Garnish with remaining basil leaf and a slice of pepper.

CHAPTER FOUR

April
SAINTS

SAINT URBAN, APRIL 2

To help us recover from the humiliation of April Fool's Day, Holy Mother Church consoles us with a feast day. St. Urban of Langres (327–390), the brother of St. Lodegaria, was consecrated Bishop of Langres in 374. Not long after, political turmoil drove him from his home and forced him to take refuge in a nearby vineyard. The vine-dressers helped him hide, and he in turn converted them to Christianity. Using their vineyards as an underground railroad, he traveled from town to town spreading the Faith. His gratitude to the vine-dressers, together with his devotion to the Precious Blood of Our Lord, made it only natural for him to become the patron saint of all who work in the wine industry and a saint invoked against blight, frost, storms, alcoholism, and faintness.

We can combine St. Urban's patronage of wine and of alcoholics with a nonalcoholic wine such as **Giesen Alcohol-Removed New Zealand Sauvignon Blanc.** This crisp, dry white wine is made from a native of France, the sauvignon blanc grape.

LAST CALL

Keep your eye out on the weather today. The Germans have an old adage:

Ist Sonnenschein am Urbanstag,
gedeiht der Wein nach alter Sag.

Which means:

If there is sunshine on St. Urban's Day,
The wine thrives afterwards they say.

SAINT BENEDICT THE MOOR, APRIL 4

Benedict the Moor (1526–1589) did not have an easy life. As a descendent of African slaves brought to Italy, he was made to suffer the prejudices of his age. Granted, he was emancipated at birth for his parents' "loyal service," but like other Italian peasants, he grew up without an education and the gift of literacy. When he was twenty-one, he was insulted for the color of his skin. A hermit noticed his humility and magnanimity in the face of such humiliation and invited him to join his community. Benedict then became a Sicilian Franciscan, nicknamed "Il Moro" because of his ebony complexion. At the age of twenty-eight, he became the leader of his community. Today he is the patron saint of African missions, African Americans, black missions and black people, and Sicily.

One of the three most common types of blood orange, the Moro is the most colorful. Its roots date back to the nineteenth century in the citrus-growing area of Lentini (Sicily, Italy). How better to honor the saintly Il Moro?

Il Moro Mocktail

Makes 1 drink

1 oz. blood orange syrup
½ oz. fresh lemon juice
2 dashes orange bitters, optional
4–6 oz. sparkling water

Pour syrup, lemon juice, and bitters (if using) into a shaker with ice and shake 40 times. Strain into a cocktail glass and top with sparkling water.

SAINT WALTER, APRIL 8

Walter of Pontoise (1030–1099), a.k.a. Walter Gaultier, was a professor of philosophy and rhetoric who has the curious distinction of being a patron saint of vintners, prisoners of war, and those suffering from job-related stress. He joined the Benedictines to escape "the temptations presented by success in his field" but was soon pressed into becoming the Abbot of Pontoise. St. Walter loathed the monastery's laxity and was worried about

becoming vainglorious himself, and so he ran away—several times. Eventually the Pope had to order him to remain in his abbey. Saint Walter was beaten and imprisoned by his fellow Benedictines for his opposition to simony within the order, but he bore his persecution with patience and even joy. He passed away on Good Friday, April 8, 1099, and is considered to be the last saint in the Western Church canonized by an authority other than the Pope.

Walter's penchant for hightailing it out of town, combined with his patronage of wine, called to mind a cocktail with a punny name:

Grape Escape

Makes 1 drink

- 4–6 grapes (preferably purple or red flesh)
- 1½ oz. Ghia Berry Apéritif
- ¾ oz. elderflower cordial (nonalcoholic)
- ¾ oz. fresh lime juice
- 2 frozen grapes on a cocktail spear (preferably frozen)

Muddle grapes in a shaker. Add liquid ingredients and ice and shake 40 times. Strain into a coupe glass and garnish with grapes.

POPE SAINT LEO THE GREAT, APRIL 11 (NOVEMBER 10)

Leo (400–461) was the first Pope to earn the epithet of Great. An aristocrat by birth, his character and wisdom were evident even as a deacon: great

figures from the East such as St. Cyril of Alexandria sought him out, and the Emperor chose him to settle a dispute between the two highest ranking officials in Gaul. He was unanimously chosen to be Pope and proved an indefatigable Pontiff. Leo was a firm opponent of heresy yet kind to repentant heretics. To resolve the controversy about Jesus Christ being one person with a fully human nature and a fully divine nature, he wrote the "Tome of Leo" and had it read to the Council of Chalcedon. After it was read, the Council Fathers cried out: "This is the faith of the fathers, this is the faith of the Apostles. So we all believe, thus the orthodox believe. Anathema to him who does not thus believe. Peter has spoken thus through Leo!"

Dom Guéranger writes of St. Leo: "As his name implies, he is the Lion of Holy Church, thus representing in his own person one of the most glorious of our Lord's titles."

Oh, where to begin. A good number of the new nonalcoholic spirits use lion's mane mushroom, an adaptogen that relaxes and enhances one's mood. Examples include:

Little Saints makes two spirits from lion's mane mushroom, St. Ember and St. Juniper.

Three Spirit's Social, a dark herbal elixir that is described as the ultimate mood elevator, is made from lion's mane mushroom, yerba mate, and damiana.

De Soi's Spritz Italiano is a harmonious blend of sweet and bitter citrus, crisp white grape, and bold gentian root, complete with rich and relaxing adaptogens L-theanine, lion's mane, and reishi mushroom.

De Soi also makes a **Golden Hour** from a blend of adaptogens like reishi mushroom, lion's mane, and L-theanine that "promotes relaxation and mental clarity in every sip."

LAST CALL

A toast: "Through the intercession of the lion-hearted Pope Leo the Great, may all his successors on the throne of Peter roar only with the voice of truth and justice."

SAINT LIDWINA, APRIL 14

Lidwina or Lydwina was fifteen years old when she broke a rib in an ice-skating accident. The Dutch girl's condition deteriorated significantly: a ceaseless pain in her side eventually became paralysis, blindness in one eye, sores on her face, and bleeding from her mouth, ears, and nose (some believe that this is one of the first documented cases of multiple sclerosis). Bedridden for thirty-eight years, Lidwina is even said to have shed body parts such as skin, bones, and intestines that her parents kept in a jar and that emitted an odor of sanctity. (Lidwina's mother eventually had to bury them because they attracted so much attention.) But through it all, Lidwina drew closer to Christ and even added to her sufferings through rigorous fasting. Before her death, she had gained a reputation as a holy healer of others.

We don't blame you if hearing St. Lidwina's story makes you never want to strap on a pair of skates again, but the good news is that you now have her on your side as a heavenly protectress when you hit the ice. And after spending a day in a winter wonderland, a hot toddy hits the spot.

LAST CALL

A toast: "May the intercession of St. Lidwina keep us from the sufferings of St. Lidwina."

Lyre's Classic Hot Toddy

Makes 1 drink

1½ oz. Lyre's American Malt
1 tbsp. honey
2–3 tsp. fresh lemon juice
4–6 oz. hot water
1 lemon slice, garnish
1 cinnamon stick, garnish

Pour liquid ingredients into an Irish Coffee glass or coffee mug and stir until honey dissolves. Garnish with lemon slice and cinnamon stick.

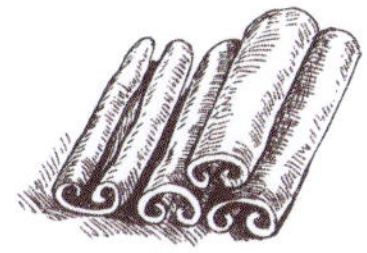

POPE SAINT LEO IX, APRIL 19

Pope Leo IX (1002–1054) was one of the great reformers of the medieval Church. He fought against simony and clerical marriage. He also combatted the errors of Berengar of Tours, who denied the Real Presence of Christ in the Eucharist. When Patriarch Michael I Cerularius of Constantinople denounced the use of unleavened bread and fasting days in the Western Church, Leo sent a delegation to Constantinople to smooth things out. Unfortunately, his legate Cardinal Humbert of Silva Candida dispensed with negotiations and excommunicated the Patriarch, thus initiating the Great Schism between the Western and Eastern churches.

Leo may have chosen the wrong man as his legate, but we still admire his reforming spirit. Tonight, go to the other holy Pope Leo (see April 11) and enjoy some libations made from lion's mane mushroom.

SAINT GEORGE, APRIL 23

George (ca. 275–303) was a native of Lydda in Palestine and a Roman soldier who received the crown of martyrdom by being beheaded after several

APRIL

unsuccessful attempts to execute him. According to one legend, his persecutors gave him poison to drink but he made the sign of the cross over it and remained unharmed. In the West, St. George is one of the Fourteen Holy Helpers, invoked for the protection of domestic animals, and in the Christian East, he is called "the Great Martyr."

And, of course, there is the medieval story of how George rescued a princess named Alexandra from a dragon who had been terrorizing a town in Libya or Syria. The princess had been chosen by lot to be the dragon's next meal; after making the sign of the cross, George fought the dragon, pinning it to the earth with his lance. He led the defeated monster into the city and told the twenty thousand townsfolk that he would kill it if they all converted to Christianity, which they did. George then beheaded the dragon with his sword.

Monin has a delightful syrup made from pitaya or dragon fruit, a Pacific Rim fruit that tastes like a combination of strawberry and pear but with lush tropical notes. Our original Dragonslayer Mocktail is a good way to use the syrup and honor St. George. Or enjoy the dragon-themed options for St. Margaret of Antioch (see July 20).

Dragonslayer Mocktail

Makes 1 drink

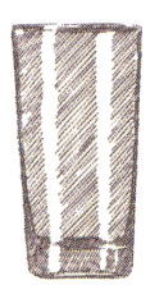

- 1 oz. Monin dragon fruit syrup
- ½ oz. fresh lemon juice
- 4–6 oz. sparkling water

Pour syrup and lemon juice in a shaker with ice and shake 40 times. Strain into a cocktail glass and top with sparkling water.

LAST CALL

Turn an old French battle cry into a toast: "Vive Monsieur Saint Georges!"

SAINT PETER CANISIUS, APRIL 27 (DECEMBER 21)

Peter Canisius (1521–1597) was a Jesuit priest, a prolific writer, and the "Second Apostle of Germany" (so-called because of his frequent and incredibly successful missions to that country). His life reads like a summary of the important events and figures of the sixteenth century. He was present at the 1557 Colloquy of Worms, where, speaking in opposition to Philip Melanchthon, he highlighted the divisions within Protestantism in such a way that the Protestants were forced to dissolve the meeting. He was an advisor of Emperor Ferdinand I, whom he solemnly warned about the dangers of apostatizing and of making concessions to Protestants in return for military support. He was a theological expert at the Council of Trent, where he gave advice on Holy Communion under both species and the Index of Forbidden Books. He was on good terms with Pope Saint Pius V and Saint Charles Cardinal Borromeo. Even the spiritual master Saint Francis de Sales sought his advice. He was a great promoter of Catholic education on all levels, and although he was a critic of Protestantism, he approached his non-Catholic brethren with charity and respect and was in return respected by them.

St. Peter was also the first Dutchman to enter the Society of Jesus, a fact that can be celebrated with something from his native land. *Anijsmelk* or "Anise-milk" is a Dutch drink made with hot milk, anise seed, and sugar that is traditionally enjoyed while ice skating on one of the many canals of Holland (it is also said to have a soporific effect). DeRuijter makes powder sticks of anise flavoring and sugar, but since these may be difficult to find in the US, here is an easy recipe you can use at home:

Anijsmelk

Makes 1 drink

1 cup milk
1 heaping tsp. anise seed (or 2 drops anise extract)
sugar or honey, to taste

Pour the milk and seeds (either loose or in a tea ball) into a saucepan and bring to a slow boil. Reduce the heat and simmer for 5 minutes. Remove the seeds (strain or remove tea ball) and add sugar or honey. Pour into a mug.

SAINT LOUIS DE MONTFORT, APRIL 28

Louis-Marie Grignion de Montfort (1673–1716) was a French priest best known for his preaching, his theological writings on the Blessed Virgin Mary, and his promotion of consecrating one's life to Mary. What is less known is that he had a short fuse when it came to drunks.

Apparently, during an outdoor sermon in the village of Roussay, a group of men deep in their cups heckled the saint with vulgar shouts and songs from a nearby café. After finishing the sermon and blessing the congregation, St. Louis marched over to the hecklers. Here is what happened next in the words of Fr. Bryce Sibley:

> They greeted St. Louis, who was a massive man, with a few derisive yet humorous comments. St. Louis, however, responded with his fists. He struck each of the men, knocking them unconscious. Then just as Our Lord drove the moneychangers out of the temple, St. Louis began tearing up the café, overturning tables, throwing chairs, smashing glasses and breaking bottles. He then walked out of the café, over the bodies of the drunken

hoodlums, and back up the street. Needless to say, he never had a problem with disruptive behavior during his homilies for the rest of his stay in that town.

Louis' fiery temper reminds us of Three Spirit's Livener Fierce Tonic.

Fierce Tonic

Makes 1 drink

- 2 oz. Three Spirit's Livener
- 4 oz. kombucha, lemonade, or sparkling water
- 1 oz. pink grapefruit juice
- soda water
- 1 orange twist, garnish
- 1 olive, garnish

Pour first 3 liquid ingredients into a large wine glass with ice and top with soda water. Stir gently and garnish with orange twist and olive.

SAINT ADJUTOR, APRIL 30

Adjutor or Ayoutre (d. 1131) was a noble Norman who fought with distinction in the Crusades for sixteen years before being captured and imprisoned in Jerusalem. He was miraculously freed by St. Mary Magdalen and St. Bernard of Tiron and returned home to become a monk. Adjutor is invoked against drowning and is the patron saint of boaters because one day he heard of a whirlpool in the River Seine that was claiming the lives of many boatmen. Rushing to the scene, he made the sign of the cross over the whirlpool and sprinkled it with holy water, making it instantly disappear.

We figure that the following cocktail is apt.

LAST CALL

At your next pool party or yacht christening make the following toast: "May the prayers of Saint Adjutor keep us afloat."

Whatever Floats Your Boat

Makes 1 drink

3/4 oz. honey syrup (1:1 ratio)
1/2 oz. fresh lemon juice
1 1/2 oz. Ghia Berry Apéritif
4 cucumber slices
1 pinch fennel pollen, garnish

Muddle 3 cucumber slices in a shaker. Add honey syrup, lemon juice, and ice and shake 40 times. Strain into an old-fashioned glass over a large ice cube. Float the Ghia Berry Apéritif and garnish with a cucumber slice floating on top and fennel pollen on the cucumber.

CHAPTER FIVE

May

SAINTS

SAINT JOSEPH THE WORKER, MAY 1

Just as the early Church co-opted various pagan festivals and converted them to good use, so too in 1955 did Pope Pius XII co-opt the neopagan Communist holiday of May Day or International Workers Day by instituting the Feast of St. Joseph the Worker. Well, he almost did: Italians jokingly refer to the day as *San Giuseppe Communista*. At any rate, St. Joseph certainly was a model worker: although he was from the royal house of David, he did not hesitate to have a blue-collar job in order to provide for the Holy Family.

A Gimlet would be an appropriate mixed drink for the occasion, since this famous cocktail is named after an auger-like hand tool most likely used by St. Joseph.

Basil Gimlet

Makes 1 drink

- 1½ oz. Lyre's Dry London Spirit
- 2 tsp. premium elderflower cordial
- ⅔ oz. mint tea syrup
- 2 tsp. fresh lime juice
- 2–3 drops peach bitters
- 6–8 fresh basil leaves

Put all ingredients except one basil leaf in a shaker with ice and shake hard 40 times. Strain into a champagne coupe glass and float remaining basil leaf on top.

Note: To make mint tea syrup, combine equal parts sugar and very strong mint tea in a saucepan over low to medium heat until sugar is dissolved. Let cool.

Gimlet

Makes 1 drink

- 2 oz. Free Spirits' The Spirit of Gin, chilled
- ¾ oz. simple syrup
- 1 lime wedge, garnish

Pour Spirit of Gin and simple syrup into a shaker with ice and shake briefly. Strain into a chilled coupe glass and garnish with lime wedge.

Fresher Optimist Gimlet

Makes 1 drink

2 oz. Optimist Fresh
½ oz. fresh lime juice
¼ oz. fresh lemon juice
1 handful arugula
½ oz. apricot jam
½ oz. jalapeño syrup

Muddle most of the arugula in a shaker, then add ice and all other ingredients. Shake 40 times and strain into an old-fashioned glass with 1 large ice cube. Garnish with remaining arugula.

SAINT MONICA, MAY 4 (AUGUST 27)

Monica (322–387), in the words of an old country Western song, was a good-hearted woman in love with a good-timin' man. Her husband Patricius had the hottest temper of any man in the village, was unfaithful to her, and exercised poor judgment as a parent: when he noticed that his son St. Augustine had entered puberty, he started bragging about all the illegitimate children his boy would soon be siring (what is Latin for creeeeepy?). Through it all, Monica gave quiet but firm witness to Christ, at last winning over her husband to the Faith. And she did the same for her son Augustine as well, praying for him ceaselessly after he became a heretic and a lecher until he finally converted. No wonder that St. Monica is the patron saint of difficult marriages and disappointing children.

There is also a story about St. Monica and drinking. When she was a little girl, Monica liked to sneak sips of wine from the cellar as she was pouring it out of the cask for the family until a servant taunted her by calling her a "wine-bibber." Monica was stunned by the rebuke and realized that she had developed a bad habit, which she instantly broke. As an adult, Augustine says, his mother's "soul was not a slave to winedrinking, nor had she any love of wine to provoke her to hatred of the truth." For this reason she has become a patroness of alcoholics even though she was not a teetotaler: she and her husband even owned a vineyard. Monica actually sounds like an ideal patron saint of the "soberish" movement.

She is, at any rate, a patroness of our With the Saints series, since our first book, *Drinking with the Saints*, came out on her feast day in 2015. Nonalcoholic wine is an obvious way to honor this holy, soberish, wine-bibber. We are going to go with a sparkling nonalcoholic wine because of its joyful associations, and Saint Monica's grief certainly gave way to great joy. **Sovi** has a delicious nonalcoholic **sparkling rosé** that comes in a can, but do not let that deter you; after all, it avoids waste.

LAST CALL

Your homework assignment is to read book nine of the *Confessions*, where Augustine describes his mother's life and death; be sure to have a box of Kleenex on hand. Then, make a toast in honor of today's saint: "To St. Monica: may she help us wine-bibbers drink soberly."

SAINT STANISLAUS, MAY 7 (APRIL 11)

Stanislaus (1030-1079) was born in Szczepanów, Poland, and earned a reputation as archdeacon to the bishop of Kraków for his eloquence, holy example, and ability to convert penitents. He became Bishop of Kraków in 1072 and eventually excommunicated King Boleslaus II the Bold over an unknown controversy. The king, in return, ordered Stanislaus executed without trial. When his soldiers refused to touch the holy bishop, the king killed Stanislaus himself while the saint was celebrating Mass. Poland was outraged, and Boleslaus the Bold found himself dethroned for his bold and wicked act, spending the rest of his life as a penitent in a Benedictine abbey.

Fittingly, Stanislaus' name means "becoming glorious," which is exactly what a martyr becomes. And since Stanislaus was martyred in the morning (since Masses were celebrated before twelve noon), a Morning Glory mocktail is the perfect choice.

Morning Glory

Makes 1 drink

- 1 oz. fresh lemon juice
- 1 egg white
- 1 tbsp. cane sugar
- 1 oz. heavy cream, well-chilled
- ⅛ tsp. orange blossom water
- 4–5 orange juice ice cubes (to make, put pulp-free o.j. in an ice-cube tray and freeze)
- 1 can Blood Orange HOPWTR, well-chilled

Combine lemon juice, egg white, sugar, cream, and orange blossom water in a shaker and dry shake (no ice) 40 times. Add about 4 orange juice ice cubes, then shake again until the ice stops rattling in the tin and the drink is frothy and very creamy (about 3 minutes; feel free to take an occasional break). Strain into a highball glass and fill nearly to the top. Place the drink in a freezer to set and harden slightly. Temperatures will vary but check it at about 7–10 minutes. As it hardens into a meringue, it will rise when the water is poured on top. Remove the drink from the freezer. Slowly pour Blood Orange HOPWTR to top. Serve with a straw.

LAST CALL

St. Stanislaus joins the ranks of John the Baptist, Thomas Becket, Thomas More, and others for their holy opposition to unjust regimes or rulers. Take the Rabbi's prayer about the czar in *Fiddler on the Roof* and adapt it to a toast: "Through the intercession of St. Stanislaus, may the Lord keep bad leaders as far away from us as possible."

SAINT DAMIEN DE VEUSTER, MAY 10/APRIL 15

Father Damien of Molokai (1840–1889) was a "martyr of charity" who succumbed to leprosy after sixteen years of caring for the spiritual and temporal needs of lepers on the state-quarantined island of Molokai in Hawaii. The lepers had been forced there by the government of what was then the

Kingdom of Hawaii (under British influence), but there was no one there to assist the lepers. When the local bishop received a desperate plea for a priest, he asked his priests for a volunteer. Three others besides Damien courageously accepted, and the bishop chose Damien. Damien explained that he did not fear death because as a member of the Congregation of the Sacred Hearts of Jesus and Mary he was already dead to the world, a funeral pall having been placed over him during his ordination to the priesthood.

Tough as nails, this son of Belgium built a chapel on the island with his own hands, instituted order and agriculture, and administered tender mercy to the suffering and dying despite the utterly deplorable things he saw, touched, and smelled—which, if we relayed here, would spoil your appetite for a drink. Damien's feast day is May 10 on the universal calendar and April 15 in the state of Hawaii.

Like St. Damien, pineapple is not native to Hawaii, but like the saint, it has become a symbol of these islands. Sentia's GABA Gold can be used in a mocktail with pineapple juice called "Golden Tropics." A second option is a phony Mai Tai, a cocktail long tied to Hawaii's tiki culture, and a third is the Missionary, a mocktail that calls to mind the tropical flavors that Christian missionaries first encountered on these islands.

Golden Tropics

Makes 1 drink

- 1½ oz. GABA Gold
- 1½ oz. pineapple juice
- ¾ oz. passion fruit syrup
- ¾ oz. fresh orange juice
- ½ oz. fresh lime juice
- 2 dashes grapefruit bitters, optional

Pour all ingredients into a shaker with ice and shake 40 times. Strain into a cocktail glass.

Lyre's Mai Tai

Makes 1 drink

1 oz. Lyre's Dark Cane Spirit
1 oz. Lyre's White Cane Spirit
1 oz. Lyre's Orange Sec
1 oz. fresh lime juice
¼ oz. orgeat syrup
¼ oz. simple syrup
1 lime wedge, garnish
1 mint sprig, garnish

Pour all liquid ingredients into a shaker with ice and shake 40 times. Strain into a highball glass with ice and garnish with lime wedge and mint sprig.

Social Strawberry Mai Tai

Makes 1 drink

1½ oz. Three Spirit's Social
½ oz. orgeat syrup
½ oz. fresh orange juice
½ oz. fresh lime juice
1–2 large strawberries, hulled and quartered
1 dried pineapple slice, garnish
1 fresh mint sprig, garnish

Pour liquid ingredients and strawberries into a shaker with ice and shake hard 40 times. Strain into a highball glass with ice and garnish with pineapple and mint.

Missionary

Makes 1 drink

2 oz. pineapple juice
1 oz. simple syrup
1 oz. sour mix
1 pineapple wedge, garnish
1 Toschi Amarena cherry, garnish

Pour all ingredients into a shaker with ice and shake 40 times. Strain into a highball glass with ice and garnish with pineapple and cherry.

LAST CALL

A good reading companion for your drink on this day is John Farrow's biography of St. Damien called *Damien the Leper: A Life of Magnificent Courage, Devotion, and Sacrifice*. Farrow, the father of actress Mia Farrow, was a film director who had heard of Fr. Damien while working on location in the South Seas and resolved to write his life's story.

OUR LADY OF FATIMA, MAY 13

Between May 13 and October 13, 1917, Our Lady appeared six times to three shepherd children. During these apparitions the Blessed Virgin told them three secrets. The first was a terrifying glimpse of Hell. The second was a call to spread devotion to the Immaculate Heart of Mary, to have the Pope consecrate Russia to her Immaculate Heart, and to have Communion of reparation on First Saturdays (failing that, Our Lady predicted the onslaught of World War II and the spread of Soviet communism). The third secret involved a "bishop dressed in white" felled by his enemies. Pope St. John Paul II interpreted the attempt on his life in St. Peter's Square on May 13, 1981 (note the date) as the fulfillment of this secret, and he credited his recovery to Our Lady of Fatima. In gratitude, he ordered that the assassin's bullet which was removed from his body be placed in the tiara of the statue of Our Lady of Fatima.

To commemorate the first secret, try this variation of a virgin Blood Mary:

Inferno

Makes 1 drink

salt
8 oz. tomato juice
2 tsp. fresh lemon juice
1 tsp. fresh lime juice
2–3 dashes hot pepper sauce
½ tsp. Worcestershire sauce
½ tsp. prepared horseradish
1 dash freshly ground black pepper
1 lemon or lime wedge, garnish

Rim a highball or old-fashioned glass by rubbing lemon or lime wedge along the edge and dipping it in salt. Fill with ice. Add all ingredients except wedge to a shaker with ice and shake vigorously 40 times. Strain into glass and garnish with wedge. (You can also get creative with garnishes of celery, olives, feta cheese, and even bacon. It's Hell, after all.)

LAST CALL

The third secret remains a hot topic: Controversy surrounds whether the Vatican revealed its full content or is holding back, whether the Pope actually consecrated Russia to the Immaculate Heart of Mary like he was supposed to, etc. If you want to catch a glimpse of the horrors of the End Times, invite a few Catholics on different sides of the issue over tonight and let them go at it. Even without alcoholic lubrication, it should prove memorable.

SAINT PEREGRINE, MAY 15

Not to be confused with St. Peregrine Laziosi (the patron saint of cancer patients), St. Peregrine of Auxerre was a third-century bishop and martyr who was sent by the Pope to evangelize parts of Gaul. He was martyred, along with his companions, when he interrupted the dedication of a new temple to Jupiter and implored the people to abandon their idols.

"San Pellegrino" is Italian for St. Peregrine, and the town of San Pellegrino Terme is the home of S. Pellegrino mineral water, which has been bottled by the San Pellegrino Company (now owned by Nestlé) since 1899. Sanpellegrino Aranciata Rossa is made from hand-picked blood oranges, a perfect tribute to our martyred saint.

Rossa Fizz

Makes 1 drink

- 1 can Sanpellegrino Aranciata Rossa
- 2 orange slices or wedges, divided
- 2 tsp. Muscovado sugar (or plain sugar)
- 1 splash soda water
- 1 rosemary sprig, garnish

In an old-fashioned with a sturdy bottom (which is called a tunc, by the way), gently muddle 1 orange slice and sugar and add 1 splash of soda water. Add ice and top with Sanpellegrino Aranciata Rossa. Garnish with the remaining orange slice and rosemary.

SAINT DUNSTAN, MAY 19

Dunstan (909–988) was an Archbishop of Canterbury whose life was dedicated to resurrecting and reforming Church and court life in England after the devastation of the Viking invasions. St. Dunstan's courageous reproach of King Edgar was so powerful that the king broke down crying and begged him to assign a suitable penance. When the holy bishop prescribed a seven-year sentence of almsgiving, fasting twice a week, and not wearing a crown, the king gladly accepted.

In the popular imagination, this English saint is remembered for his legendary cunning in outwitting the devil. On one occasion, when Dunstan was working as a smith making church bells, Old Nick appeared to him in all his ugly savagery. Rather than cower, Dunstan took a pair of red-hot pincers and grabbed the fiend by the nose. On another occasion, Satan visited Dunstan's workshop and asked him to shoe his cloven feet. The quick-thinking Dunstan told him that he would have to first bind him to the wall. The saint then made the shoeing process so painful that the devil begged him for mercy, which Dunstan granted on condition that the Evil One never enter a house where a horseshoe was placed above the door. From this yarn arises the superstition of horseshoes having good luck.

"I'm your huckleberry" was a nineteenth-century way of saying that you are just the right person for a given role. Apparently, Dunstan is our huckleberry for keeping the Devil at bay. Here is a mocktail, then, in his honor.

Huckleberry Diablo

Makes 1 drink

- 2½ oz. Free Spirit's The Spirit of Tequila
- ¼ oz. huckleberry syrup
- ½ oz. fresh lime juice
- 3 oz. ginger beer
- 1 lime wheel, garnish
- 1 dried chile, garnish

Pour all liquid ingredients (except the ginger beer) into a shaker with ice and shake 40 times. Strain into a highball glass with ice, top with ginger beer, and stir gently. Garnish with lime wheel and chile.

LAST CALL

Here's a nice little folk rhyme for the occasion:

St. Dunstan, as the story goes,
Once pull'd the devil by the nose
With red-hot tongs, which made him roar,
That he was heard three miles or more.

To which you can add by way of a toast: "Through the intercession of St. Dunstan, may we always be one step ahead of the devil."

SAINT RITA, MAY 22

Rita of Cascia (1386–1456) was a remarkable woman. As a girl she greatly desired to become a nun, but her parents married her off to a cruel and ill-tempered man at the age of twelve. Despite this, Rita was a model wife and mother for eighteen years. When her husband was murdered, her twin sons vowed revenge. Unable to dissuade them, Rita prayed that God take their lives rather than allow them to commit a mortal sin. Both sons died a year later, fully reconciled to God and the Church.

Rita then wished to enter the convent, and after numerous difficulties finally prevailed. One day as she was meditating on a crucifix, she received a wound on her forehead as though a thorn from the Crown of Thorns had pierced her flesh. This stigmata remained with her until her death, and it was not only very painful but repulsive to some of her fellow nuns, as the wound festered and developed worms. St. Rita took all of this in stride. She light-heartedly referred to the worms as her "angels," since they aided in her sanctification, and she spent the last fifteen years of her life in her cell to avoid giving offense to others. Her incorrupt body (with the wound still visible) may be seen in a glass reliquary in the Basilica of Cascia.

Tonight we allude to Rita's name with a mocktail marga-rita. And to commemorate Rita's "angels," rim the glass with *sal con gusano* (a.k.a. agave worm salt), a salt made from the worm (larva) found in bottles of mezcal.

Spirited Rita's Spiritless Margarita

Makes 1 drink

1 can Spiritless Margarita Pour Over
1 lime wedge, garnish
sal con gusano

Rim a margarita glass by rubbing the edge with lime wedge and dipping it in sal con gusano. Fill with ice. Pour can of Spiritless Margarita Pour Over into glass and garnish with lime wedge.

SAINT PHILIP NERI, MAY 26

Even as a layman, Philip of Neri (1515–1595) was a force for the good as he visited the rough quarters of Rome and struck up conversations with people that would change their lives. After being ordained a priest, he founded the Congregation of the Oratory (the "Oratorians"). St. Philip could prophesy, read others' hearts, and see heavenly spirits. He also had a brilliant and wry sense of humor, which he combined with psychologically astute spiritual instruction. When a vain and macho nobleman, wishing to test his own powers of endurance, asked for the saint's permission to wear a hair-shirt, Philip said yes but on one condition: he had to wear it on the *outside* of his clothing.

But St. Philip's greatest attribute was his burning love of God, and we mean that literally. Once during prayer, a mystical ball of fire entered his mouth and lodged in his chest, causing his heart to be so aflame with divine fervor that the saint had to rip open his clothes and cool himself on the stone floor. After his death, it was discovered that two of his ribs were dislodged over his heart, which had expanded with the love of God. On different occasions, St. Philip's heart would become so filled with joy and consolation that he would roll on the ground and cry out, "No more, my Lord! No more!"

We can think of no more social saint than Philip Neri. Three Spirit's Summer Cup (an homage to Pimm's Cup) contains their Social Elixir, a dark herbal elixir that is billed as the ultimate social companion and mood elevator.

Nor can we think of a better patron of pedestrians and boulevardiers (a person who frequents boulevards) than St. Philip, since he loved to haunt the city streets and convert souls. The Boulevardier cocktail is essentially a Negroni with whiskey instead of gin; here are some nonalcoholic options.

St. Philip's Summer Cup

Makes 1 drink

2 oz. Social Elixir
2 tsp. fresh lemon juice
citrus soda (regular soda will do)

Pour Social Elixir and lemon juice into an old-fashioned glass with ice, top with soda, and stir.

Lyre's Boulevardier

Makes 1 drink

1 oz. Lyre's American Malt
1 oz. Lyre's Apéritif Rosso
1 oz. Lyre's Italian Orange
1 orange slice, garnish

Pour liquid ingredients into an old-fashioned glass with ice and stir briefly. Garnish with orange slice.

Free Spirits' Boulevardier

Makes 1 drink

1½ oz. The Spirit of Bourbon
1½ oz. The Spirit of Milano
1½ oz. The Spirit of Vermouth Rosso
1 orange twist, garnish
1 Toschi Amarena cherry, garnish

Pour liquid ingredients into an old-fashioned glass with 1 large ice cube and stir briefly. Garnish with orange and cherry.

LAST CALL

St. Philip considered cheer to be more authentically Christian than melancholy, and he lived by this conviction. The great German author Goethe was even able to devote an entire book to St. Philip Neri's *joie de vivre* which he entitled *The Humorous Saint*. Tonight (and every night), let good cheer and Christian joy animate your time with friends and family. Use these words of St. Philip to make a toast: "A joyful heart is more easily made perfect than a downcast one."

SAINT GERMANUS, MAY 28

Germanus (496–576) was a Benedictine monk who was almost generous to a fault. When he became abbot of Saint-Symphorien at the age of thirty-four, he gave away so many alms that his monks feared he was bankrupting them and rebelled. In the year 555, Germanus was unanimously chosen to be the Bishop of Paris. He proved to be an excellent shepherd: he made the king more devoutly Christian, stamped out pagan practices, curbed excesses at festivals, and promoted peace, all the while continuing to live an austere and ascetical life. A church that he built was eventually named after him, St. Germain-des-Prés. The title was also applied to the neighborhood in Paris where the church still stands.

St. Germain is a French liqueur made from elderflowers harvested in the French Alps, and in honor of this patronage, here is a Germanus Light using elderflower syrup as well as a couple of other tasty recipes.

Germanus Light

Makes 1 drink

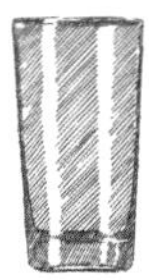

1 oz. elderflower syrup
½ oz. fresh lemon juice
4–6 oz. sparkling water

Pour syrup and lemon juice in a shaker with ice and shake 40 times. Strain into a cocktail glass and top with sparkling water.

Garden & Elderflower Tonic

Makes 1 drink

2 oz. Seedlip Garden 108
4 oz. elderflower tonic
1 cucumber ribbon, garnish

Pour Seedlip Garden and tonic into a highball with ice and stir gently. Garnish with cucumber.

Meyer Lemon Ginger Gin Drop

Makes 1 drink

3 oz. Free Spirits' The Spirit of Gin
1½ oz. elderflower syrup
½ oz. Meyer lemon juice
3–4 slices fresh peeled ginger
1 Meyer lemon peel, garnish

Muddle ginger in a shaker, then add ice and all liquid ingredients. Shake 40 times and strain into a champagne coupe glass. Garnish with lemon peel.

SAINT JOAN OF ARC, MAY 30

Joan (1412–1431), the "Maid of Orléans," was a peasant from eastern France who led the French army in several important victories against the English.

At the age of thirteen she had a vision of Sts. Michael, Catherine of Alexandria, and Margaret of Antioch in which she was instructed to drive out the English and bring Charles VII to Reims for his coronation. Voices from above persisted, and she gradually learned that she was being called to lead the French army. She was also guided by these voices to find an ancient sword buried behind the altar of a chapel.

After successfully completing her military mission, St. Joan was captured by the Burgundians, betrayed to the English, put on trial for heresy, and burned at the stake at the age of nineteen. Twenty-five years later, however, Pope Calixtus III declared her innocent of the charges. She was canonized in 1920 and made one of the patron saints of France.

The French 75 is a swank cocktail developed during WWI that was said to have the kick of the powerful French 75 mm field gun. True, the latter was not St. Joan's weapon of choice, but French soldiers did carry her image in the trenches of the Great War, and we're confident some of those images found their way onto a French 75.

Zero Proof French 75

Makes 1 drink

1½ oz. nonalcoholic gin
½ oz. fresh lemon juice
2 tsp. simple syrup
5 oz. nonalcoholic champagne (e.g., Freixenet Nonalcoholic Sparkling Wine)
1 lemon twist, Toschi Amarena cherry, orange slice, optional garnishes

Pour gin, lemon juice, and simple syrup into a shaker filled with ice and shake 40 times. Strain into a champagne flute or champagne tulip and top with champagne. Garnish with lemon and/or cherry and orange slice.

MAY

Lyre's French 75

Makes 1 drink

1 oz. Lyre's Dry London Spirit
¾ oz. fresh lemon juice
½ oz. simple syrup
2 oz. Lyre's Classico (a homage to sparkling wine)
1 lemon twist, garnish

Pour Dry London Spirit, lemon juice, and simple syrup into a shaker with ice and shake 40 times. Strain into a champagne flute or champagne coupe glass and top with Classico. Garnish with lemon twist.

LAST CALL

Mark Twain considered his best work to be the *Personal Recollections of Joan of Arc.* The novel betrays the anti-clerical bias of a nineteenth-century American liberal, but it is still a riveting read. After you are done, add a toast to the liberty of the Church against the encroachments of nationalist or secular politicking.

CHAPTER SIX

June

SAINTS

SAINT ELMO, JUNE 2

If the name Elmo triggers images of a cloying Muppet, we are happy to enrich your mind with a manlier set of associations. St. Elmo or Erasmus was an Italian bishop martyred around 303 A.D. According to legend, the saint was preaching when lightning suddenly struck the ground next to him; unfazed, he continued his sermon, much to the astonishment of his audience. Elmo's fearlessness became an inspiration for sailors, who soon began to invoke his name when a thunderstorm threatened their ship. They took the harmless corona discharge around the masts of their vessels as an indication that God had heard their prayers. Today that static discharge is known as St. Elmo's Fire. The courageous saint was martyred by being disemboweled with a windlass.

Not far from St. Elmo's Campania is the region of Calabria, which grows the special lemons that are in **St. Agrestis'** cans of **Phony Limone Negroni**. This nonalcoholic take on limoncello is tart but refreshing and ideal for summer.

Saint Elmo was nowhere near the coast of Cornwall, England, but with his connection to the sea, he would appreciate Pentire's efforts to capture the flavors of the Cornish coast with native plants in their alcohol-free spirit **Seaward**.

Similarly, Elderleaf Marine has been designed to capture marine flavors such as tropical sea buckthorn. It too works well in a G&T.

Seaward and Tonic

Makes 1 drink

2 oz. Pentire Seaward
5 oz. tonic water
1 grapefruit wedge, garnish

Pour Pentire Seaward into a highball glass with ice, top with tonic water, and stir gently. Garnish with grapefruit wedge.

Elderleaf's G&T

Makes 1 drink

1 oz. Elderleaf Marine
3 oz. tonic water
2 lime slices, garnish

Pour Elderleaf and tonic into a wine glass with ice and stir gently. Put 1 lime slice in the drink and garnish the rim with the other.

LAST CALL

A traditional sailor's toast is "Fair winds and following seas," which expresses the wish that your ship will have good winds and favorable waves. Using this nautically-rich toast will help dispel the suspicion that you are a pathetic landlubber, and ending it with "through the intercession of St. Elmo" will dupe others into thinking that you are pious.

SAINT NORBERT, JUNE 6

Norbert of Xanten (1080–1134) was a cleric at the court of the Archbishop of Cologne who had succumbed to worldliness when a near-death experience in a storm prompted him to change his ways. He sold his goods and eventually founded a religious community of canons regular called the Order of Premonstratensians, better known as the Norbertines. Later St. Norbert was appointed Archbishop of Magdeburg, which at the time was one of the outposts of Christendom.

One of St. Norbert's symbols in Christian art is a spider. As the story has it, he was celebrating Mass when he noticed a venomous spider crawl into the Precious Blood but drank It anyway rather than pour It out, even though he did not have to. At least according to a later set of rules, he could have removed the spider, burned it after the Mass, and thrown the ashes into the sacrarium.

It is difficult not to be inspired by St. Norbert's heroic virtue. Our mocktail combines the red of the blood, the legend of the spider, and the possible bitterness of consuming said spider ("amaro" is Italian for bitter).

Norbert and the Spider

Makes 1 drink

- 1 bottle St. Agrestis Amaro Falso
- 1 lemon wheel, garnish
- 1 plastic black spider ring, garnish

Pour Amaro Falso into an old-fashioned glass with ice. Garnish with lemon wheel and affix spider to the rim of the glass.

Note: Other options for the garnish include novelty ice cubes with a fake spider in them and spider-shaped candy (gummies or sprinkles).

SAINT MARGARET OF SCOTLAND, JUNE 10 (NOVEMBER 16)

Margaret (1045–1093) was an English princess and the great niece of St. Edward the Confessor. After her land had been overrun by invaders, she fled to the court of King Malcolm III of Scotland, who soon fell in love with her. St. Margaret bore him eight children and was an exemplary wife and mother. She had a civilizing effect on her rough husband—who is accurately portrayed by Shakespeare as the man who killed the infamous MacBeth—and what she did for him, she did for the country. She embroidered priests' vestments herself, and it is said that she is the one who introduced tartans to Scotland in an effort to cheer the place up.

According to one report, it was the law at St. Margaret's table "that none should drink after dinner who did not wait the giving of thanks. Hence the origin of the phrase known throughout Scotland of the Grace Cup." And, we might add, Margaret is also said to have spread the prayer after meals, "We give Thee thanks, Almighty God, for all Thy benefits, Who livest and reignest forever and ever. Amen."

For this pearl of great price ("Margaret" means pearl, by the way), enjoy the **margaritas** from another St. Margaret (see February 22). Or, enjoy a glass of **Feragaia**, Scotland's first alcohol-free scotch-like spirit made from fourteen botanicals including seaweed, bay leaf, and chamomile. It is great on the rocks, with a tonic, or with **Fever Tree's** ginger beer (simply mix to taste).

SAINT BASIL THE GREAT, JUNE 14 (JANUARY 2)

Born in Caesarea, Cappadocia, Basil the Great (ca. 329–379) came from a remarkable family. His grandfather was a martyred saint, and he had four siblings recognized as saints: Gregory of Nyssa, Macrina the Younger, Naucratius, and Peter of Sebaste. He was also a lifelong friend of St. Gregory of Nazianzus, who along with Basil and St. John Chrysostom are honored in the Eastern churches as the Three Holy Hierarchs.

As a monk, St. Basil wrote the *Rule of St. Basil*, which the monasteries of the East still follow, and as Bishop of Caesarea, despite severe health problems, he stood firm against both the Arian heresy and imperial bullying. When a prefect of the Emperor, an Arian sympathizer, threatened to tear out Basil's liver if he did not comply, Basil smiled and said, "Good. My liver's been giving me trouble for years." When the astonished prefect, who was accustomed to Arian bootlickers, said that no one had ever talked to him like that before, Basil replied, "Perhaps you've never talked to a *Christian* bishop before."

Basil and his monks lived an ascetical vegetarian life. "Our daintiest meal," he wrote to St. Gregory of Nazianzus, are herbs and "vegetables with coarsest bread, and vapid wine." Curious Elixir's Curious No. 4 has been described as "a Sicilian Blood Orange Green Mandarin Spritz," and it also contains "holy basil to reduce stress." Our abstemious and holy Basil would have liked that. You can also continue with the basil theme with a Peach Basil Cooler featuring Sentia's fragrant GABA Gold.

Basil's Curious No. 4

Makes 2 drinks

1 bottle Curious No. 4, chilled
2 orange slices, garnish

Pour Curious No. 4 into 2 wine glasses (to honor Basil's diet of "vapid wine") and garnish with orange.

Peach Basil Cooler

Makes 1 drink

¾ oz. GABA Gold
¾ oz. peach puree
½ oz. fresh lime juice
½ oz. agave nectar
4–5 fresh basil leaves
elderflower tonic water
1 peach slice, garnish

Muddle basil leaves in a shaker, then add ice, GABA Gold, peach puree, lime juice, and agave nectar. Shake 40 times and strain into an old-fashioned glass with ice. Top with elderflower tonic and garnish with peach.

SAINT VITUS, JUNE 15

The little that is known of Vitus (Guy in French and Guido in Italian) has been supplemented by holy lore. A native of Sicily in the third century, he is said to have been martyred at the age of twelve by being boiled in a cauldron of oil. Prior to that, Angels were seen dancing with him in prison. Consequently, Vitus is a patron saint of dancers (and by extension, anyone involved in show business, such as comedians and actors). And as one of the Fourteen Holy Helpers, he is invoked against epilepsy and other nervous disorders such as "St. Vitus' Dance" (Sydenham's chorea). Vitus was also known for his early rising, and so he is also the patron saint of those who have difficulty getting up in the morning—a good saint to know for those who have overused our previous cocktail books.

Do you remember the "dancing raisins" science experiment as a kid, when you placed raisins in a glass filled with soda water? The point was to demonstrate the principle of buoyancy and the transfer of energy. The raisins sink to the bottom because they are denser than the surrounding liquid, but when carbon dioxide bubbles from the soda water attach themselves to a raisin, the raisin floats up to the surface and, once the bubbles pop, sinks back down again. Seems safe enough, but one website that promotes fun learning for kids warns that "This science experiment should be done with adult supervision at all times." Really? What, pray tell, is the danger here—that some soda water may be spilled? No worries, dear website: some soda water will get that out.

Anyway, if you are brave enough to take the risk, we recommend our own dancing raisins drink in honor of today's saint. We use tonic water along with sparkling because tonic water contains quinine, and quinine glows in the presence of black light (a nice symbol for the luminous Angels dancing with St. Vitus, or perhaps of the lightning from which he protects us). The raisins, of course, are the Angels dancing (we suggest nine for the nine orders of celestial spirits), and since lavender is a traditional aid to better sleep, we add lavender simple syrup for this patron of aspiring early birds. Finally, we add three dashes of angostura bitters for the blood of martyrdom.

St. Vitus' Angel Dance

Makes 1 drink

½ oz. fresh lime juice
½ oz. lavender simple syrup
3 oz. tonic water (the colder the better; if ice is added, the raisins can't dance to the top)
3 oz. sparkling water (also cold)
3 dashes angostura bitters, optional
9 individual raisins (be sure they are not clustered together or they will not dance with you—just like a group of girls at a high school dance)

Pour lime juice, simple syrup, tonic water, and soda water into a highball with no ice and stir gently. Top with angostura bitters (optional). Drop the raisins into the glass and enjoy the show.

Note: To make lavender simple syrup, heat 1 cup water, 1 cup sugar, and 1 tablespoon fresh lavender blossoms in a saucepan over medium heat until the sugar dissolves. Strain into a sterilized jar and let cool.

LAST CALL

A toast: "May St. Vitus help us get up refreshed and early, and may we dance only for joy and not from disease."

SAINT JOHN FRANCIS REGIS, JUNE 16

John Francis Regis (1597–1640) came from a privileged French background, but he gave it all up to become a Jesuit priest whose passion was helping the poor, orphans, and at-risk women. In addition to founding a confraternity that helped the wealthy donate to the less fortunate, he founded hostels for prostitutes to train them as lacemakers. St. Regis had a simple and direct style of preaching that connected with the uneducated and resulted in numerous conversions.

Talk about ironic naming. The patron saint of common folks like medical social workers, lacemakers, and illegitimate children has lent his name to a chain of luxury resort hotels thanks to an accident of history. John Jacob Astor IV built the posh St. Regis Hotel in

1904 as a sister property of the Waldorf-Astoria and named it after the Upper St. Regis Lake in the Adirondack mountains, the summer playground of America's nineteenth- and early twentieth-century elite. Whatever the logic, it is a good opportunity to enjoy a bottle of **St. Regis Non-Alcoholic Shiraz Rosé**, a light, smooth blend lovely on its own or with your favorite cheeses.

SAINT EPHREM, JUNE 18 (JUNE 9)

Ephrem the Syrian (306–373) was a deacon, the greatest of the Syriac Church Fathers, and a Doctor of the Church. Also known as St. Ephrem of Edessa, his numerous hymns, poems, sermons, and biblical commentaries were so popular that for centuries later other authors wrote under his name.

Ephrem's magnificent hymns, of which more than four hundred still exist, earned him the sobriquet "Harp of the Holy Spirit." Many of these hymns were written to help his flock understand orthodox Christianity and reject its heretical impostors, and some of them are among the first in history to attest to the Christian belief in the total purity of the Blessed Virgin Mary, a belief undergirding the doctrine of the Immaculate Conception.

One of Ephrem's hymns, written in praise of virginity, has some choice words about the power of wine to lead a chaste maiden away from her virtue.

> Be afraid of Wine in that it disgraced Noah the Precious;
>
> He that had conquered the Deluge of water was himself conquered by a handful of wine;
>
> The Flood that was outside him did not overcome him, but the wine that was within him in silence did steal.
>
> If wine disgraced and cast down Noah, the head of families and tongues, forsooth, O lonely one, how it will conquer thee!

You heard the man: only nonalcoholic wine tonight! Let the Spirit (or local availability) move you to the right selection.

VENERABLE MATT TALBOT, JUNE 19

A man was on his way to Mass on Trinity Sunday, June 7, 1925 when he suddenly dropped dead on the streets of Dublin. Upon examining the body, doctors discovered to their astonishment chains and cords wrapped around his waist and limbs, a symbol of his total surrender and enslavement to Mary, the Mother of God. The mysterious man was Matt Talbot.

Matthew Talbot was born in Dublin to an alcoholic father who worked on the docks. At the age of thirteen, after he landed a job as a messenger for some liquor merchants, he became an alcoholic as well, and he stayed that way for fifteen years.

Matt was a dockworker like his father, and although he spent every dime on drink (and once pawned his boots for a pint), his bad habits did not interfere with his putting in a good day's work. His father tried to get him to stop drinking, going so far as to beat him and force him to change jobs. But it was when Matt had run out of money and his so-called friends snubbed him instead of buying him a drink that something changed. He came home that day early and sober, much to the surprise of his mother and sister, and said he was going to Take the Pledge for three months. That three months turned into forty-one years.

Matt had to change his routine to stay on the straight and narrow, avoiding certain companions after work and filling his life with prayer, Holy Communion, weekly confession, spiritual reading, fasting, and service. He encouraged others to quit drinking, and when he did go to a pub, he drank only mineral water. Venerable Matthew Talbot is now a popular patron saint for alcoholics.

Some of our favorite sparkling mineral waters include Mexico's **Topo Chico**, Italy's **S.Pellegrino**, France's **Perrier**, and Germany's **Gerolsteiner**

(Ireland has Ballygowan and Classic Mineral Water, but they do not export to the US). Try your favorite mineral water by itself or in one of these Ranch Water recipes:

Cut Above Ranch Water

Makes 1 drink

2 oz. Cut Above Agave Blanco
½ oz. fresh lime juice
6 oz. Topo Chico (or your favorite mineral water)
1 strawberry, lime, or summer fruit, garnish

Pour all liquid ingredients into a highball glass with ice and stir. Garnish with summer fruit.

Seedlip Ranch Water

Makes 1 drink

2 oz. Seedlip Notas de Agave
¼ oz. fresh lime juice
4 oz. soda water
1 lime wedge, garnish

Pour Seedlip and lime juice into an old-fashioned glass with ice and top with soda water. Stir gently and garnish with lime wedge.

Spiritless Ranch Water

Makes 1 drink

12 oz. Topo Chico, chilled
2 oz. Spiritless Jalisco 55
½ oz. fresh lime juice
Tajín seasoning
1 lime wedge, garnish

Pour out (or better, drink) 2 ounces Topo Chico straight from the bottle. Add the tequila then lime juice to the Topo Chico bottle. Rub the mouth of the bottle with lime wedge and dust with Tajín.

LAST CALL

A toast: "Through the intercession of Ven. Matt Talbot, may our only enslavement be to Our Lord Jesus Christ and His Mother."

SAINT ALOYSIUS GONZAGA, JUNE 21

Nobody expected, or wanted, Aloysius Gonzaga (1568–1591) to become a priest. As the eldest son of a noble family, Aloysius was expected to learn the art of war and inherit his father's title and estate. Initially, it looked like things were going according to plan: the little boy loved going to military camp at the age of five. His father was thrilled to see him leading the march of a platoon of soldiers, though his mother was less than pleased with the new words he had picked up.

But eventually, Aloysius felt the call to be a priest, and worse, a Jesuit, for entering a religious order meant renouncing all claims to his family's inheritance, a move that had to be confirmed by the Emperor. Aloysius struggled in his new vocation because of poor health (probably brought on by his severe asceticism), but that did not stop him from joining his Jesuit brethren in helping the victims of a plague that broke out in 1591 in Rome. Although he confessed to his spiritual director St. Robert Bellarmine that he was repulsed by the sight of the plague victims, he never showed it, helping them tirelessly until he himself was infected. St. Aloysius died at the tender age of twenty-three and is now recognized as a patron saint of youth and students.

For this holy son of Italy during the dog days of summer, an Italian-style refreshment will hit the spot. **De Soi** makes a **Spritz Italiano**, a harmonious blend of sweet and bitter citrus, crisp white grape, and bold gentian root, complete with rich and relaxing adaptogens L-theanine, lion's mane, and reishi mushroom. Enjoy it on the rocks with a wheel of orange or lemon.

SAINT JOHN THE BAPTIST, JUNE 24

John the Baptist has the distinction of being the only other person besides Our Lady and Our Lord whose earthly birthday is a Church feast (his heavenly birthday, or martyrdom, is observed on August 29). This no doubt has something to do with the Baptist's miraculous conception, his unique role as the "Precursor of the Lord," and most of all, his uncommon holiness. According to an ancient tradition, St. John, like the prophet Jeremiah, was cleansed of original sin while still in the womb at the moment his mother St. Elizabeth met the Blessed Virgin (Luke 1:45).

And, of course, John is the Bible's most famous teetotaler. While he was still in the womb, Saint Gabriel predicted that he would taste neither wine nor strong drink (Luke 1:15). This restraint, combined with John's holiness and wild-man status, indicate that he took a vow of the Nazarite. During the duration of this vow, a "Nazarite" (*nazir* is the Hebrew word for consecrated or set apart) could not cut his hair, drink alcohol, or ingest anything from the grape, or touch corpses and graves. Most Nazarite vows were temporary, but three biblical figures made a lifelong vow: Samson, Samuel (see Judges 13:4–7; 1 Samuel 1:11), and John the Baptist.

John the Baptist is a patron saint of Puerto Rico, the national drink of which is the Piña Colada. Here are some options.

JUNE

Virgin Piña Colada

Makes 1 drink

1 cup frozen pineapple chunks
1/3 cup coconut cream
1/2 cup pineapple juice
1 pineapple wedge, garnish
1 Toschi Amarena cherry, garnish

Mix frozen pineapple chunks, coconut cream, and pineapple juice in a blender and blend at high speed until smooth. Pour into a Piña Colada glass or Poco Grande glass or Hurricane glass (or a highball) and garnish with pineapple wedge and cherry.

Lyre's Piña Colada

Makes 1 drink

2 1/2 oz. Lyre's White Cane Spirit
2 1/2 oz. fresh young coconut water
3/4 oz. simple syrup
6 fresh pineapple chunks
1 pineapple wedge, garnish
1 mint sprig, garnish

Muddle pineapple chunks in a shaker. Add liquid ingredients and ice and shake vigorously 40 times. Strain into a Piña Colada glass or Poco Grande glass or Hurricane glass (or a highball) and garnish with pineapple wedge and mint sprig.

Caleño's Piña Colada

Makes 1 drink

2 oz. Caleño Light & Zesty
1 1/2 oz. pineapple juice
1 1/2 oz. coconut cream
1/2 oz. fresh lime juice
1 pineapple wedge, garnish
1 pineapple leaf, garnish

Pour liquid ingredients into a shaker with ice and shake vigorously 40 times. Strain into a Piña Colada glass or Poco Grande glass or Hurricane glass (or a highball) with crushed ice and garnish with pineapple wedge and leaf.

Little Saints' Mushroom Piña

Makes 1 drink

1 cup fresh pineapple
3 oz. St. Ember
½ cup oat milk
1 pineapple wedge, garnish

Put all ingredients except pineapple wedge into a blender. Add ice and blend until smooth and creamy. Strain into a Piña Colada glass or Poco Grande glass or Hurricane glass (or a highball) with crushed ice and garnish with pineapple wedge.

LAST CALL

A toast to John the Baptist: "May he help keep our faith and our wits about us even if we lose our heads."

SAINT JOSEMARÍA ESCRIVÁ, JUNE 26

During the Spanish Civil War, Josemaría Escrivá de Balaguer (1902–1975) often had to hide from Republican troops with orders to kill priests. On one occasion militiamen apprehended a man whom they thought was Josemaría and hanged him outside the house of Josemaría's mother. But Father Josemaría survived, and so too did Opus Dei, the organization he had founded in 1928. Latin for the "Work of God," Opus Dei is a prelature of laypersons and clergy dedicated to the universal call to holiness and the sanctification of work. "The Work," as it is often called, is currently in sixty-six countries with over sixty thousand members from eighty different nationalities.

Folks in the Work refer to St. Josemaria Escriva as "our Father" or the "Founder," but the saint used to stress that it was God, not he, who founded Opus Dei. Alluding to a Spanish brandy named *Fundador* (Founder), he liked to joke, "the best Founder I know comes in a bottle."

JUNE

St. Josemaría Escrivá was renowned for his fidelity to the Magisterium and his obedience to the Church, but that does not mean he lacked a lighter side. Among his many charming qualities was his great fondness for donkeys. He liked the idea of the donkey as a faithful pack animal and as the beast of burden that carried Christ into Jerusalem. The humble monsignor even called himself a "mangy donkey" frequently, and he used the image of a donkey turning a waterwheel to teach how one can achieve holiness in the fulfillment of one's ordinary duties.

There aren't many drinks named after the donkey, but thanks to the Moscow Mule, there is more than one named after the donkey's half-brother. **Little Saints** has a canned **Ginger Mule** that is "a mood-lifting blend of reishi mushroom and aromatic terpenes." Or you can try the following.

Ginger London Mule

Makes 1 drink

1½ oz. Wilfred's Aperitif
3 oz. ginger beer
1 lime wedge, garnish
1 ginger slice, garnish

Pour Wilfred's into a highball glass with ice and top with ginger beer. Squeeze some of the juice from the lime wedge into the drink and stir. Garnish with lime wedge and ginger slice.

Seedlip Mule

Makes 1 drink

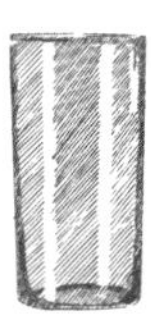

2 oz. Seedlip Spice 94
½ oz. ginger nectar
½ oz. fresh lime juice
4 oz. soda water
1 lime slice, garnish

Pour Seedlip, nectar, and lime juice into a highball glass with ice and top with soda water. Stir gently and garnish with lime slice.

TJ's Spiritless Kentucky Mule

Makes 1 drink

2 oz. Spiritless Kentucky 74
4–6 oz. ginger beer
1 squeeze lime
1 dehydrated lime, garnish

Pour all liquid ingredients into a highball glass with ice and garnish with lime.

Optimist's Smokey Mule

Makes 1 drink

1½ oz. Optimist Smokey
1 oz. fresh lemon juice
1 oz. passion fruit syrup
1–2 dashes Firewater tincture
4 slices cucumber, divided
2 oz. hibiscus ginger beer
1 pinch cayenne pepper
1 candied ginger, garnish

Muddle syrup in a shaker with 3 cucumber slices. Add Smokey, lemon juice, tincture, and ice and shake 40 times. Strain into an old-fashioned glass and top with ginger beer. Dust the top with cayenne pepper and garnish with candied ginger and remaining cucumber slice.

LAST CALL

The Founder viewed members of the Work as his children, and often he addressed them teasingly, "with the naturalness of a father and friend." Here is an example of his playfulness to one of his children down with an illness: "Dear Michael—may Jesus safeguard you for me. I called you a scoundrel in my last letter, but I didn't go far enough, you boozer. Here's to sherry!" Paraphrase this impish note thusly: "Here's to St. Josemaría Escrivá! And may Jesus safeguard us (current/former) boozers through his intercession."

SAINTS PETER AND PAUL, JUNE 29

The "twin" founders of the new Christian Rome, Peter and Paul are said to have been martyred on the same day in the Eternal City in A.D. 68. Paul was a Roman citizen who received the relatively humane execution of decapitation while Peter, a mere Galilean fisherman, was sentenced to be crucified. According to legend, Peter escaped jail and fled so quickly that a bandage around his leg fell off that was covering a sore caused by his chains (we suspect that this is the reason he is the patron of foot problems—that, or a fossilized footprint of the saint allegedly made during the same incident). After he cleared the walls of Rome, Peter saw Jesus Christ walking towards the city. "Where are you going, my Lord?" he asked. "To be crucified again," Jesus replied. Peter realized that he was called to martyrdom and returned to face it. Feeling unworthy to die like Our Lord, he asked to be crucified upside down (that last detail is historically accurate).

Christ gave Peter the keys to the kingdom. According to its co-founders Karishma and Tekla, KEY is a natural and "long-lasting Ketone Energy Drink that is pure and delicious" and that helps you get into ketosis. If Saint Peter had had KEY, he could have used it to power up on Pentecost morning while baptizing the multitude. (Then again, at $45 for a twelve-pack, the Apostle who said "Gold and silver have I none" might not have been able to afford it.) We can put our KEY, which comes in grapefruit peach, pineapple passion fruit, and ginger lime, in a highball on the rocks: the "rocks," of course, are for the rock that is Simon Peter. For a cocktail spear, use a bamboo pick with a knot at the end: the knot is a nod to Peter's Christ-given power to bind and loosen. On the other hand, if you want to honor St. Paul as well, use a cocktail sword, since his symbol is a sword. Bringing the portmanteau to a new low, we call this concoction a Petosis.

JUNE

Petosis

Makes 1 drink

- 12 oz. KEY
- 1 slice grapefruit, pineapple, or lime, depending on the flavor of KEY
- 1 knotted bamboo cocktail stick or cocktail sword spear

Pour KEY into a highball filled with ice and garnish with fruit speared by bamboo or sword spear.

In the same vein, we made a simple mocktail with stone fruit syrup in tribute to Peter as the rock of Christ's Church. For the full package, add one ounce of Ketohol Raw Concentrate by Hard Ketones (for more on Ketohol, see January 20).

Keys and Stones

Makes 1 drink

- 1 oz. Monin stone fruit syrup
- 1 oz. Ketohol Raw Concentrate, optional
- ½ oz. fresh lemon juice
- 4–6 oz. sparkling water

Pour everything but sparkling water into a shaker with ice and shake 40 times. Strain into a cocktail glass and top with sparkling water.

LAST CALL

A good toast can be made from the traditional Collect of the vigil of the feast: "May almighty God, who has made us solid on the rock of Apostolic faith, never allow us to be busted up by trouble."

CHAPTER SEVEN

July

SAINTS

JULY

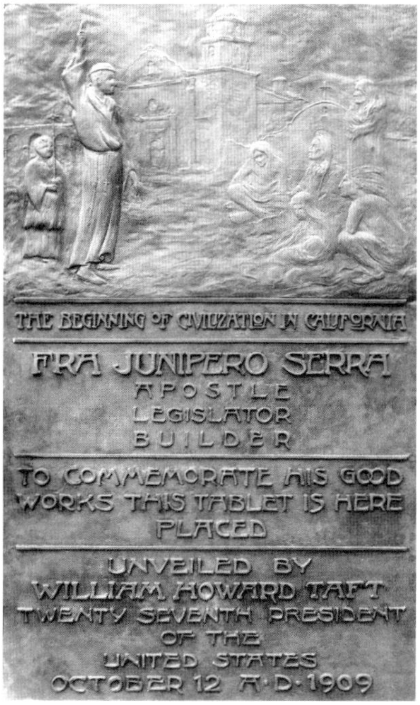

SAINT JUNIPERO SERRA, JULY 1

Franciscan friar Fr. Junipero Serra (1713–1784) was a highly regarded professor of philosophy in Spain when he joined the missionary college of San Fernando in Mexico and then volunteered for mission work among the native Americans. He went to great lengths to call his Indian congregation to repentance during his sermons, such as pounding his breast with a stone, scourging himself, and applying a lit torch to his bare chest. He also learned their language and translated the catechism for them. Serra was appointed superior of a group of fifteen Franciscans and went on to found the twenty-one California missions, going as far north as Sonoma. He traveled on foot despite a chronic and painful leg injury and bravely resisted the policies of the government, which sought to exploit the native population. Saint Junipero passed away on August 28, but his feast is observed on July 1, the date that he first set foot in what is now San Diego.

Father Serra's religious name is Junipero or Juniper, which he took in honor of an early Franciscan saint. Juniper (the plant) is the main ingredient in gin and in a growing number of nonalcoholic spirits. We include several options, but special mention must be made of **Little Saints**, which produces a spirit named after our saint (intentionally or not, we know not). The company describes their St. Juniper in the following way: "Herbaceous juniper meets a woodsy, citrusy blend of cucumber, birch and yuzu for an experience that's equal parts bright and complex. Powered by organic lion's mane mushroom and damiana, St. Juniper was formulated to lighten minds and open hearts."

We also include a recipe that uses **FreeGlider** by the prestigious English gin distiller **Sipsmith**. Sipsmith experimented with 189 prototypes and over 100 ingredients to create the ultimate alcohol-free spirit, and they passed the cost of all that R&D onto the customer with a price that no Franciscan could ever afford: $175 for a 700ml bottle.

Little Saints' Gin and Tonic

Makes 1 drink

1½ oz. Little Saints' St. Juniper
4 oz. tonic water
1 lemon slice, garnish

Pour all liquid ingredients into a highball glass and stir 40 times. Add ice and garnish with lemon slice.

Lyre's Gin & Tonic

Makes 1 drink

1½ oz. Lyre's Dry London Spirit
4 oz. tonic water
3 dashes aromatic bitters
1 pink grapefruit slice
1 rosemary sprig, garnish

Put all ingredients except rosemary into a highball glass and stir 40 times. Add ice and garnish with rosemary sprig.

Cut Above Gin & Tonic

Makes 1 drink

2 oz. Cut Above Gin
3–4 oz. premium tonic water
1 lime or lemon wedge, garnish

Pour Cut Above and tonic water into a highball glass filled with ice and stir gently. Garnish with lemon wedge.

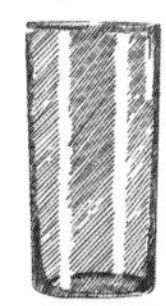

Monday Galaxy Gin and Soda

Makes 1 drink

1½ oz. Monday Gin
2 oz. Tangerine Topo Chico
2 oz. butterfly pea flower tea, chilled
1 lemon

Pour Monday Gin and Topo Chico into a highball glass with ice and top with butterfly pea flower tea. Squeeze lemon on top and watch the deep blue turn into a lavender galaxy.

FreeGlider and Tonic

Makes 1 drink

1¾ oz. Sipsmith's FreeGlider
3½ oz. premium tonic water, chilled
1 grapefruit twist, garnish

Pour FreeGlider and tonic water into a highball glass with ice and stir gently. Garnish with grapefruit twist.

Cranberry Orange Gin and Tonic

Makes 1 drink

5–6 cranberries
2½ oz. Free Spirits' Spirit of Gin
2–3 oz. soda water
1 orange slice, garnish

Muddle the cranberries in a highball glass. Add ice, Spirit of Gin, and soda water and stir gently. Garnish with orange slice.

SAINT THOMAS THE APOSTLE, JULY 3

While the traditional calendar keeps the Feast of St. Thomas on December 21 (the day of his martyrdom), the new calendar keeps it on July 3 (the day his relics were transferred from India to Syria). Even if you already celebrated St. Thomas' feast in December, in the spirit of the doubting Thomas you have to ask yourself: are you *sure* you celebrated it? How do you know that it wasn't just a dream? Wasn't it the year before that you are remembering and not last year? And did you really celebrate it properly?

To hedge your bets, let Thomas' adopted homeland provide the refreshment for tonight. Aam panna is a traditional and delicious Indian summer beverage made from raw mangoes.

Aam Panna

Makes 1 drink

- 2 large raw mangoes
- 1/2 cup sugar
- 1 tsp. roasted cumin powder
- 1/2 tsp. black salt
- 1 tsp. black pepper powder
- 10–12 fresh mint leaves
- 4 cups water

Wash and boil raw mangoes in 2 cups water until soft. Let cool, peel, and extract the pulp. Blend the pulp until smooth. Mix mango pulp with sugar, cumin powder, black salt, black pepper powder, and mint leaves. Blend again. Add 2 cups water, then adjust sweetness and salt. Pour into glasses, with or without ice, and garnish with mint leaves (optional).

SAINT PIER GIORGIO FRASSATI, JULY 4

Pier Giorgio Frassati (1901–1925) was in many ways unremarkable: a lackluster student, an avid mountain-climber, a practical joker. Yet this son of Turin, Italy wanted holiness for himself and his friends, and he got it. He tirelessly promoted the Faith among the youth, bravely resisted the rise of fascism in Italy, and generously helped the poor. When he was unexpectedly struck down in the prime of life by polio at the age of twenty-four, thousands of people (to his parents' astonishment) showed up at his funeral to show their respect to their son; and it was the poor who first petitioned for his canonization.

What makes Frassati so appealing today is that he is relatable. As Cristina Siccardi writes: "his sanctity gets through to young people today because of the concreteness of his life; Pier Giorgio faced the everyday problems of all young men: the weariness of study, the joy and enthusiasm of being with friends, playing sports, communing with nature . . . and then his healthy appetite, his desire to sing and have fun, his way of being authentic without pretense and hypocrisy, with a pipe in his mouth, and a billiard cue in his hand, and a glass of beer" (*Pier Giorgio Frassati: A Hero for Our Times*, Ignatius, 251).

Tonight, on this Fourth of July, enjoy a nonalcoholic beer. As of this writing, Italian nonalcoholic beer is not available in the US, but anything by **Athletic Brewing Company** would be appropriate given that St. Frassati was a great sportsman.

The motto most associated with St. Frassati is *Verso l'Alto* or "Towards the Top." You can pay homage to this inspiring motto with a bottle of **Alta** by the **Casamara Club.** Alta is a delicious Italian-style botanical soda perfect for a hot summer's day. Casamara Club also makes an Alpine botanical soda called **Como**.

Finally, for a native Italian option, enjoy a bottle of Crodino. This non-alcoholic aperitif was created way back in 1964 and has since become an Italian classic. It is available for purchase online and perhaps at your nearest Italian grocery store.

LAST CALL
A toast: "Verso l'Alto!"

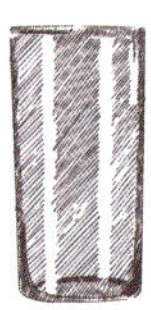

Crodino Spritz

Makes 1 drink

1 bottle Cordino
1 orange slice, garnish

Pour Cordino into a highball glass or goblet with ice and garnish with orange.

SAINT ELIZABETH OF PORTUGAL, JULY 8 (JULY 4; JULY 5 IN THE US)

Elizabeth (a.k.a. Isabel or Isabella in Spanish and Portuguese) (1271–1336) was named after her great aunt St. Elizabeth of Hungary. Even as a girl, Elizabeth said the entire Divine Office, went to High Mass at least once a day, fasted and did penance, and avoided frivolous amusement. She was married

young to a dissolute king who kept a corrupt court. Elizabeth maintained her virtue and went to extraordinary lengths to help the poor. Her goodness incurred jealousy, and she was falsely accused by a page of infidelity with another page. The enraged king ordered a lime-burner to throw into his furnace the first page who came to him and then sent the accused page to the lime-burner. On the way, however, the good page stopped for Mass. Impatient over the lack of any news, the king sent the wicked page to see what had happened, and the lime-burner threw *him* into the furnace. The astonished king interpreted these events as a divine confirmation of Elizabeth's innocence.

Elizabeth was also renowned for her skills in peacemaking. She once reconciled her son Affonso and her husband when Affonso, tired of his father's preferences for his illegitimate children, rebelled. Elizabeth rode in between the two opposing armies and made peace before the battle was met. After her husband died, Elizabeth tried to become a tertiary in a convent of Poor Clares that she had founded earlier, but her religious retirement was interrupted when Affonso, now king of Portugal, marched against the king of Castile. Despite her age and weakness, the holy queen dowager again rushed out to where the two armies were drawn up and helped establish peace. This last exertion proved too much for her, and she died "full of heavenly joy" soon after.

You can pay tribute to the lime-burning incident with a lime-cooling drink. Lime cordials, which consist of lime juice, sugar, and water, are a good refreshment during these hot summer days. An easy option is **Rose's Sweetened Lime Juice**, the world's first commercially produced fruit concentrate. Or you can make your own if you have a good kitchen scale. Your local supermarket may have food grade citric acid (in the canning aisle), or you can order online. Finally, companies like Sentia and Free Spirits offer several options.

Lime Cordial

Makes 1 drink

250 grams sugar
8 oz. very hot water
8 grams freshly grated lime peel (from 1–2 limes)
1½ oz. fresh lime juice
25 grams citric acid
1–2 limes, grated

Combine all ingredients in a blender on medium speed for thirty seconds. Let cool. For a delicious lime soda, use 1 oz. lime cordial and 3 oz. soda water or ginger beer.

Lime Rickey

Makes 1 drink

1 oz. lime cordial (see above)
sparkling water
1 dash grenadine
1 mint sprig, garnish

Pour lime cordial into a highball glass with ice, top with sparkling water, add grenadine, and stir gently. Garnish with mint.

Golden Lime Soda

Makes 1 drink

¾ oz. Sentia GABA Gold
¾ oz. fresh lime juice
4–6 oz. soda water
1 lime wedge, garnish

Pour GABA and lime juice into a shaker with ice and shake 40 times. Strain into a highball glass with ice, top with soda water, and stir gently. Garnish with lime.

Ginger Lime

Makes 1 drink

3/4 oz. Sentia GABA Gold
1/2 oz. fresh lime juice
4–6 oz. ginger beer
1 dehydrated orange wheel, garnish

Pour GABA and lime juice into a shaker with ice and shake 40 times. Strain into a highball glass with ice, top with ginger beer, and stir gently. Garnish with orange wheel.

Cherry Lime Gin Rickey

Makes 1 drink

2 1/2 oz. Free Spirits' The Spirit of Gin
4–5 fresh pitted cherries
half a lime, squeezed
4–6 oz. soda water
3 dashes All The Bitter New Orleans Bitters, optional

Muddle the cherries in a highball glass. Add Spirit of Gin, lime juice, and bitters, and fill with crushed ice. Top with soda and stir gently. Garnish with the spent lime husk.

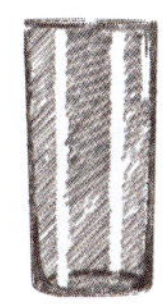

LAST CALL

Someone can raise a glass and say, "To St. Elizabeth: Blessed are the peacemakers!" To which the rest answer: "For they shall be called the children of God!" Some mention of "peace on earth" would also be appropriate, as the phrase has a good biblical pedigree; but "world peace" is a cliché best left to hippies and beauty pageant contestants.

SAINTS JOHN FISHER AND THOMAS MORE, JULY 9 (JUNE 22)

John Fisher (1459–1535) was a cardinal and the Bishop of Rochester who was beheaded on June 22, 1535, for his opposition to King Henry VIII. A learned and holy man, he was arguably the only virtuous bishop in all of England

when that "miserable monarch" (to quote the Baronius Missal) established his own church.

St. John Fisher was a humble man, and so he won't mind if we focus more on his holy "partner in crime." Thomas More (1478–1535) was the most successful private lawyer in the country and the most celebrated Renaissance humanist of the day when he agreed to become the Chancellor of England under King Henry VIII. More was incredibly versatile in his writing and thinking; he could be, in the words of one contemporary, "a man of marvellous mirth" as well as a man of "sad gravity." If you don't believe it, buy yourself a copy of More's *Utopia*—a word that he coined—or his *Dialogue Concerning Heresies*, which C. S. Lewis called the best Platonic dialogue ever written in English.

Thomas More is most famous for refusing to sign the Act of Supremacy that recognized Henry VIII as the head of the Church in England, a refusal that led to his martyrdom on July 6, 1535—fittingly, the then-Octave Day of the Feast of Sts. Peter and Paul. Even on the gallows, More kept his gentle humor, asking the executioner if he could remove his beard from the chopping block, since *it* had not been convicted of high treason. More's reputation for integrity and conscience has stood the test of time. More's friend Erasmus famously described him as a "man for all seasons," meaning that More was the kind of friend you wanted for every conceivable situation.

Erasmus also gives an interesting profile of Thomas More's eating and drinking habits. It turns out that the saint was almost a teetotaler.

> I have never seen any person less fastidious in his choice of food. As a young man, he was by preference a water-drinker, a practice he derived from his father. But, not to give annoyance to others, he used at table to conceal this habit from his guests by drinking, out of a pewter vessel, either small beer almost as

> weak as water, or plain water. As to wine, it being the custom, where he was, for the company to invite each other to drink in turn of the same cup, he used sometimes to sip a little of it, to avoid appearing to shrink from it altogether, and to habituate himself to the common practice. . . . But he does not shrink from things that impart an innocent pleasure, even of a bodily kind.

More also chose to go to the gallows without a parting glass. As he was being led to his execution, a woman pushed passed the soldiers and offered him some wine. More, however, refused on the grounds that Jesus Christ at His passing had no wine but gall and vinegar.

It is easy for us to emulate More's drinking habits. "Small beer" was inexpensive, low-alcohol beer consumed by children, servants, and manual laborers as a way of escaping water-transmitted diseases (the alcohol in the water was just enough to kill pathogens but not enough to make you groggy). Tonight, enjoy your favorite no- or low-alcoholic beer, such as something from the **Athletic Brewing Company**. Or try **HOPWTR**, an alternative to beer made with sparkling water, hops, stress-relieving adaptogens such as ashwagandha, and cognition-boosting nootropics such as L-Theanine. Maybe you'll even inch a little closer to St. Thomas More's impressive IQ.

LAST CALL

A toast to the faithful Fisher and the merry More with an adaptation of the latter's last words: "To the king's good servants, and God's first!"

SAINT JOHN GUALBERT, JULY 12

John Gualbert (ca. 995–1073) was an Italian nobleman whose only brother had been murdered. Swearing revenge, John chanced to come upon his brother's killer face-to-face in a narrow passageway on Good Friday. When John drew his sword to slay him, the man "besought him by the passion of Jesus Christ, who suffered on that day, to spare his life." The memory of Christ, who prayed for his murderers on the cross, greatly affected Saint John, and lifting his brother's killer from the ground, said to him: "I can refuse nothing

that is asked of me for the sake of Jesus Christ. I not only give you your life, but also my friendship forever. Pray for me that God may pardon me my sin."

John then went to a nearby monastery to pray, and as he knelt before the crucifix begging forgiveness for his sins, Christ on the cross bowed his head three times, signaling His approval. St. John eventually became an exemplary monk, the founder of his own religious community at Vallombrosa in Italy, and a courageous opponent of the simony and clerical immorality plaguing the Church at the time. St. John's powerful story of repentance and anti-corruption is a reminder that true reform, like charity, begins at home.

Ghia has a delicious mocktail called "You Had Me at Hi." In honor of St. John's conversion—and in his forgiving spirit—we hope they will forgive us for renaming it to suit the occasion. The red color betokens the Precious Blood shed on Good Friday, while the lime symbolizes the bitterness of the Passion.

You Had Me at Jesus

Makes 1 drink

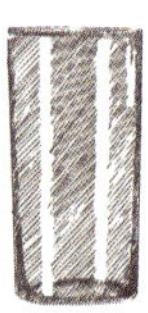

- 1½ oz. Ghia Apéritif
- 1 oz. cranberry juice
- 2 oz. sparkling water
- 1 lime wheel, garnish

Pour liquid ingredients into a highball glass with ice and stir gently. Garnish with lime wheel.

OUR LADY OF MT. CARMEL, JULY 16

The Feast of Our Lady of Mt. Carmel began in the fourteenth century as a way of thanking the Blessed Virgin Mary for her protection of the Carmelite Order during its difficult first years. The order, which was founded in Europe in the twelfth century, carries on a tradition that quite possibly stretches back to the prophet Elijah on Mount Carmel in the Holy Land. Later on, the feast came to be associated with what is formally called the Scapular of Our Lady of Mt. Carmel and what is more commonly known as the brown scapular. It is believed that this sacramental was given by our Lady to St. Simon Stock, the English general of the Carmelite order in 1251, along with the promise that whoever wears the brown scapular and fulfills several other conditions will not suffer damnation.

The brown scapular and the Feast of Our Lady of Mt. Carmel are also linked in popular imagination to the so-called "Sabbatine Privilege," the belief that our Lady will rescue her special disciples from Purgatory on the first Saturday after they have died. Technically, this belief is not attached to the brown scapular per se but to members of the Carmelite order, and moreover, the belief about a first Saturday deliverance has received an icy reception from the Magisterium. But hey, folk belief is folk belief. Sweeten your devotion to Our Lady of Mt. Carmel with one of these drinks:

Salted Caramel White Russian Mocktail

Makes 1 drink

2 oz. water
1 tbsp. salted caramel sauce
1 tsp. espresso powder
1/4 tsp. unsweetened baking cocoa
1 1/2 oz. whipped cream
salted caramel sauce, for garnish

Dip the rim of an old-fashioned glass into salted caramel sauce and fill with ice. Pour water, caramel sauce, espresso powder, and baking cocoa into a mixing glass and stir 40 times. Pour mixture into the old-fashioned glass and top with whipped cream.

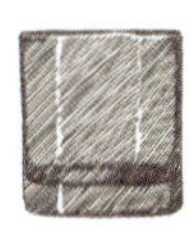

Lyre's Salted Caramel Espresso Martini

Makes 1 drink

1½ oz. Lyre's Coffee Originale
½ oz. Lyre's Spiced Cane Spirit
1½ oz. cold drip or fresh espresso
½ oz. salted caramel syrup
1 caramel popcorn cluster, garnish

Pour all liquid ingredients into a shaker without ice and dry shake 40 times. Add ice, shake briefly, and strain into a champagne coupe glass. Garnish with popcorn.

Spiritless Caramel Espresso Martini

Makes 1 drink

2 oz. Spiritless Jalisco 55
1 oz. Cheeky Cocktails Espresso Syrup
1 oz. caramel syrup
caramel cold foam
caramel, garnish
coffee beans, garnish

Pour Jalisco, espresso syrup, and caramel syrup into a shaker with ice and shake 40 times. Strain into a champagne coupe glass. Top with caramel cold foam, drizzle caramel onto the foam, and add coffee beans.

Note*:* To make caramel cold foam, combine 2 ounces heavy cream, 1 ounce 2% milk, 1½ ounces caramel syrup, and ¼ teaspoon fine sea salt. Beat until foamy.

SAINT MARGARET OF ANTIOCH, JULY 20

Margaret, also known as Marina or Marine (d. 304), was a beautiful Christian maiden whom the Roman prefect at Antioch wished to marry, but since the proposal also came attached with a demand to apostatize, Margaret refused. She was tortured and eventually executed. Colorful stories abound about St. Margaret, the most famous being that Satan, in the form of a dragon, swallowed her but was forced to cough her up because the tiny cross she carried irritated his innards. Consequently, she is now a patron saint of pregnant women! St. Margaret is one of the saints who spoke to St. Joan of Arc, and she is one of the Fourteen Holy Helpers.

Monin has a delightful syrup made from pitaya or dragon fruit, a Pacific Rim fruit that tastes like a combination of strawberry and pear but with lush tropical notes. A dragon fruit lemonade hits the spot on a hot summer's day as well as honors this surprising dragonslayer.

The second option is our original Dragonslayer Mocktail, which we also pair with St. George (see April 23).

Third, enjoy a margarita from another St. Margaret (see February 22).

Finally, try one of these three recipes. Spiritless' Dragon Fruit Margarita captures the names of both Margaret and her nemesis. And we thought a skinny margarita was appropriate on the assumption that either St. Margaret was petite or the dragon was exceedingly large to swallow her whole.

Dragon Fruit Margarita

Makes 1 drink

2 oz. Spiritless Jalisco 55
2 oz. dragon fruit syrup
1 oz. fresh lime juice
½ oz. orange liqueur
coarse salt, garnish
1 lime wedge, garnish

Rim a margarita or cocktail glass by rubbing the edge with lime wedge and dipping it in salt. Pour liquid ingredients into a shaker with ice and shake 40 times. Strain into glass and garnish with lime wedge.

JULY

Dragon Fruit Lemonade

Makes 1 drink

7 oz. lemonade
¾ oz. Monin Dragon Fruit Syrup
1 lemon slice or dragon fruit slice, garnish

Fill a highball with ice. Pour liquid ingredients into glass, then pour the mixture into an empty shaker and back again into the highball glass. Garnish.

Skinny Margarita

Makes 1 drink

1½ oz. Lyre's Agave Blanco Spirit
1 oz. fresh lime juice
½ oz. Lyre's Orange Sec
1 dash orange bitters, optional
salt
1 lime wedge, garnish

Rim a margarita or cocktail glass by rubbing the edge with lime wedge and dipping it in salt. Pour liquid ingredients into a shaker with ice and shake 40 times. Strain into glass and garnish with lime wedge.

SAINT MARY MAGDALENE, JULY 22

The story of this notorious sinner-turned-saint is well-known thanks to the New Testament. Mary Magdalene's contrition before our Lord inspired so many medieval portraits of her weeping that it led to the term "maudlin" (a British pronunciation of "Magdalene") for something that is mawkish. "Maudlin" has even been defined as overly sentimental *because of drunkenness*: "To drink maudlin" is an obsolete phrase for reaching the stage of inebriation where one becomes tearfully emotional.

Thanks to this book, we can easily drink to the Magdalene instead of drinking maudlin. A Slutty Mary is the name given to a Bloody Mary that has tequila instead of vodka. Following this logic, a Blood Mary with phony tequila is a No Longer Slutty Mary, just like our saint today.

No Longer Slutty Mary

Makes 1 drink

1½ oz. nonalcoholic tequila
3 oz. tomato juice
1 dash fresh lemon juice
½ tsp. Worcestershire sauce
2–3 drops Tabasco hot sauce
salt and pepper
lemon or lime wedge, celery stick, or olives for garnish, optional

Place all ingredients except garnishes into a shaker with ice and shake 40 times. Strain into an old-fashioned glass or highball glass with ice. Garnish.

LAST CALL

St. Anselm has a beautiful "Prayer to Mary Magdalene" that will make you weepy without drunkenness.

SAINT APOLLINARIS, JULY 23 (JULY 20)

Apollinaris of Ravenna (ca. 200) was born in Antioch. When he became the first Bishop of Ravenna, he preached the Gospel in the face of tremendous persecution, being exiled, beaten, scalded with hot water, stabbed, imprisoned, and starved at various times before being martyred at Classe. The magnificent Basilica of Sant'Apolliare in that city is believed to be built on the site of his martyrdom.

JULY

Apollinaris mineral water is named after today's saint. Georg Kreuzberg had bought a vineyard in Germany's Eifel region in 1852 and was disappointed when its grapes did not thrive. Literally wanting to get to the bottom of things, he dug down fifty feet and discovered an underground spring of naturally carbonated mineral water. Kreuzberg named the spring after St. Apollinaris, a patron saint of wine. Today Apollinaris is billed as the "Queen of Table Waters."

Apollinaris is great in a variety of drinks, including a Classic Grape Cooler and a Limeade that was popular during Prohibition.

Classic Grape Cooler

Makes 1 drink

- Apollinaris classic mineral water
- 6 seedless red grapes
- 2 tsp. brown sugar
- 4 lemon balm leaves (a.k.a. balm mint or lemon mint)

Crush the red grapes, lemon balm leaves, and brown sugar in a glass. Fill the glass with crushed ice and Apollinaris and stir. Garnish with lemon balm leaves.

Limeade

Makes 1 drink

- 3 limes, squeezed (approximately 3 oz.)
- 1 tbsp. sugar
- 4–6 oz. Apollinaris classic mineral water

Pour lime juice and sugar into a shaker without ice and dry shake 40 times. Pour into a highball glass with ice, top with Apollinaris, and stir gently.

SAINT JAMES THE GREATER, JULY 25

James (d. 42 or 43) was the brother of St. John the Apostle, both of whom our Lord nicknamed "Sons of Thunder." James is also given the epithet "the

Greater" to distinguish him from "James the Lesser" (or the Younger), another Apostle who was Our Lord's cousin. Together with Sts. Peter and John, James the Greater was one of the three Apostles given the special privilege of witnessing the Transfiguration of Jesus Christ on Mount Tabor and His Agony in the Garden. St. James was beheaded in Jerusalem on the orders of Herod Agrippa.

St. James is the patron saints of several causes and places, including the Diocese of Brooklyn, New York. Tonight, let the canned or bottled beverages of Brooklyn-made **St. Agrestis** refresh the palate. The owners formed the name Agrestis from the Latin word for a field (*ager*) to indicate that they use only the world's best, raw ingredients to make their natural spirits. And "St." is an ode to the brand's Italian culture. Another tie-in is that St. James' final resting place in Spain is called Santiago de Compostela, *Campus Stellae* being Latin for "field of the star."

And speaking of Santiago, here is a virgin Caesar by that name. A Caesar, incidentally, is a Bloody Mary made with clamato instead of tomato juice.

Santiago Caesar

Makes 1 drink

4 oz. Mott's Clamato Juice
3 dashes Cholula hot sauce
4 dashes Worcester sauce
3 dashes salt & pepper
Caesar seasoning salt rimmer such as Mott's
1 lime wedge, etc., garnish

Rim a highball by rubbing lime wedge along the edge of the glass and dipping it in seasoning salt. Add ice, liquid ingredients, salt, and pepper to glass and stir 40 times. Garnish extravagantly. Options include celery sticks, pepperoni sticks, pearl onions, olives (green or black), dill pickle chunks, lime wedges, pickled asparagus spears, etc.

SAINT CHRISTOPHER, JULY 25

July 25 boasts of two great saints, the first bearing the title of great, the other being great in size. According to legend, Reprobus was a giant of a man (7½ feet tall) from the third century who wanted to serve the greatest king ever. He enlisted in the service of a mighty potentate, but when he noticed that the man was afraid of the devil, he left him to serve the Prince of Darkness. That did not last long, however: when Reprobus noticed that the devil was afraid of a roadside cross, he rightly reasoned that Christ was the mightiest of all.

After converting, Reprobus sought the advice of a holy hermit. The hermit told him to fast: Reprobus said he couldn't. The hermit told him to offer many prayers. Ignorant of how to pray, Reprobus again asked for something else. Finally, the hermit suggested that he put his large stature to good use and ferry people across a dangerous river on his shoulders. Reprobus happily agreed to the task until one night he was awakened by a small child asking for passage. As they crossed the river, Reprobus almost collapsed and drowned under the little one's weight. When the exhausted giant complained after they reached the other side, the child replied: "Be not astonished: thou bearest him who beareth the world." As proof, the Child commanded Reprobus to plant his staff in the ground, at which point it blossomed into a palm tree with leaves and dates. Our Lord then baptized Reprobus personally, changing his name from Reprobus (Latin for "rejected") to Christopher (Greek for "Christ-bearer"). The Christ-bearer went on to suffer martyrdom for his fearless preaching of the Gospel.

Saint Christopher is one of the Fourteen Holy Helpers, a group of saints popular during the Middle Ages for their specific powers of intercession. Christopher was invoked as a patron against sudden death, especially the Plague. There was a rumor going around that anyone who saw an image of the saint would not die suddenly that day. As a result of this belief, images of Saint Christopher were placed near the doors of houses or churches, sometimes on the inside and—for the benefit of passersby—sometimes on the outside. According to one tally, there are more images of Saint Christopher on the walls of old English churches than of any other saint except the Blessed Virgin Mary.

Because his staff burst into bloom, the saint was designated a patron of gardeners. Christopher's patronage of travelers was extended to motorists in the early twentieth century and caught on quickly, especially since traffic accidents are in some sense the modern plague, taking as many lives as epidemics of old and in even more sudden a manner. Blessing automobiles on Saint Christopher's Day used to be a common Catholic custom, and Saint Christopher medals or statuettes are still standard on many a Catholic dashboard.

Tonight, you can toast to Christopher as a patron of motorists or of gardeners with one and the same beverage. The makers of Ghia chose their name in part because of the automobile design firm Carrozzeria Ghia, which made beautifully designed cars that were approachable, like the sleek Karmann Ghia. That's the connection to motorists; the connection to gardeners is from the delicious content of this drink.

LAST CALL

The French have a saying, often put on their St. Christopher medals, that makes a nice toast: "Look at St. Christopher and go on reassured."

Dusk in the Garden

Makes 1 drink

2 oz. Ghia Apéritif
5 blackberries
¼ oz. orange blossom water
¼ oz. fresh orange juice
1 dried mandarin wheel or dried calendula flower petals, garnish

Gently muddle blackberries in a shaker. Add ice and all liquid ingredients. Shake 40 times and strain into chilled coupe glass. Garnish with dried mandarin orange wheel or dried calendula flower petals. Or both!

SAINT MARTHA, JULY 29

What an honor to have been Martha, Mary, or Lazarus, the three siblings in Bethany whom Jesus loved to visit when he was in Judea. On one of these occasions, Martha was hustling to make her Guest comfortable while her younger sister Mary sat at the Lord's feet, absorbing every word. When Martha asked Jesus to make her sister help her, He replied: "Martha, Martha, thou art careful and art troubled about many things: but one thing is necessary. Mary hath chosen the best part, which shall not be taken away from her" (Luke 10:41–42). Martha and Mary came to be seen in the Christian tradition as embodiments of the active life and contemplative life, respectively. The active life is by no means bad, but the contemplative life, which everyone is called to have at least some share of, is closer to the bliss of the Beatific Vision.

Of course, being active has its merits too. According to the *Golden Legend*, Martha moved to southern France in a rudderless ship. At the time, a river dragon was terrorizing the locals; one of the monster's more peculiar features is that when it was being chased it defecated on its pursuers an ordure half an acre wide that was like glass and that made whatever it touched burn like fire. The townsfolk begged Martha to intervene, which she did: she found the dragon and stopped him from eating a man by sprinkling holy water on it and showing it the cross. The dragon then became docile, allowing St. Martha to leash it with her girdle and lead it back to the people, who then ganged up on it and stabbed it to death (not exactly the happy ending of St. Francis and the Wolf of Gubbio!). The dragon's name was Tarasconus, and ever since the town in France has been called Tarascon. Since 1474, Tarascon has had an annual festival celebrating Martha's defeat of the dragon. The story is slightly farfetched, but so is the *Golden Legend*'s other claim that St. Martha abstained from all wine while in the south of France.

Tarascon is not far from the French Riviera, and the **Casamara Club** makes a refreshing Riviera botanical soda called **Sera** that is perfect after a hot day taming dragons. You can also borrow a drink from St. Margaret of Antioch (see July 20).

LAST CALL

Give the Martha in your life a break today by helping out with serving; or, if you are the Martha, choose the better part and sit at the Master's feet while someone else frets over the details. One thing is necessary, that you and your friends be filled with the merriment of fellowship in Christ as you bend the elbow together. Then, raise a glass and say, "To choosing the better part!"

SAINT IGNATIUS OF LOYOLA, JULY 31

Íñigo López de Loyola (1491–1556) was born in the castle of Loyola above Azpeitia, Spain, located in Basque Country. He is described as being "of a somewhat fiery and warlike nature," which is a nice way of saying that he was a poster boy for Latino machismo, coupled with powerful family connections to get him out of trouble for gambling, quarreling, and swordplay (oh, and he also had an eye for the ladies). Not surprisingly, Ignatius became a military officer. After a battle in which he was wounded by a cannon ball, his leg did not heal properly and had to be broken and reset (without anesthesia). The leg healed this time, but with a bony protrusion below the knee. Ignatius found this unacceptable, as it made it impossible to wear the tight-fitting boots and hose of a courtier, so he ordered the doctors to *saw off* the offending knob (again without anesthesia). Who knew that the wages of vanity could be so high?

During his long recuperation, Ignatius wanted to read romance novels, but since the family castle had none, he had to settle for a book on the life of Christ and a book on the saints. The effect on him was dramatic. St. Ignatius abandoned his worldly ways and founded the Society of Jesus. Better known as the Jesuits, the order became renowned for its notable educators, missionaries, and scientists.

One of the Jesuits' many accomplishments was naming a certain New World flower after the Passion of Our Lord Jesus Christ. The passion flower, from which passion fruit syrup is made, reminded Jesuit missionaries of the details of Jesus' suffering (see Passion Sunday in Lent for more details). To us, it is the quintessence of Jesuit piety and inquiry at its best, and so we honor Ignatius with drinks made with passion fruit. To begin, **HOPWTR Passion Fruit** is "packed with Citra, Amarillo, Mosaic, and Azacca hops, delivering a tropical, tangy flavor with a strong hint of hops, all with no calories and no sugar." An easy homemade solution is an Italian cream soda; or you can try a mocktail with nonalcoholic spirits.

Passion Fruit Italian Cream Soda

Makes 1 drink

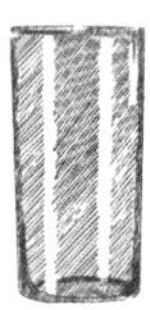

8 oz. soda water

3/4 oz. passion fruit syrup

3/4 oz. cream

Build in a highball glass half-full of ice. Stir when ready to drink.

Passion Fruit Mojito

Makes 1 drink

2 oz. Lyre's White Cane Spirit

3/4 oz. fresh lime juice

3/4 oz. passion fruit puree

3/4 oz. simple syrup

3/4 oz. soda water

8–10 mint leaves

1 passion fruit half, garnish

1 mint sprig, garnish

Gently muddle mint leaves in an old-fashioned glass. Pour liquid ingredients into glass, add ice, and stir gently. Garnish with half a passion fruit and mint sprig.

JULY

Garden Booch

Makes 1 drink

1½ oz. Seedlip Garden 108
passion fruit kombucha
1 mint sprig, garnish

Pour Seedlip into an old-fashioned glass with ice and top with kombucha. Stir gently and garnish with mint.

Spicy Passion Fruit Margarita

Makes 1 drink

2 oz. Spiritless Jalisco 55
¾ oz. orange liqueur
¾ oz. fresh lime juice
2–3 jalapeño slices
½ passion fruit, scooped out
½ oz. passion fruit syrup
spicy salt
1 passion fruit wheel, garnish

Rim a margarita or old-fashioned glass by rubbing passion fruit wheel on the edge and dipping it in spicy salt. Put lime juice, half a passion fruit, passion fruit syrup, and jalapeño slices into a shaker and muddle. Add orange liqueur, Jalisco 55, and ice and shake 40 times. Strain into the glass and garnish with passion fruit wheel.

LAST CALL

A toast: "To St. Ignatius: through his intercession, may our passion bear fruit for the greater glory of God."

CHAPTER EIGHT

August

SAINTS

LAMMAS DAY, AUGUST 1

In the universal calendar before 1960, today was the Feast of St. Peter in Chains. In the post-Vatican-II calendar, it is the Feast of St. Alphonsus Ligouri. But in medieval and Renaissance England, the first of August was better known among simple folk as "Loaf Mass Day," or Lammas Day for short.

Lammas Day was a wheat harvest festival in which a loaf of bread made from the recent crop would be brought to church and blessed. Lammas Day was a time of merriment: the town of Ballycastle in Northern Ireland, for example, has been celebrating Ould Lammas Fair for the past four hundred years. And the holiday once had a curious impact on our language. It was used to demarcate time: in *Romeo and Juliet* we learn that Juliet's fourteenth birthday is on "Lammas-eve at night" (I.iii.19). And it was used to designate property: "Lammas lands" were the fields used in common for winter grazing, while "Lammas wheat" was winter wheat, presumably planted in early August.

What better way is there to give thanks to almighty God for the gift of wheat than with a nonalcoholic **wheat beer**? These beers are brewed with a large proportion of wheat (sometimes as high as 50%) in addition to barley. In Germany, wheat beers are known as *weissbier* ("white beer"). The Bavarian *weissbier* is probably the best known, especially its *hefeweizen* ("yeast wheat") variety.

Here are some options:

The **Ceria Brewing Company** in Denver has **a Grainwave Belgian-Style Wheat Ale** that is made with blood orange peel and coriander.

Grüvi, also in Denver, has a **Weekday Wit** that emulates Belgium's wheat beers.

Rightside Brewing out of Los Angeles offers a fruity citrus wheat beer called **Golden Road NA Mango**.

Untitled Art Florida in Waunakee, Wisconsin has a **Weisse** that is similar to a fruited Berliner Weiss-style sour ale.

Weihenstephaner in Freising, Germany has been brewing for centuries. Its **Hefeweissbier Alkoholfrei** lives up to its legacy.

Wellbeing Brewing Victory Wheat is from St. Louis, Missouri and made with electrolytes and other nutrients for post-sweat refreshment and replenishment.

LAST CALL

One curious byproduct of Lammas Day is a whimsical term for "not ever." A "latter Lammas" is a day that will never come, and "at latter Lammas" means never. To the bewilderment of your friends, spend the day casually incorporating obsolete Lammas terms into the conversation. Then, spend the evening offering toasts involving the words "latter Lammas."

OUR LADY OF THE SNOWS, AUGUST 5

The Feast of the Dedication of the Church of Our Lady of the Snows commemorates the great Roman basilica better known as St. Mary Major. According to tradition, our Lady foretold the church's location to a Christian nobleman in a dream, instructing him to build wherever he saw snow the next morning (in Rome on a hot August day no less). The man awoke and found to his amazement a blanket of snow on the Esquiline Hill.

Enough said.

Snow Day

Makes 1 drink

2½ oz. Three Spirit's The Spirit of Gin
½ oz. Meyer lemon cordial
1 egg white
crunchy-baked meringue or fresh meringue
1 dehydrated lemon or freshly grated Meyer lemon zest, garnish

Pour gin, lemon cordial, and egg white into a shaker without ice and dry shake 40 times vigorously. Add ice and shake briefly until chilled. Strain into an old-fashioned glass or champagne coupe glass. Top with meringue, and garnish with grated Meyer lemon zest or dehydrated lemon.

Note: To make Meyer lemon cordial, squeeze the juice from 3 pounds of Meyer lemons and strain into a saucepan. Add 2 cups of cane sugar and heat over medium heat until sugar dissolves, stirring occasionally. Let cool. You should have almost 3 cups of cordial, plenty for a party.

SAINT JOHN MARY VIANNEY, AUGUST 9 (AUGUST 4)

Jean-Marie Vianney (1786–1859) almost did not become a priest. His Latin scores were terribly low, and he had to dodge a couple of drafts into Napoleon's armies. But it's a good thing he prevailed. Once this unassuming man became the pastor or curé of Ars, he not only transformed the tiny French village of 253 people but enriched the entire Church. The "Curé d'Ars" was an indefatigable priest, spending up to sixteen hours a day in the confessional and having the gift of reading people's hearts. The devil was not pleased with the saint's success and plagued him for what could possibly be the longest period of diabolical infestation in Church history. For decades, Satan kept the saint awake at night with terrifying noises, once even setting his bed on fire. St. John Mary took it all in stride. The devil spent so much time at the rectory, the Curé once quipped that "we're practically friends."

St. Jean-Marie Vianney is the patron saint of priests. Since a parson is an old name for a parish priest, make a Parson's Particular in honor of the Curé d'Ars.

Parson's Particular

Makes 1 drink

- 2 oz. fresh orange juice
- 1 oz. fresh lemon juice
- 4 dashes grenadine
- 1 egg yolk
- 1 lemon wheel, garnish

Pour all ingredients into a shaker with ice and shake 40 times.

Strain into an old-fashioned glass and garnish with lemon wheel.

LAST CALL

St. John Vianney wrote a beautiful prayer to our Lord that can be used to begin a celebration of this holy priest's life and legacy:

> **I love You, O my God, and my only desire is to love You until the last breath of my life.**
>
> **I love You, O my infinitely lovable God, and I would rather die loving You than live without loving You.**
>
> **I love You, Lord, and the only grace I ask is to love You eternally.**
>
> **My God, if my tongue cannot say in every moment that I love You, I want my heart to repeat it to You as often as I draw breath.**

SAINT LAWRENCE, AUGUST 10

Lawrence of Rome (c. 225–258) was born in Spain and became the archdeacon of Rome. In August 258, the Emperor Valerian commanded that all Catholic clergy be executed. When Lawrence was arrested, he asked for three days to assemble the Church's wealth. The prefect of Rome, eager for lucre, agreed. Lawrence then gave away as much money as he could to the poor, and on the third day appeared before the prefect with a delegation of the poor, the crippled, and the blind. "Behold the true treasures of the Church,"

Lawrence told the stunned prefect. Enraged, the prefect ordered him to be slowly roasted alive on a gridiron, but even here the fearless deacon got the last laugh. After a long period of suffering, St. Lawrence declared, "You can turn me over; I am done on this side." Not to be outdone in dark humor, the Church has made St. Lawrence the patron saint of comedians and cooks.

Wölffer Estate Vineyard in Long Island, New York produces **Spring in a Bottle**, a nonalcoholic rosé made from Saint Laurent grapes—along with Pinot Noir, Pinot Meunier, and Dornfelder grapes. The well-balanced blend has strawberry, peach, and lemon notes.

Lawrence is also a patron saint of Canada, the Gulf of St. Lawrence having been discovered on his feast day in 1534 by Jacques Cartier (which, believe it or not, is French for Jimmy Carter). Tonight, honor St. Lawrence's adopted country with some maple syrup in a St. Lawrence mocktail. The maple leaf, after all, is the sweet symbol on the national flag of Canada.

St. Lawrence Mocktail

Makes 1 drink

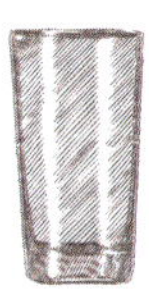

- 2 oz. fresh grapefruit juice
- 1 oz. fresh lime juice
- 1 oz. simple syrup
- ½ oz. maple syrup
- sparkling water
- 1 lime wheel, garnish

Pour grapefruit juice, lime juice, simple syrup, and maple syrup in a shaker filled with ice and shake 40 times. Strain into a cocktail glass and top with sparkling water. Garnish with a lime wheel.

LAST CALL

St. Lawrence's feast is a time to celebrate the sometimes macabre yet humorous aspects of Catholic life that adorn its many virtues. Why not throw a comedy or joke-telling party in honor of the saint? You can call it a Roast.

THE ASSUMPTION OF THE BLESSED VIRGIN MARY, AUGUST 15

The infallible dogma that Mary the Mother of God was "assumed" or taken up into Heaven body and soul was not solemnly defined until 1950 by Pope Pius XII, but the belief itself stretches back to the earliest centuries of Christianity and has been celebrated liturgically since the sixth century. Among Catholic and Orthodox Christians, the only real debate has been whether the Blessed Virgin Mary died and was then assumed into Heaven or whether she was taken up to Heaven alive like Elijah. Pius XII circumvented this controversy by simply stating that the Blessed Virgin Mary, "having completed the course of her earthly life, was assumed body and soul into heavenly glory."

Traditionally the Assumption is one of the greatest feasts of the year, accompanied by grand processions and festivities. One custom is particularly interesting: the blessing of herbs and fruits, for which there is a detailed ceremony in the traditional *Roman Ritual*. In honor of Our Lady and this ancient tradition, how about something with strawberry? In medieval art the strawberry is a symbol of, among other things, Mary's fruitful virginity because the plant both flowers and fruits at the same time. **GT's** has a Synergy line of raw kombucha that includes **Strawberry Serenity**, a fitting choice for today's feast because Our Lady has been described as a model of serenity. The label boasts that one sixteen-ounce bottle contains 9 billion living probiotics, which are excellent for gut health. It reminds us of Our Lady's soul, which contains the hearts and thoughts of many (see Luke 2:35).

Serenity on the Rocks

Makes 2 drinks

8 oz. Synergy Strawberry Serenity Raw Kombucha

Swirl the bottle gently to distribute the probiotics evenly, but do not shake (it is carbonated and will fizz up if you do). Pour into 2 old-fashioned glasses filled with ice and serve.

Strawberry Feels

Makes 1 drink

1 can De Soi's Champignon Dreams, chilled
1 strawberry slice, garnish
1 grapefruit peel, garnish

Pour Champignon Dreams into a pretty glass with ice, then garnish with grapefruit peel and strawberry.

Sweet Strawberry Tonic

Makes 1 drink

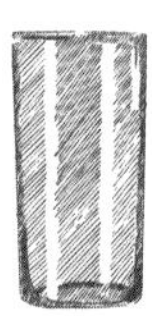

2 oz. Spiritless Jalisco 55
4 oz. Owen's Tonic Water
1 oz. strawberry simple syrup
strawberry ice

Combine all ingredients in a highball glass and stir.

Note #1: To make strawberry simple syrup, slice 8 ounces strawberries and remove stems, then put in a saucepan along with 1 cup water and 1 cup sugar. Bring to a boil and then reduce to a simmer, stirring occasionally for 20 minutes or until the liquid is very red. Strain into a sterilized jar and let cool.

Note #2: To make strawberry ice, place small strawberries in an ice cube tray, fill with water, and freeze.

Strawberry Mojito

Makes 1 drink

2 oz. Lyre's White Cane Spirit
3/4 oz. fresh lime juice
3/4 oz. strawberry puree
3/4 oz. simple syrup
2 oz. soda water
8–10 mint leaves
1 strawberry slice, garnish
1 mint sprig, garnish

Slap mint leaves against wrist to release flavors (or gently muddle in an old-fashioned glass). Put mint and liquid ingredients except soda water into an old-fashioned glass with ice, top with soda water, and stir gently. Garnish with strawberry slice and mint sprig.

LAST CALL

Adapt today's Collect into a toast: "To our glorious Mother the Blessed Virgin Mary, taken up this day to Heaven body and soul: may she help keep us intent on heavenly things, and thus obtain a share in the glory of her Assumption."

SAINT JOACHIM, AUGUST 16 (JULY 26)

Anne and Joachim were a childless elderly couple who prayed to God for offspring and were rewarded with a daughter, the Blessed Virgin Mary. Devotion to Our Lord's grandparents grew considerably in the Latin Church during the Middle Ages and early modern period, with some pious but misguided enthusiasts even going so far as to suggest that Anne conceived without the so-called marital embrace because a kiss from her husband sufficed. In 1677 the Holy See condemned this error, but the claim, outlandish as it is, at least pays Joachim the singular compliment of having one heckuva smooch. In honor of this grandfather's potent pucker, grandly reputed to have helped create a living soul in his wife's womb, try a Pucker Me Golden with Sentia's GABA Gold, which has the best nose or bouquet of anything we have tried.

Joachim's Pucker Me Golden

Makes 1 drink

1 oz. fresh grapefruit juice
¾ oz. GABA Gold
½ oz. ginger syrup
soda water

Pour grapefruit juice, GABA Gold, and ginger syrup into a shaker with ice and shake 40 times. Strain into a cocktail glass and top with soda water.

Note: To make ginger syrup, heat equal parts sugar and water in a saucepan and stir until sugar is dissolved. Add an equal part of ginger slices (which are easier to strain than grated ginger) and bring to a light boil. Cover, reduce heat, and allow to simmer for about 15 minutes. Remove from heat and let cool for about 1 hour. Strain out the ginger and store in a sealed jar.

SAINT BERNARD TOLOMEI, AUGUST 20

In the eyes of the world, Giovanni Tolomei (1272–1348) was a great success. After receiving an excellent education, Tolomei became a professor of law at the University of Siena, a knight in the army of King Rudolph I of Germany and, after his return to his hometown of Siena, one of the city's ruling elite. But Giovanni's worldly success came to an abrupt halt when he was struck by blindness. The Sienese luminary prayed to the Blessed Virgin Mary, and he regained his sight. Eternally grateful, Tolomei and two companions formed a small religious community on a mountain that his family owned. Giovanni took the religious name of Bernard, after St. Bernard of Clairvaux (whose feast day, coincidentally, is also today). Bernard Tolomei eventually founded the Congregation of the Blessed Virgin of Monte Oliveto (the Olivetans), which quickly spread throughout Italy. The Olivetans reacted heroically to the Plague of 1348, leaving their monasteries to serve the sick. Saint Bernard Tolomei and eighty-two of his fellow monks perished as a result.

The Olivetans are considered a branch of the "white monks" of the Benedictine Order because they wear white habits instead of black and follow the *Rule of St. Benedict*. Their compliance with the Rule, however, is not total. The Olivetans were extreme in their asceticism. They fasted more than the Church required, practiced several corporal mortifications in public, ate only bread and water, slept on straw, wore wooden sandals and habits made out of coarse fabric, and slept little. They were also, as one biographer puts it, "fanatical total abstainers." St. Benedict's *Rule* guarantees a portion of wine each day to a monk. The Olivetans not only rejected this provision, but they uprooted all the vineyards and destroyed all the wine-presses and vessels on the property. But such zealotry is difficult to sustain. Eventually, the order lightened up, and not only did they replant their vineyards, but later Constitutions stipulated that they keep the best wine for themselves and sell the rest! That sounds hedonistic, but the idea was that all food and drink on the table should be of the same (good) quality so that older or more prestigious monks could not claim the best portions for themselves.

The story of St. Bernard and his Olivetans is a good reminder to appreciate the virtues and rewards of abstinence but without begrudging others their own choices or acting like a bull in a china shop at your local liquor store.

Saint Bernard named his congregation after the Mount of Olives because the mountain on which he lived had olive trees and in memory of Christ's agony in the garden. Olive drinks are an obvious choice for tonight, such as the following two:

Olive You

Makes 1 drink

2 oz. Ghia Apéritif, chilled
¼ oz. olive brine, chilled
1 Castelvetrano olive, garnish
fresh black pepper, garnish

Pour Ghia and olive brine into a cocktail glass. Add 1 large ice cube and garnish with Castelvetrano olive and a dusting of fresh black pepper.

Lemon Olive Oil Elixir

Makes 1 drink

2 lemons, sliced
2 tbsp. olive oil
2 tbsp. honey
3 cups water
1 small knob ginger
2 oz. Spiritless Jalisco 55 or Kentucky 74
lemon zest, garnish
salt

Rim a cocktail glass by rubbing the edge with lemon and dipping it in salt. Put lemons (peels and all), olive oil, honey, ginger, and water in a blender and blend until smooth. Strain into a shaker with ice and add Spiritless. Shake 40 times. Strain into rimmed cocktail glass and top with a dash of olive oil and lemon zest.

THE IMMACULATE HEART OF MARY, AUGUST 22 (SATURDAY AFTER THE SACRED HEART OF JESUS)

Devotion to the Immaculate Heart of Mary is at least as old as St. John Eudes (1601–1680), and a feast to the Pure Heart of Mary was celebrated in some places in the nineteenth century. But it was not until Pope Pius XII consecrated the entire human race in the midst of World War II to Mary's Immaculate Heart that he instituted a universal feast for "peace among nations, freedom for the Church, the conversion of sinners, the love of purity, and the practice of virtue."

Theories vary on the origin of the Bloody Mary cocktail, but most agree that the name itself is an unflattering epithet for Queen Mary Tudor (ruled 1553–1558), the Catholic monarch whose efforts to restore the Faith in England after the shenanigans of her father Henry VIII included the execution of Protestant heretics. We are changing all that right here, right now. We don't want to canonize Queen Mary (even though she wasn't the villain her detractors have made her out to be), but we do want to commandeer the drink and dedicate it to a Mary whose immaculate heart bleeds for us from the "sword of sorrow" that pierced it (Luke 2:35). And we feel justified in doing so, since the British use of "bloody" as a vulgar adjective is actually believed by some to come from "By our Lady," an invocation of the Mother of God.

Bloody Marys are a popular morning and brunch drink, possibly because they are (erroneously) reputed to cure hangovers or simply because they taste really good on a sunny morning. Almost all liquor stores carry nonalcoholic Bloody Mary mix, which may be a good idea if you are hosting a large number of people. Or you can make your own drinks from scratch. The standard name for a nonalcoholic Bloody Mary is a Virgin Mary. It usually involves nothing more than deleting the vodka from your favorite Bloody Mary recipe. Here is ours:

Virgin Mary

Makes 1 drink

- 4–6 oz. tomato juice
- 1 dash lemon juice
- ½ tsp. Worcestershire sauce
- 2 or 3 drops Tabasco hot sauce
- salt and pepper
- lemon or lime wedge, celery stick, or olives for garnish, optional

Place all ingredients except garnishes in a shaker with ice and shake 40 times. Strain into an old-fashioned glass filled with ice. Garnish.

LAST CALL

Mix yourself and your friends a virgin Bloody Mary, raise it high, and exclaim, "By our Lady, Mary! Through her Immaculate Heart may we have peace among nations, freedom for the Church, the conversion of sinners, the love of purity, and the practice of virtue."

SAINT LOUIS, AUGUST 25

The Crusader King Louis IX of France (1214–1270) was brought up right by his mother Queen Blanche, who once said to him, "I love you, my dear son, as much as a mother can love her child, but I would rather see you dead at my feet than ever have you commit a mortal sin." Louis took these words to heart. As an adult, he asked a friend if he would rather contract leprosy or commit a mortal sin. Without hesitation the friend chose sin. The King replied, "This is a wild, foolish answer. When a man dies, all his sicknesses end, but mortal sin is a terrible disease which does not end with death. If you love me, I beg you to choose any suffering rather than give in to mortal sin!" To make sure that he himself would never do so, St. Louis daily assisted at two Masses and prayed for several hours. St. Louis ruled his kingdom justly and fought corruption in the administration of royal justice, setting up a court that would eventually become Parliament. He participated in two Crusades, the second of which took his life through illness.

This take on a Kir Royale is a fitting tribute to our holy monarch.

Royal Berry Spritz

Makes 1 drink

½ oz. raspberry syrup
4 oz. nonalcoholic sparkling wine

Pour cordial into a flute or wine glass and slowly top with nonalcoholic sparkling wine. The sugar in the cordial will cause the wine to fizz, so pour carefully. Garnish with fresh, seasonal berries.

LAST CALL

We Catholics can get indifferent to what an ugly business sin really is, either because we slowly drift with the culture into defining deviancy down or because we take the sacrament of confession for granted. The words of Queen Blanche and St. Louis are a good slap across the face. Screw up your courage and say the following toast: "To St. Louis: may he help us choose death before sin!" Of course, you may need a bracer in order to make that toast, and therein lies the conundrum.

SAINT AUGUSTINE, AUGUST 28

Augustine of Hipp (354–430) is famous for converting to the Catholic faith after a lascivious life involving two consecutive mistresses and an illegitimate son. He went on to become the Bishop of Hippo Regius in modern-day Algeria, a devastating opponent of the schisms and heresies of his day, and the most influential and important of the Church Fathers (which is saying a lot).

Augustine's autobiography, *Confessions,* is a spiritual masterpiece. In it we learn that fruit trees played an interesting role in Augustine's life. The book includes a lengthy reflection on when Augustine stole pears from a neighbor's tree as a teenager; and when Augustine finally does convert, he tells us that it was under a fig tree.

We can put these two fruits together into a delicious mocktail.

St. Augustine's Fig and Pear Mocktail

Makes 1 drink

2 oz. pear juice
1 oz. fig-thyme simple syrup
½ oz. fresh lemon juice
2 oz. ginger beer
1 sliced pear, garnish
1 thyme sprig, garnish

Pour pear juice, fig-thyme simple syrup, and lemon juice into a shaker filled with ice and shake 40 times. Strain into a coupe glass or cocktail glass. Top with ginger beer and garnish with sliced pear and a sprig of thyme.

Note*:* To make fig-thyme simple syrup, combine half a cup water, 2 tablespoons of fig jam, and 1 sprig of thyme in a saucepan over medium heat and stir occasionally until jam dissolves. Strain and let cool.

LAST CALL

Borrowing a famous line from the *Confessions*, make the following toast: "Through the intercession of St. Augustine, the Doctor of Grace, may our restless hearts find rest in God."

SAINT FIACRE, AUGUST 30 (SEPTEMBER 1 IN FRANCE AND IRELAND)

Fiacre of Breuil (d. 670) was an Irish priest who lived in a hermitage in County Kilkenny. Disciples flocked to him, but preferring solitude, he moved to what is now Saint-Fiacre, France, and there built an oratory to the Blessed Virgin Mary. When visitors again came knocking on his door, he established a hospice for strangers and served them from his well-kept garden. Fiacre was renowned for his mastery of herbal medicines and had the power of healing by the laying on of hands. An old French word for hemorrhoids is a pun on his name: *le fic* (small tumor) *de S. Fiacre.*

Fiacre's mastery of herbal remedies also gave him the dubious patronage of sexually transmitted diseases.

The perfect drink for this patron saint of gardeners, florists, horticulturists, and costermongers (vegetable vendors) is something made from V8 Vegetable Juice, which was invented in 1933 in response to the nutritional crisis caused by the Great Depression and named after the powerful V8 engine. The juice is comprised of eight vegetables: beets, celery, carrots, lettuce, parsley, watercress, spinach, and tomato. A Bloody Mary made with V8 instead of tomato juice is called a Bloody Eight or an Eight Ball. We're calling our nonalcoholic version St. Fiacre's Feast, and we suggest that you be lavish with the vegetable garnishes.

St. Fiacre's Feast

Makes 1 drink

4–6 oz. V8 Vegetable Juice
1 dash lemon juice
½ tsp. Worcestershire sauce
2 or 3 drops Tabasco sauce
salt and pepper

Add ice, liquid ingredients, salt, and pepper to glass and stir 40 times. Garnish extravagantly. Options include celery sticks, pepperoni sticks, pearl onions, olives (green or black), dill pickle chunks, lime wedges, pearl onions, pickled asparagus spears, etc.

LAST CALL

You can make a toast about hemorrhoids, but it may not sit well with some of your guests. Or you can make a toast about STD testing, but the results may not be positive. A safer bet is the following: "To St. Fiacre, the patron saint of gardeners: through his intercession, may both our hearts and our gardens be free of weeds and full of good produce."

CHAPTER NINE

September

SAINTS

POPE SAINT PIUS X, SEPTEMBER 3 (AUGUST 21)

The future Pope Pius X (1835–1914) was born Joseph Sarto in Riese, Italy, the son of the town mailman. The family's humble circumstances did not stop little Giuseppe from being generous to a fault. His sisters had to hide his laundry because when "Beppi," as he was called, came across a poor person, he would literally give him the shirt off his back! Joseph grew up to be a fine parish priest, bishop, patriarch of Venice, and pope.

As Supreme Pontiff, Pius X worked to restore the liturgy to its proper place in peoples' hearts. He promoted Gregorian chant, frequent reception of Holy Communion, and active participation (a concept much misunderstood these days, but that's not his fault). St. Pius X also declared war on the heresy of Modernism, the infatuation with all things modern to the detriment of the ancient and unchanging Faith.

In honor of the redoubtable foe of Modernism and the stalwart promoter of the ancient liturgy, what could be better than that timeless classic, the Old Fashioned? Here is a generic option followed by some brand-specific recipes.

Old Fashioned Mocktail

Makes 4 drinks

- 2 cups water
- 2 black tea bags
- 1 oz. maple simple syrup
- 8 dashes Angostura bitters
- 4 orange peels or Toschi Amarena cherries, garnish

Steep the tea in the hot water for 3–5 minutes. Let tea cool completely. In the meantime, make maple simple syrup by heating equal parts maple syrup and water until syrup dissolves. Let cool completely. Once both tea and syrup are cool, make the cocktail. For each serving, pour ¼ cup tea, ¼ ounce simple syrup, and 2 dashes bitters into an old-fashioned glass with ice and stir. Garnish with an orange peel or cherry.

SEPTEMBER

Spiritless Old Fashioned

Makes 1 drink

2¼ oz. Spiritless Kentucky 74
¼ oz. simple syrup (or Spiritless Horse's Kick Ginger Syrup for a spicier kick)
3 dashes All The Bitter Aromatic Bitters
1 orange peel, garnish

Pour liquid ingredients into an old-fashioned glass with ice and stir. Garnish with orange peel.

Lyre's Old Fashioned

Makes 1 drink

2 oz. Lyre's American Malt
¼ oz. simple syrup
2 dashes aromatic bitters
1 orange peel, garnish

Pour liquid ingredients into an old-fashioned glass with ice and stir. Garnish with orange peel.

Ritual Zero Proof's Old Fashioned

Makes 1 drink

2 oz. Ritual Whiskey Alternative
1–2 dashes aromatic bitters
¼ oz. simple syrup
1 dash water
1 orange slice, garnish

Pour liquid ingredients into an old-fashioned glass with ice and stir 40 times. Garnish with orange slice.

Pathfinder's Old Fashioned

Makes 1 drink

2 oz. The Pathfinder Hemp & Root Spirit
½ oz. demerara simple syrup
4 dashes aromatic bitters
1 orange peel, garnish

Pour liquid ingredients into an old-fashioned glass with ice and stir 40 times. Garnish with orange peel.

Note: To make demerara simple syrup, combine equal parts demerara sugar and water in a saucepan over medium heat until sugar dissolves. Let cool and pour into a sterilized jar.

LAST CALL

Pope St. Pius X's papal motto, "To restore all things in Christ" (Ephesians 1:10), also makes a good toast, as in: "To Pope St. Pius X: may his prayers and intercession help us in the great privilege of restoring all things in Christ."

St. Pius X required all clergy to take the "Oath Against Modernism," which can easily be found online. Test your orthodoxy and those of your friends by reading it aloud. Guests who flunk have to do the dishes—oh, and recant their heresy immediately.

NATIVITY OF THE BLESSED VIRGIN MARY, SEPTEMBER 8

Usually in the liturgical calendar, a saint's "birthday" is the day that he passed from this earthly life to his eternal reward in Heaven. On this day, however—nine months after the Feast of the Immaculate Conception—the Church directs our attention to the earthly birthday of the Mother of God. As such, Mary is one of only three persons to receive this distinction (Jesus Christ and John the Baptist being the other two).

Today's feast is the occasion for a grape harvest festival in the wine regions of France. Winegrowers bring their best grapes to church for a blessing and tie some of these first fruits to a statue of the Blessed Virgin. A festive meal is then held during which the grapes are consumed. French winemakers and wine-growers refer to this holy day as "Our Lady of the Grape Harvest." Feel free to enjoy a nonalcoholic wine tonight (see our list of nonalcoholic wines in Appendix I).

But the most popular tradition associated with the Nativity of Our Lady is the blessing of seeds and seedlings for the autumn planting season. The old *Roman Ritual* contains a beautiful blessing for the occasion, which we cite below.

And with gardens on our mind, we propose the following:

Secret Garden

Inspired by John Van Lieslo

Makes 1 drink

1¾ oz. Little Saints' St. Ember
1 oz. green juice
½ oz. fresh lime juice
½ oz. agave nectar
chipotle salt
1 dried orange wheel, garnish

Pour liquid ingredients into a shaker with ice and shake 40 times. Strain into a cocktail glass. Add a pinch of chipotle salt on top and garnish with orange.

Spiritless Flowers

Makes 1 drink

2 oz. Spiritless Kentucky 74
4 oz. Owen's Sparkling Cranberry Juice
2–3 floral ice cubes
1 edible flower, garnish

Pour Kentucky 74 into an old-fashioned glass with floral ice cubes and top with Owen's Sparkling Cranberry Juice. Gently stir and garnish with edible flower.

Note*:* To make floral ice cubes, place small edible flowers (e.g., dandelions, violets, etc.) in an ice cube tray, fill with water, and freeze.

LAST CALL

The following toast is adapted from the *Ritual*'s charming Blessing of Seeds and Seedlings: "Through the intercession of the Blessed Virgin Mary, whose birthday we celebrate today, may almighty God our merciful Father, who sows and cultivates the heavenly Word and who tills the topsoil of our hearts with spiritual rakes, always look upon us with merry eyes and a cheerful countenance."

SAINT NICHOLAS OF TOLENTINO, SEPTEMBER 10

The Augustinian friar Nicholas (1246–1306) was famous for comforting and sometimes healing the dying; for freeing souls from Purgatory by his prayers; for extinguishing fires; and for healing sick animals by giving them "St. Nicholas' bread," bread over which he had invoked the blessings of the Blessed Virgin Mary. One of the miracles attributed to St. Nicholas occurred after he was given a roasted fowl for dinner. A vegetarian, St. Nicholas made the sign of the cross over the bird, and it flew out the window.

LAST CALL

A toast: "Through the intercession of Saint Nicholas, may our use of this book take time off Purgatory."

Since we can't think of a drink for a flying roasted bird, let's stick with the theme of Purgatory.

Purgatorio

Makes 4 drinks

- 1 cup raspberries
- 2 cups crushed ice
- 1 cup prune juice
- ¾ cup cranberry juice
- 2 tbsp. fresh lime juice
- 1 cup ginger ale
- ¾ cup sparkling lemonade
- 1 piece peeled ginger (1–2 inches) sliced thinly, garnish

Distribute raspberries and crushed ice evenly in 4 highball glasses. Pour prune juice, cranberry juice, and lime juice into a mixing glass and stir 40 times. Pour into glasses and top with ginger ale and sparkling lemonade. Garnish with ginger.

FEAST OF THE HOLY NAME OF MARY, SEPTEMBER 12

If you are wondering why there is a feast honoring the name of the Mother of God, recall the story about St. Francis compelling the devil to admit what he was afraid of. The devil mentioned three things: the Holy Name of Jesus, the brown scapular, and the Holy Name of Mary.

The first Feast of the Holy Name of Mary took place in 1513 on September 15, the octave day of her nativity (as faithful Jews, Sts. Joachim and Anne would have named their daughter Mary eight days after her birth). Over time, however, the feast moved around to various dates, eventually landing on September 12, thanks in large part to the Battle of Vienna in 1683.

On September 12 of that year, the Polish king and warrior Jan III Sobieski saved the city of Vienna, Austria, from the Turkish army in a spectacular military victory that changed the course of history. Sobieski made a bold assault over a mountain range, and when the shouts of his Hussar cavalry "made known that the 'Northern Lion' was on the field . . . the Turks fled, panic-stricken." After the battle, a curious Capuchin friar named Blessed Marco d'Aviano used coffee beans left behind by the hastily retreating Turks to brew himself a cup. Because he found the taste too bitter, he added milk, and thus the cappuccino or "little Capuchin," was born.

Little Saints has a canned **Espresso Martini** that will not disappoint, or try any of the following:

Sentia's Espresso Martini

Makes 1 drink

1¼ oz. GABA Black
1 oz. espresso
¾ oz. agave syrup
crushed chocolate-covered espresso beans, optional garnish

Pour all liquid ingredients into a shaker with ice and shake 40 times. Strain into a coupe glass. Optional: rim the glass with crushed chocolate-covered espresso beans.

Lyre's Espresso Martini

Makes 1 drink

1½ oz. Lyre's Coffee Originale
½ oz. Lyre's White Cane Spirit
1½ oz. premium cold drip or fresh espresso, chilled
2 tsp. vanilla syrup (not vanilla extract) or simple syrup
coffee bean, garnish

Pour all liquid ingredients into a shaker with ice and shake 40 times. Strain into a champagne coupe glass or cocktail glass and float coffee bean on top.

Spiritless Chocolate Espresso Martini

Makes 1 drink

2 oz. Spiritless Jalisco 55
4 oz. Owen's Espresso Martini Mix
chocolate syrup
cocoa powder
1 chocolate-covered strawberry, garnish

Rim a champagne coupe or cocktail glass with chocolate syrup and cocoa powder. Pour all liquid ingredients into a shaker with ice and shake 40 times. Strain into the glass and garnish with chocolate-covered strawberry.

LAST CALL

For a toast, you can use Sobieski's *"Veni, vidi, Deus vicit"* ("I came, I saw, God conquered") or a verse taken from the Litany of Divine Praises: "Blessed be the name of Mary, Virgin and Mother." Heck, why not use both?

THE SEVEN SORROWS OF OUR LADY, SEPTEMBER 15

The day after the Feast of the Holy Cross, the Church celebrates the Blessed Virgin Mary's Seven Sorrows, that is, 1) the prophecy of Simeon (Luke 2:34–35); 2) the flight into Egypt (Matthew 2:13–14); 3) the loss of the Child Jesus in the temple (Luke 2:43–45); 4) the meeting of Jesus and Mary on the Way of the Cross; 5) the Crucifixion; 6) the taking down of the Body of Jesus from the Cross, and 7) the burial of Jesus. In the traditional (1962) calendar, the Church also commemorates the Seven Sorrows on the Friday before Good Friday: while Good Friday recalls the Passion of the Christ, the Seven Sorrows recall the Compassion of His mother. Compassion literally means a "suffering with," and nobody suffered with Jesus like Mary, who watched in horror as her Son underwent unspeakable torments. The sinless Man of Sorrows had His passion, and so did the sinless Mother of Sorrows. "And while His accomplished everything," Frank Sheed writes, "hers was not for nothing. It was part of the design of the Redemption that while the Divine Person suffered

the Passion that redeemed us, a human person should suffer a passion parallel with His."

We should not be surprised about this parallel: according to St. Paul, all Christian suffering shares in the redemptive suffering of Our Lord (see Colossians 1:24). How much more significant, then, is the suffering of Mary, who has a special role in the economy of salvation? When at the wedding of Cana Mary tells Jesus that the wine has run out, He does not ask what that has to do with Him but rather, "Woman, what is that to Me and to thee? My hour is not yet come." (John 2:4). The Blessed Virgin Mary is somehow an ongoing part of the Plan.

So let us toast to Mary's compassion for her Son, and her compassion for us as well. GT's has a Synergy line of raw kombucha that includes Passionberry Bliss. The label boasts that one sixteen-ounce bottle contains 9 billion living probiotics, which are excellent for gut health. It reminds us of Our Lady's soul, pierced by a sword, out of which the thoughts of many are revealed (see Luke 2:35).

Kompassion on the Rocks

Makes 2 drinks

16 oz. Synergy Passionberry Bliss Raw Kombucha

Swirl the bottle gently to distribute the probiotics evenly, but do not shake (it is carbonated and will fizz up if you do). Pour into 2 old-fashioned glasses filled with ice and serve.

LAST CALL

Today's Collect can be modified and used as a toast. "Let us toast to the most sweet soul of Mary, which was pierced by a sword of sorrow at the Passion of Our Lord, as foretold by the prophet Simeon. And may her Divine Son grant that we who honor her sorrows may reap the happy fruit of His Passion."

SAINT HILDEGARD OF BINGEN, SEPTEMBER 17

Known as the "Sibyl of the Rhine" for her poetic prophecies, Hildegard of Bingen (1098–1179) was born to a noble German family and entered the cloister of Disibodenberg before founding her own convents at Rupertsberg and Bingen. Her reputation for prophecy and holiness spread (against her will), and soon Hildegard was corresponding with kings and popes. In addition to authoring over three hundred letters, Hildegard also composed several dozen hymns and fifteen books ranging from theology to science. Most of Hildegard's works are still available today, including over one hundred albums that feature her musical compositions. In 2012, Pope Benedict XVI declared St. Hildegard a Doctor of the Church, the fourth woman in history to receive that honor.

As you would expect from a Doctor of the Church, Hildegard was an exceptionally wise person, with a keen insight into moral psychology and an avid interest in numerous subjects, including medicine. Although she often recommends beer or wine for various ailments, she was also a master of nonalcoholic wine tonics, which more and more people are coming to realize actually work. To make the tonics, Hildegard mixed regular wine with other ingredients and then boiled the mixture until the alcohol had evaporated.

Parsley wine is one of Hildegard's recommend wine tonics and probably the most popular today. The simple concoction is used to treat minor heart conditions, rheumatism, chronic inflammation, and insomnia. "Whoever suffers from pain in the heart, spleen or side, drink this wine often (daily) and it will heal him," Hildegard writes. She recommends three ounces a night for chest tightness, heart pain, and other circulatory discomfort and half a cup before bedtime for better sleep.

Hildegard is also the first known person to recommend in writing the use of hops in beer. **Hoplark's 0.0 Really Really Hoppy** lives up to its name. This nonalcoholic craft brew is made with no malt and double-dried Simcoe and Citra hops.

St. Hildegard's Parsley Wine

Makes 1 drink

1 bunch parsley
1 bottle wine (preferably organic)
2 tbsp. white wine vinegar
3/4 cup honey

Put parsley in a medium saucepan and pour in the other ingredients. Bring to a boil and boil for 10 minutes. Let cool, strain, and pour back into the bottle.

Note: The alcohol in the wine should have evaporated after 10 minutes, but there may be trace amounts left.

And if any saint knew about the power of plants, it was Hildegard. Three Spirit makes a botanical elixir called Social that harnesses lion's mane mushroom, yerba mate, and damiana. It goes great in a Plant Power.

Plant Power

Makes 1 drink

- 1 oz. Social Elixir
- 1 oz. pineapple juice
- 1 oz. pomegranate juice
- ½ oz. orgeat
- ½ oz. turmeric juice
- ½ oz. ginger juice
- soda water
- 1 mint leaf, garnish
- 1 tropical fruit, garnish

Pour all ingredients (except soda and garnishes) into a shaker with ice and shake 40 times. Strain into a chilled old-fashioned glass, top with soda water, and garnish with mint leaves and tropical fruit.

SAINT MATTHEW, SEPTEMBER 21

Before becoming one of the twelve Apostles and one of the four evangelists, Matthew was a publican or tax collector. Never a profession popular with the rest of society, it was particularly loathed in Matthew's day for two reasons: the taxes went to the hated conquerors, the Romans, and the tax collectors usually squeezed more than their fair share out of the taxpayer in order to skim off the top. But Matthew was probably an honest guy even before he became an Apostle of Our Lord, and he responded to our Lord's summons to follow Him so quickly that he did not even stop to take any of his money.

Understandably, Matthew is a patron saint of accountants, bankers, customs officers, tax collectors, and the like. In 1934, the Pope put security guards at banks under Matthew's protection: we suspect that during the Great Depression the Holy Father thought they could use a little extra help against desperados. But perhaps the most fitting pairing of all is that Matthew was chosen to be the sole patron of the Archdiocese of Washington, D.C., which of course includes that great magnetic center of tax collection known as our nation's capital.

Here is our original mocktail to honor St. Matthew, which is very loosely based on a vintage cocktail called the Income Tax.

Duty-Free Mocktail

Makes 1 drink

- 1½ oz. orange juice
- 1 oz. blood orange juice
- ¼ oz. peach nectar
- 1 dash aromatic bitters
- 1 dehydrated orange wheel, garnish

Pour all ingredients into a shaker with ice and shake 40 times. Strain into a cocktail glass and garnish with orange wheel.

LAST CALL

A toast: "May the intercession of St. Matthew keep our tax collectors honest and our taxes minimal. And may the taxpayer money that is collected be used in conformity with God's law and for the sake of the good, the true, and the beautiful."

SAINT PIO OF PIETRELCINA, SEPTEMBER 23

The Capuchin priest Francesco Forgione (1887–1968) is better known to the world as Padre Pio of Pietrelcina. As a boy, he was already eager for the ascetical life (his mother had to stop him from sleeping on the floor with a stone pillow), and he was already having mystical visions: he had two-way conversations with Jesus, the Blessed Virgin, and his guardian angel, and he was surprised to learn that not everyone else did too.

The first priest to receive the stigmata (St. Francis of Assisi was a deacon), Padre Pio was renowned even in his lifetime for his bilocation and miracles, his spiritual suffering, his reading of people's hearts, and his physical battles with the devil and other demons. The devil tried mightily to overthrow Padre Pio, appearing in benign forms like Padre Pio's ecclesiastical superior or even our Lord and our Lady, or in terrifying forms such as an ugly black cat or a repugnant animal.

Another name for the verbena plant is devil's bane because it was believed to have been used to staunch Our Lord's wounds after He was taken down from the cross. Padre Pio can certainly be called a bane of the devil, and he also bore Christ's wounds through the stigmata. Methinks we found our drink for tonight.

Devil's Bane Mocktail

Makes 1 drink

2 oz. Bax Botanics Verbena
½ oz. fresh lime juice
½ oz. simple syrup
10 mint leaves

Gently muddle leaves in a shaker. Add remaining ingredients and ice and shake 40 times. Strain into a highball glass with ice.

LAST CALL

In the words of St. Pio, "May Jesus be always in your mind, in your heart, and before your eyes." Another option: "To Padre Pio, vanquisher of the black devil by the grace of God."

NORTH AMERICAN MARTYRS, SEPTEMBER 26 (OCTOBER 19)

Note: In the new Roman calendar, September 26 is the feast date for the North American martyrs in Canada while October 19 is the date in the US. In the traditional calendar, the date is September 26 in both the US and Canada.

Also known as the Canadian Martyrs and the Martyrs of New France, the mostly Jesuit North American Martyrs are Sts. Jean de Brébeuf, Noël Chabanel, Antoine Daniel, Charles Garnier, René Goupil, Isaac Jogues, Jean de Lalande, and Gabriel Lalemant. Missionaries to the Huron Indians, they were brutally tortured and killed by the Hurons' enemy, the Iroquois, between 1642 and 1649. The National Shrine of the North American Martyrs in Auriesville, New York, is located near where three of the martyrs—Sts. René Goupil, Isaac Jogues, and Jean de Lalande—were killed.

We won't go into all the graphic details of their martyrdom (and boy are they graphic), but we need to mention one. An Iroquois woman sawed off the thumb of St. Isaac Jogues with a clam shell. When he escaped and returned to France, he had to receive special permission from the Pope to celebrate Mass since he lacked a "canonical digit," a finger necessary to hold the Sacred Host. The Pope granted the dispensation immediately, saying, "It would be unjust if a martyr of Christ should not drink the blood of Christ." Incredibly, Jogues returned to the mission territory of New France, where he was again taken prisoner and this time tomahawked by a Mohawk.

Let's drink to these brave soldiers of Christ and bearers of the Light to the North American continent. Clamato juice is a New York invention that is popular in Canada, so both sides of the border can claim it for their own. "Clamato" is a portmanteau of "clam" and "tomato," its two main ingredients. That's right: you can contemplate St. Isaac Jogues' bloody thumb and the instrument of its removal as you drink tonight. Or, forget that we said that and just focus on the US-Canadian connection. And think of the tomato as betokening the New World that these martyrs evangelized, for it is native to this hemisphere.

In Canada, clamato juice is used chiefly to make a Bloody Mary–like beverage called a Caesar. Here is a simple recipe:

Virgin Caesar

Makes 1 drink

2 dashes Tabasco Sauce
4 dashes Worcestershire sauce
3 dashes salt & pepper
4 oz. Mott's Clamato Juice
Caesar seasoning salt rimmer such as Mott's

Rim a highball by rubbing lime wedge along the edge and dipping it in seasoning salt. Add ice, liquid ingredients, salt, and pepper to glass and stir 40 times. Garnish extravagantly. Options include celery sticks, pepperoni sticks, pearl onions, olives (green or black), dill pickle chunks, lime wedges, pearl onions, pickled asparagus spears, etc.

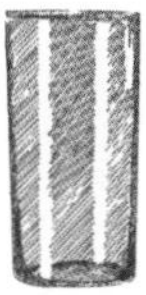

SEPTEMBER

LAST CALL

In 1662, the Jesuits convinced the French government to ban alcohol as a bartering item in the fur trade because the native population was not faring well with strong drink. Tonight, toast to a time when the Society of Jesus exercised good judgment, promoted virtue, and spread the Gospel—and pray that they will do so again.

Or, since one of the martyrs (St. René Goupil) is the patron saint of anesthesiologists, knock yourself out tonight with jokes about anesthesiologists.

SAINT MICHAEL, SEPTEMBER 29

From the Middle Ages to the nineteenth century, the Feast of Saint Michael, or "Michaelmas" (pronounced MICK-el-mus), was celebrated as a major holy day. Michaelmas fairs, parades, plays, etc. would be held in honor of the great Archangel who cast Satan into Hell. Michael is further honored as the guardian angel of the Church militant, the "banner bearer" who conducts souls to Purgatory and Heaven, and the *Praepositus* or "governor" of Heaven (in contrast to Lucifer who is the "ruler" of Hell).

Having a drink has long been a customary part of Michaelmas festivity. *Michelsminne*, or St. Michael's Love, was the name given in some parts of northern Europe for wine consumed on St. Michael's Day. The custom has been especially popular in Denmark.

In *Drinking with the Saints*, we recommend St. Michael's Sword, a concoction made with blackberry brandy. The blackberry hearkens to an old Irish legend: when St. Michael cast Lucifer out of Heaven, the devil fell on a blackberry bush and cursed and spat on the blackberries, thereby rendering them sour after September 29. Consequently, folks would eat blackberries on Michaelmas but not after. Our mocktail, the St. Michael's Dagger, pays homage to this legend, and so do the other recipes here. You can also try a delicious glass of mora, a drink from Costa Rica where blackberries grow in abundance, and three new mocktails involving blackberries.

Mora

Makes 4 drinks

2 cups ripe blackberries
½ cup granulated sugar, more to taste
3 cups cold water

Wash blackberries, cover with sugar, and refrigerate overnight. Place berries and sugar in a blender and blend until very smooth. Strain with a fine mesh strainer, pushing juice out of the pulp; when you can get no more juice, pour the water onto the pulp and push more. Taste and add more sugar or water as needed.

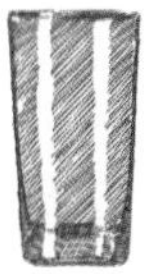

St. Michael's Dagger

Makes 1 drink

1 oz. blackberry syrup
½ oz. fresh lemon juice
4–6 oz. sparkling water
1 Toschi Amarena cherry, garnish

Pour syrup and lemon juice in a shaker with ice and shake 40 times. Strain into a cocktail glass and top with sparkling water. Garnish with a cocktail sword and a cherry to symbolize Michael's victory over Lucifer, who like the cherry is red with rage and shame.

Lyre's Blackberry Smash

Makes 1 drink

2 oz. Lyre's American Malt
½ oz. fresh lime juice
½ oz. simple syrup
5 blackberries, divided
8 mint leaves
1 mint sprig, garnish

Muddle 4 blackberries and mint with simple syrup in a shaker. Add liquid ingredients and ice and shake 40 times. Strain into an old-fashioned glass with ice and garnish with mint sprig and remaining blackberry on a cocktail spear.

Peachy Keen

Makes 1 drink

1 can De Soi's Purple Lune
1 peach slice, garnish
1 blackberry, garnish

Pour Purple Lune into a pretty glass with ice, then garnish with a slice of peach and a blackberry.

Blackberry Whiskey

Makes 1 drink

2 oz. Monday Whiskey
4–5 fresh blackberries
½ oz. fresh lemon juice
½ oz. simple syrup
1 orange peel, garnish
1 blackberry, garnish

Muddle the blackberries with lemon juice and simple syrup in a shaker. Add Monday Whiskey and ice and shake 40 times. Strain into an old-fashioned glass with ice and garnish with orange peel and blackberry.

SAINT JEROME, SEPTEMBER 30

This patron saint of biblical scholars and librarians, who gave the Church the Latin Vulgate translation of the Bible, used a rock as a pillow and spent the last thirty-four years of his life in a hermit's cell outside Bethlehem. Jerome (347–420) was also notoriously grouchy, even towards fellow saints. He called St. Ambrose of Milan "a jackdaw who decks himself in other birds' showy feathers" and accused him of writing "bad things in Latin taken from good things in Greek." His correspondence with St. Augustine is legendary for its acrimony, with the two theological heavyweights sparring round after round.

That Jerome is a canonized saint should give hope to all curmudgeons of the world. And what better way to celebrate the memory of this acerbic ascetic than with a Whiskey Sour. Here are three cocktail options. Or, enjoy a can of **0.0 Hop Sour** by **Hoplark**, their take on a Kettle Sour–style beer.

Sentia Sour

Makes 1 drink

- 1½ oz. GABA Red
- ½ oz. agave
- ¾ oz. fresh lemon juice
- ¾ oz. aquafaba (chickpea juice) or 1 egg white (we prefer egg white)

Pour all ingredients into a shaker with ice and shake 40 times. Strain into a chilled glass or an old-fashioned glass with ice.

Note: 1 egg white suffices for 2 cocktails.

Lyre's Whiskey Sour

Makes 1 drink

- 2 oz. Lyre's American Malt
- 1 oz. fresh lemon juice
- ½ oz. egg white, aquafaba (chickpea juice), or 4 drops foaming agent
- 2 tsp. simple syrup
- 2 dashes aromatic bitters
- 1 orange wedge, garnish
- 1 Toschi Amarena cherry, garnish

Pour all liquid ingredients into a shaker without ice and dry shake briefly. Add ice, shake 40 times vigorously, and strain into an old-fashioned glass with ice. Garnish with orange and cherry.

Spiritless' Kumquat Whiskey Sour

Makes 1 drink

2 oz. Kentucky 74
1 oz. fresh lemon juice
1 oz. ginger syrup
3 kumquats, divided
2 sprigs rosemary, divided

Combine 2 kumquats, 1 sprig of rosemary, and ginger syrup in a shaker and muddle well. Add Kentucky 74 and lemon juice. Shake 40 times and strain into a cocktail glass filled with 1 large ice cube. Slice the remaining kumquat and float on top. Garnish with remaining rosemary sprig.

LAST CALL

"May God, through the intercession of our patron St. Jerome, have mercy on all of us cranks, hotheads, and grumps."

CHAPTER TEN

October

SAINTS

GUARDIAN ANGELS, OCTOBER 2

Every individual has his own Guardian Angel, and it is also believed that many groups do as well, such as families, churches, dioceses, and nations. Our Guardian Angels protect us from harm and from the wiles of the devil, and so we owe them a vote of thanks, or at least a toast. And since, according to St. Thomas Aquinas, they will remain with us as companions in Heaven, we might as well get used to them.

Blue Angel Low Alcohol Cocktail

Makes 1 drink

2 oz. blue curacao liqueur
2 oz. fresh lemon juice
1 oz. brown sugar
2 lemon wedges
4 mint leaves, divided
1 dram water
sparkling water
1 lemon slice, garnish

Muddle ½ of the curacao, lemon juice, brown sugar, lemon wedges, and 2 mint leaves in a shaker. Add 1 large ice cube and a little water. Shake 40 times. Pour remaining curacao into a highball glass. Using a Black and Tan spoon, layer the contents of the shaker into the glass. Using the same technique, layer sparkling water into the glass. Gently lower several ice cubes into the drink and garnish with lemon slice and remaining mint leaves.

Note: Contains alcohol.

LAST CALL

Thank your Guardian Angel tonight for the near-misses in your life and ask him to keep up the good work.

SAINT THÉRÈSE OF LISIEUX, OCTOBER 3 (OCTOBER 1)

One of the most popular saints of the twentieth century, Thérèse of Lisieux (1873–1897) was a French Carmelite nun who is most famous for her spirituality of the Little Way: rather than conquer Heaven through martyrdom or extreme asceticism or heroic acts of virtue, she resolved to perform little acts of mortification to help her on the path to holiness.

Thérèse is affectionately known as the Little Flower, and so we propose the following drink in her honor.

Little Flower Power

Makes 1 drink

1½ oz. Ghia Apéritif
1½ oz. elderflower tonic
grapefruit or lemon zest

Pour Ghia and elderflower tonic into an old-fashioned glass with ice and stir gently. Garnish with zest. Serve in lowball glass on the rocks.

SAINT FRANCIS OF ASSISI, OCTOBER 4

Francis was born Giovanni di Pietro di Bernardone (ca. 1181–1226), but his father nicknamed him Francesco, the "Frenchman." This great saint, who dramatically converted to a life of radical poverty after hearing proclaimed the Gospel passage, "Take neither gold nor silver," was exceedingly humble. Even though he was the founder of the Franciscan Order, he refused to be ordained a priest, remaining a deacon throughout his life.

Francis is usually pictured communicating with a bird, but perhaps the most memorable critter associated with this patron saint of animals and the environment is a wolf. The town of Gubbio was being terrorized by a ravenous wolf, and so St. Francis went out to meet it. After chastising "Brother Wolf" and making the sign of the cross over it, he convinced the wolf to stop his raids on the townsfolks' livestock. In return, because the wolf had only attacked out of hunger, the saint made the townspeople promise to feed the wolf. The wolf and the citizens of Gubbio became friends from that day on, and they even mourned when the wolf eventually died.

Tonight, honor this miracle with a Sound and Furry or a San Francisco.

Sound and Furry

Makes 1 drink

- 2¼ oz. Spiritless Kentucky 74
- ¼ oz. Liber & Co. Pineapple Gum Syrup
- ¼ oz. Runamok Vanilla & Cinnamon Maple Syrup
- 1 dash All The Bitters Aromatic Bitters
- 1 dash Lion's Mane Tincture
- 1 candied pineapple, garnish

Pour all liquid ingredients into a shaker with ice and shake 40 times. Strain into an old-fashioned glass with ice and garnish with candied pineapple.

San Francisco

Makes 2 drinks

- 1 oz. fresh orange juice
- 1 oz. grapefruit juice
- 1 oz. pineapple juice
- 1 oz. sour mix or fresh lemon juice
- 1 egg white, optional
- sparkling water
- 2 dashes grenadine
- 2 Toschi Amarena cherries, garnish
- 2 orange slices, garnish

Pour egg white and all liquid ingredients except sparkling water into a shaker with ice and shake 40 times. Strain into a highball glass with ice, top with sparkling water, and stir gently. Garnish with cherry and orange slices.

LAST CALL

St. Francis of Assisi used to call his body "Brother Ass." Like any jackass or jenny ass, the body sometimes needs a stick and sometimes a carrot, and sometimes even a sugar cube. Tonight, give Brother Ass the sugar cube.

OUR LADY OF THE ROSARY, OCTOBER 7

A "rosary" or *rosarium* is literally a garland of roses, but it is more familiar to Catholics as a special garland of prayers offered to the Blessed Virgin Mary. Developed in the Middle Ages, the rosary is one of the Church's most powerful weapons in her spiritual arsenal.

The Feast of the Holy Rosary was instituted to commemorate the spectacular victory of the outnumbered armada of the Holy League over the mighty Ottoman navy at the Battle of Lepanto in 1571. Pope St. Pius V instructed all of Italy to pray the rosary as the battle took place off the coast of Greece. As the Turks were being defeated, the Pope was in a meeting with his cardinals in Rome over six hundred miles away. Suddenly, he stopped working, opened a window, looked at the sky, and cried out, "Now is not the time to talk business any more but to give thanks to God for the victory He has granted to the arms of the Christians." The holy Pontiff attributed this victory, which turned the tide of Islamic dominance in the Mediterranean Sea, to the rosary and to Our Lady's intercession.

LAST CALL

Tonight, after praying the rosary, of course, read Chesterton's magnificent poem "Lepanto."

Rose Water Gin Cocktail

Makes 1 drink

2 oz. Monday Gin
1 oz. fresh lemon juice
1 oz. rose water syrup
soda water
3 rose petals, garnish

Pour Monday Gin, lemon juice, and rose water syrup into a shaker with ice and shake 40 times. Strain into an old-fashioned glass and top with soda water. Garnish with rose petals.

Note: To make rose water syrup, combine 1 cup sugar and 1 cup water in a saucepan over medium heat until the sugar dissolves. Let cool and add 1 teaspoon rose water.

SAINT JOHN HENRY NEWMAN, OCTOBER 9

John Henry Newman (1801–1890) was the most famous intellectual in the Church of England when he shocked all of Great Britain and converted to the Catholic faith. Newman lost many friends because of his decision, but his loyalty to the Church was eventually rewarded when he was made a cardinal by Pope Leo XIII. Newman was the greatest theologian of the nineteenth century and a keen critic of the liberalism of his day. Canonized a saint in 2019, we will bet our bar tab that he will one day be declared a Doctor of the Church.

Cardinal Newman was not a phony, he did not hail from Mexico nor from Milan, and yet our thoughts turn to St. Agrestis' Phony Mezcal Negroni, mainly because its brilliant color reminds us of the color of the cardinal's hat that he so eminently deserved. In those days, the Pope used to place the red wide-brimmed hat, called a galero, on the recipient's head in order to make him a cardinal, but because Newman was too old to travel, Leo XIII shipped it to him instead—which is also how we received our bottles of St. Agrestis. The beverage is also bittersweet, like Newman's turn to Rome. Or for groups, enjoy a Cardinal Punch.

Newman's Galero

Makes 1 drink

- 1 bottle of St. Agrestis Phony Mezcal Negroni
- 1 strawberry, garnish
- 1 tinsel tassel toothpick, for the tassels on a galero

Pour St. Agrestis into an old-fashioned glass with ice and garnish by spearing the strawberry with the toothpick and putting it in the glass.

Cardinal Punch

Makes as much as you like

- 1 part cranberry juice
- 1 part ginger ale
- 1 splash fresh orange juice
- 1 dash fresh lemon juice
- 1 dash simple syrup

Pour ingredients into a punch bowl with ice and stir.

LAST CALL

Newman stands out in this book because he is the only one on record for proposing a toast. Here is the full passage, from his *Letter to the Duke of Norfolk*:

> **Certainly, if I am obliged to bring religion into after-dinner toasts (which indeed does not seem quite the thing), I shall drink—to the Pope, if you please—still, to Conscience first, and to the Pope afterwards.**

As for Newman's opinion about the incompatibility of religion and after-dinner toasts, our own well-formed conscience compels us to dissent.

And so, a toast: "To Conscience first, and to Saint John Henry Newman and the Pope afterwards."

SAINT GUMMARUS, OCTOBER 11

The Belgian Saint Gummarus or Gomer (717–744) was happy serving at the court of King Pepin until he got married. His wife Guinimaria was described as "extravagant and perverse in her ways, cruel, capricious and altogether unteachable." Gummarus strove to make his wife agreeable to reason and religion, but he was called away to war for eight years. When he returned, he found the place in shambles thanks to Guinimaria's cruelty and incompetence. Apparently, "she was so mean that she even refused beer to the reapers at harvest!" Gummarus made full restitution to the servants and tenants she had wronged (which is why, we suspect, he is the patron of cowherds and so forth), and his example even affected Guinimaria for a while. However, her good behavior did not last long and she soon reverted to her old ways. Gummarus finally gave up and founded a hermitage around which the town of Lierre grew over time.

St. Gummarus' most famous miracle is the time that he wrapped his belt around a felled tree and caused it to bloom again. As a result, the saint is invoked for help with a wide array of fractures (including hernias) and is a patron saint of foresters, lumberjacks, and woodcutters.

Everleaf has a botanical spirit that captures the flavors of the forest and pairs well with today's feast.

Everleaf Old Fashioned

Makes 1 drink

2 oz. Everleaf Forest
3 dashes nonalcoholic bitters
¼ oz. maple syrup
1 orange peel, vanilla pod, maple leaf, or cinnamon, garnishes

Pour all liquid ingredients into an old-fashioned glass with ice and stir gently. Garnish at will.

LAST CALL

Tonight, be extra nice to your spouse as you recall Shakespeare's ominous line: "Better well-hanged than ill-wed." Then, offer the following toast: May the prayers of St. Gummarus keep us from the marital woes of St. Gummarus.

SAINT WILFRID, OCTOBER 12

Wilfrid, Bishop of York (634–709), may have never become a saint were it not for his mean stepmother. The hag made his life at home miserable, so when he had a chance to join the court of King Oswy in Northumbria at the tender age of fourteen, he leaped at it. From there he went to the famous Monastery of Lindisfarne and then to the Continent, where he received an education in Rome and Lyons. When he returned to England, Wilfrid promoted the Benedictine order and total obedience to the Holy See. This was unhappy news to the Irish monks who had evangelized the region and had a different modus operandi. Nor did Theodore, the Archbishop of Canterbury, like the new model. When Theodore divided Wilfrid's diocese into smaller sections for the sake of reform, Wilfrid went over his head and complained to Rome; the case was decided in Wilfrid's favor. And two different kings of Northumbria did not care for Wilfrid either; first Ecgfrith and then Aldfrith alternated between imprisoning and exiling the troublesome bishop whose several appeals to Rome complicated everybody's lives. When he was not annoying other leaders, Wilfrid promoted the *Rule of St. Benedict*, brought religious treasures to England, improved the quality of the liturgy, built several monasteries, and began the Anglo-Saxon evangelization of the Germanic peoples.

Wilfred's (different spelling) Nonalcoholic Aperitif is a delight. A carefully crafted blend of distilled and extracted natural botanicals, it is made with zesty bitter orange, aromatic rosemary, and just a hint of rhubarb. It can be enjoyed over ice but is even better with tonic water. Wilfred's website also has several different cocktail recipes. To honor today's saint, who strikes us as a slightly bitter fellow who liked to tattle to Rome, we recommend a Lime Sour Fred's.

Lime Sour Fred's

Makes 1 drink

- 2½ oz. Wilfred's Aperitif
- ¾ oz. fresh lime juice
- ½ oz. simple syrup
- ¾ oz. egg white or aquafaba (chickpea water)
- 1 mint leaf, garnish

Pour all liquid ingredients into a shaker with ice and shake 40 times. Strain into a cocktail or champagne coupe glass. Garnish with mint or another edible leaf.

SAINT EDWARD THE CONFESSOR, OCTOBER 13

Since he was the eighth son of his father Ethelred the Unready, Saint Edward the Confessor (1003–1066) never expected to be king. Worse, his family's defeats at the hands of the Danes meant that he had to live in exile in Normandy from ages ten to forty. Edward learned early on the vanity of political ambition and turned his attention to the cultivation of piety. He assisted at Mass and the Divine Office every day, after which he would go out hunting, his favorite sport.

When he finally took the throne, Edward was welcomed with great joy by the English people; even the Danish carpetbaggers liked him, owing to "his gentle saintly character." During his lifetime, Edward was renowned for his holiness and miraculous powers. Scrofula (*tuberculous lymphadenitis*) is an ugly skin disease that was once called "the king's evil" because it was believed that a monarch's touch could cure it. The custom of a king touching victims of this disease goes back to King Clovis in France in 496, but Edward was the first English monarch to practice the "royal touch," and for him it actually worked. Many cures are attributed to his miraculous intervention.

Earl Grey tea is oh-so-English, and so is Bax Botanics, English makers of alcohol-free spirits. Their Verbena is made from a plant also known as the devil's bane because it is said to have staunched Our Lord's wounds after He was taken down from the cross. Put these together, and you get the King's Touch.

The King's Touch (a.k.a., Verbena Iced Tea)

Makes 1 drink

2½ oz. Earl Grey tea
1¾ oz. Bax Botanics Verbena
½ oz. apple juice
2 tsp. simple syrup
1 lemon wheel, garnish

Make a strong brew of Earl Grey tea, cool, then chill in the fridge. Pour all liquid ingredients (including tea) into a mixing glass with ice and stir 40 times. Strain into an Irish Coffee glass or tea glass with ice and garnish with lemon wheel.

SAINT TERESA OF ÁVILA, OCTOBER 15

When she was a little girl, Teresa (1515–1582) and her brother dreamt of becoming martyrs, and so they set off for the land of the Moors. Their plan for an easy access to Heaven was thwarted, however, by an uncle who met them on the way and quickly brought them back to their worried mother. They next resolved to become hermits, but they could never find enough stones to build their hermitages in the family garden.

Saint Teresa recounted these stories later in her life, for she had a lovely, self-deprecating sense of humor. Teresa was a good girl, but after her pious mother's death at the age of fourteen, she became immoderately attached to popular fiction and her personal appearance. This frivolity ended when she was educated by Augustinian nuns and introduced to books on Franciscan spirituality. But after eighteen months with the Augustinians, Teresa became seriously ill. It was during that time that she began to understand the ways in which she was resisting God.

Teresa later joined the Carmelite convent at Ávila, but after seeing how lax they had become regarding the rules of cloister, she founded along with Saint John of the Cross the Order of Discalced Carmelites. At the same time, Teresa's intimacy with God grew. She began to experience mystical visions and religious ecstasy. Teresa learned that there is one reliable litmus test for mystical experiences: if it leads to the love of God *and* neighbor, it is real; if it does not, it is not. The saint was named the first female Doctor of the Church in 1970 by Pope Paul VI and praised by Pope Benedict XVI as "one of the peaks of Christian spirituality of all time."

We keep it simple tonight for this saint who loved simplicity with a Nun and Coke, "nun" being a pun on "none," for the amount of alcohol therein.

Nun and Coke

Makes 1 drink

- 2 oz. Lyre's Dark Cane Spirit Non-Alcoholic Rum
- 4 oz. cola
- 1 lime wedge, garnish

Fill a highball halfway with ice. Build the other ingredients and garnish with lime.

LAST CALL

As mentioned, St. Teresa had a wonderfully dry sense of humor and is reputed to have once said, "Lord, save me from sour-faced saints." Make this prayer your own tonight by turning it into a toast as you vow never to confuse life-giving sanctity with buzz-killing sanctimoniousness.

SAINT LUKE, OCTOBER 18

Luke the Evangelist is the author of the third Gospel and the Acts of the Apostles. He did not know our Lord personally, but he was a disciple of St. Paul and, it is believed, a confidant of Our Lady, which may be why his Gospel includes so many details about Christ's infancy and childhood that are not found elsewhere.

St. Luke is also credited with having painted or "written" a number of important icons of the Madonna and Child, such as Our Lady of Czestochowa in Poland, the icon *Salus Populi Romani* ("Protectoress of the Roman People") in Rome's Basilica of St. Mary Major, and the Theotokos of Vladimir in Russia. The liqueur amaretto was invented by a beautiful Italian innkeeper who posed for a Madonna painting by the Renaissance artist Bernardino Luini. Like the little drummer boy, the lovely model showed her gratitude to Luini for this honor by doing what she did best, and so she perfected a liqueur from almonds and apricots.

Amaretto is not to be confused with Amaro, a bitter Italian herbal liqueur that is commonly consumed as an after-dinner *digestivo*. But because we suspect that confusion reigns when it comes to attributions of St. Luke's paintings, we feel that confusion is exactly what is warranted here. Thus we turn to the aptly named Amaro Falso by St. Agrestis.

OCTOBER

St. Luke's True/False Madonna Mocktail

Makes 1 drink

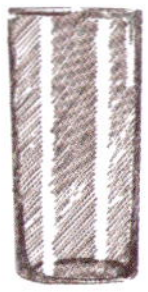

1 bottle St. Agrestis Amaro Falso
1 lemon twist, garnish

Pour St. Agrestis into a highball glass with ice and garnish with lemon twist.

BLESSED KARL OF AUSTRIA, OCTOBER 21

Karl Franz Joseph Ludwig Hubert Georg Otto Marie (1887–1922) was also known as Charles I of Austria and Charles IV of Hungary, the last ruler of the Austro-Hungarian Empire, the last Emperor of Austria, the last king of Hungary, the last king of Bohemia and Croatia, the last king of Galicia and Lodomeria, and the last monarch of the famed house of Hapsburg-Lorraine. In addition to these august titles and distinctions, Bl. Karl is known within the Catholic fold as a just ruler who strove to implement the principles of Catholic social teaching in the face of an insane world war. His conduct during World War I was exemplary: he was the only major political leader in the conflict to support Pope Benedict XV's eminently reasonable peace efforts. After the defeat of his empire, Karl steered his homeland clear of civil war but was banished from it as a result. The leader of a once-great Catholic Empire ended his days on the island of Madeira in exile and in poverty at the age of thirty-four. His feast day on the calendar is rare in that it marks not his earthly passing but the anniversary of his wedding to his faithful wife, Princess Zita.

As of this writing, there are no good nonalcoholic substitutes for Madeira, a fortified wine akin to Port. Better then to turn to a good, hearty nonalcoholic red like **St. Regis Cabernet Sauvignon**.

LAST CALL

Bl. Karl's motto was: "I strive always in all things to understand as clearly as possible and follow the will of God, and this in the most perfect way." Strive to work this beautiful sentiment into a worthy toast.

SAINT ANTHONY MARY CLARET, OCTOBER 23 (OCTOBER 24)

Antonio María Claret y Clara (1807–1870) was a great preacher and author of 150 books. He founded the Missionary Sons of the Immaculate Heart of Mary, better known as the Claretians. For a while he was Archbishop of Santiago in Cuba, during which time he denounced slavery and racism, developed agricultural methods that he tested himself, and instituted trade schools and credit unions for the poor. Anthony was equally at home at the upper end of the social spectrum and was made confessor of Queen Isabella II of Spain. When the queen was exiled, he was placed under house arrest and died in the Cistercian monastery at Fontfroide, France.

The mojito, Cuba's most famous mixed drink, is made from ingredients native to the island and can be traced in some form or another as far back as the sixteenth century. Here are some nonalcoholic variations.

Spindrift Nojito

Makes 1 drink

8 oz. Spindrift Nojito
3 fresh mint leaves, garnish
1 lime wheel, garnish

Pour Nojito into an old-fashioned glass filled with ice and garnish with mint leaves and lime.

OCTOBER

Blueberry Mojito

Makes 1 drink

2 oz. Bax Botanics Verbena
9 large basil leaves, divided
3/4 oz. fresh lemon juice
2 tsp. simple syrup

Muddle 8 basil leaves in a shaker, then add ice and the liquid ingredients. Shake 40 times and strain into an old-fashioned glass with ice. Garnish with remaining basil leaf.

Lyre's Mojito

Makes 1 drink

2½ oz. Lyre's White Cane Spirit
1 oz. fresh lime juice
½ oz. simple syrup
8–10 mint leaves
1 oz. soda water
1 lime wheel, garnish
1 mint sprig, garnish

Add mint leaves and all liquid ingredients to a highball glass with ice and stir 40 times. Top with soda, stir more, and garnish with lime wheel and mint sprig.

LAST CALL

The Claretians have a special devotion to the Blessed Virgin Mary. Tweak their motto into a toast: ***"Her sons rose up and proclaimed her most blessed throughout the world."***

SAINT MINIATUS, OCTOBER 25

Miniatus or Minias is revered as the first Christian martyr of Florence. It is believed that Miniatus was either a soldier in the Roman army or a member of Armenian royalty on pilgrimage when he was martyred in A.D. 250.

Another Florentine treasure is the Negroni cocktail, invented by Count Camillo Negroni in 1919. As Orson Welles once put it, "The bitters are excellent for your liver, the gin is bad for you. They balance each other."

We need not worry about gin when there is an abundance of options for today. **Curious Elixir's Curious No. 1** is a riff on the Negroni, "with the added benefit of rhodiola and gentian to boost energy." **St. Agrestis** likewise has a **Phony Negroni,** a **Phony Mezcal Negroni**, and a **Phony Espresso Negroni** that come in bottles or cans. With these products, all you have to do is pour the product into an old-fashioned glass with ice and garnish with an orange wheel.

And here are some do-it-yourself options:

Zero Proof Negroni

Makes 1 drink

- 1¾ oz. Wilfred's Aperitif
- ½ oz. fresh grapefruit juice
- 1 squeeze fresh lemon
- 3 dashes nonalcoholic bitters (Angostura bitters is also possible but has a small trace of alcohol)
- 1 orange peel, garnish

Pour liquid ingredients into an old-fashioned glass with large ice cube and stir 40 times. Garnish with orange peel twirl.

Negroni Sbagliato-no

Makes 1 drink

1¾ oz. Wilfred's Aperitif
2½ oz. sparkling nonalcoholic Prosecco
1 dash nonalcoholic sweet vermouth, or a few drops nonalcoholic bitters
1 orange slice, garnish

Pour liquid ingredients into a wine glass ice and stir 40 times. Garnish with an orange slice.

Lyre's Negroni

Makes 1 drink

1 oz. Lyre's Dry London Spirit
1 oz. Lyre's Apéritif Rosso
1 oz. Lyre's Italian Orange
1 orange slice, garnish

Pour liquid ingredients into an old-fashioned glass with 1 large ice cube and stir 40 times. Garnish with orange slice.

No-Groni Sour

Makes 1 drink

1½ oz. Free Spirits' The Spirit of Gin
1 oz. The Spirit of Milano
¾ oz. fresh lemon juice
¼ oz. orange juice
¼ oz. simple syrup
1 blob of egg white or aquafaba
3 dashes Angostura bitters

Add the lemon juice and egg white to a shaker without ice and dry shake 40 times. If using aquafaba you can skip this step. Add the remaining liquid ingredients (except the bitters) and ice and shake briefly. Strain into an old-fashioned glass with ice, float the bitters on top, and garnish with orange peel.

PF Negroni

Makes 1 drink

1 oz. The Pathfinder Hemp & Root Spirit
1 oz. nonalcoholic gin
1 oz. Campari
1 orange peel, garnish

Pour liquid ingredients into an old-fashioned glass with 1 large ice cube and stir 40 times. Garnish with orange peel.

Not-A-Groni

Makes 1 drink

1½ oz. Little Saints' St. Ember
¾ oz. Lyre's Aperitif Rosso
¾ oz. Pathfinder
2 dashes cardamon bitters
1 orange peel, garnish

Add St. Ember, Lyre's, Pathfinder, and bitters to a mixing glass with ice and stir 40 times. Strain into an old-fashioned glass with a large ice cube, and garnish with orange peel.

LAST CALL

The great Italian poet Dante was born and raised in Florence, but after being exiled by his enemies, he harbored a hatred of the city and signed off his letters with, "Dante: a Florentine by birth but not by character." Ouch! Work this into your daily correspondence as well.

SAINT BEAN, OCTOBER 26

We know not much about the eleventh-century St. Bean or Beóán except that he was the first of the three known bishops of Mortlach in Scotland and that his name means "lively one." St. Bean got the job of bishop after God delivered Scotland from those nasty Scandinavians (read: Vikings).

Three Spirits makes a botanical spirit called Livener, which promises to energize. Their Euphoric Spritz is a good way to honor today's lively saint.

OCTOBER

Euphoric Spritz

Makes 1 drink

1½ oz. Three Spirit's Livener
2½ oz. lemonade
2½ oz. kombucha
1 cucumber ribbon, garnish
1 mint sprig, garnish

Cut cucumber ribbon with a lemon peeler and place in a large wine glass, affixing it with a large ice cube. Pour in liquid ingredients and garnish with mint sprig.

LAST CALL

Now is the time to modify the theme song from Rowan Atkinson's "Mr. Bean" and sing: Ecce sanctus, qui est faba! (Behold a saint, who is a bean.)

SAINTS SIMON AND JUDE, OCTOBER 28

Simon and Jude were both chosen by our Lord to be among His original twelve Apostles. Both, it is believed, were martyred in Persia after the former had preached the Gospel in Egypt and the latter in Mesopotamia. Simon is called the Zealot in the Bible either because he belonged to a virulently anti-Roman Jewish sect by that name or because he was zealous in following his new Master. Jude Thaddeus is the author of a brief and strongly-worded New Testament epistle which mentions, among other things, the curious detail that St. Michael the Archangel and the Devil fought over the remains of Moses (Jude 9).

But St. Jude is most famous for being the patron saint of desperate or hopeless causes. This role is relatively recent, dating back to 1929 when a Fr. James Tort, C.M.F., encouraged the devotion to his parishioners in southeast Chicago, most of whom were laid-off steel workers. The devotion grew rapidly; on the final night of a solemn novena held on St. Jude's feast, there was an overflow crowd outside the church of a one thousand people. The next day, the stock market crashed, and soon more Americans were turning to St. Jude during the Great Depression and World War II. There isn't much else to tie St. Jude to hopeless causes, although it has been speculated that because of the similarity of St. Jude's name to Judas Iscariot, people wouldn't pray to the "forgotten Apostle" unless all else failed!

Regardless of how he got the job, St. Jude is now an everyman's saint. And for an everyman's saint, have a mixed drink that is evocative of the working-class Boilermaker.

Boilermaker

Makes 1 drink

1 oz. Spiritless Kentucky 74
8 oz. nonalcoholic beer

Pour the Kentucky 74 into a shot glass. Fill a pint glass halfway with beer. Drop the shot glass into the beer.

LAST CALL

Turn a popular prayer to St. Jude into a toast, and toss in his fellow Apostle St. Simon: "To Saints Simon and Jude, and may the Sacred Heart of Jesus be adored, glorified, loved, and preserved throughout the world now and forever."

SAINT NARCISSUS, OCTOBER 29

No, this saint was not so obsessed with his good looks that he perished while staring at his own reflection; indeed, no saint could fit such a description. Narcissus (99–216) was an astonishing eighty years old when he was elected Bishop of Jerusalem. Together with the other bishops of Palestine, he helped

determine that Easter should always be celebrated on a Sunday. Everyone loved Narcissus except the wicked, who chafed at his strict religious discipline. Three men accused the saint of a terrible crime, each making a vow. The first said that if he were lying, he wished he would perish by fire. The second said that if he were lying, he wished he would die of leprosy. And the third said that if he were lying, he wished he would go blind.

As the saying goes, be careful what you wish for. The first liar perished in a house fire, along with his whole family. The second contracted leprosy and died soon after. After seeing the demise of his friends, the third grew terrified and publicly confessed the conspiracy against Narcissus, weeping so much that he lost his eyesight.

We combine the fate of these three false witnesses with Narcissus' role in shaping the Easter holiday with a Comeuppance Cucumber Cocktail—the cucumber, curiously enough, being a symbol of the Resurrection (see Easter Sunday).

Comeuppance Cucumber Cocktail (a.k.a. Green Goddess)

Makes 1 drink

- 1¾ oz. Bax Botanics Verbena
- 2 tsp. cucumber juice
- 1 small handful mint leaves
- ½ oz. fresh lime juice
- 3 oz. lemonade

Juice half a cucumber in a liquidizer and strain through a fine sieve. Muddle the mint and lime juice in a shaker. Add cucumber juice, Bax Botanics, lemonade, and ice and shake 40 times. Strain into an old-fashioned with ice and garnish with lime.

LAST CALL

A toast: "Through the intercession of St. Narcissus, may we never become narcissistic."

ALL HALLOWS' EVE, OCTOBER 31

If you have been observing Sober October and have made it this far, congratulations! Either way, you deserve an appropriate beverage for the occasion. For a group function, we recommend a spooky punch. Our Witch of Endor's Sorceress Comfort is made with simple ingredients and dry ice, that mysterious solid form of carbon dioxide which creates an eerie mist when wet. If you are lucky, your local supermarket carries dry ice, especially around Halloween. You should purchase it an hour or two before your event (lest it evaporate) and store it in a cooler with the lid cracked (lest the gasses build up). Dry ice should *not* be consumed, but it is safe in drinks.

As for the name of our punch: It may surprise you to learn that there are no canonized witches in the Catholic Church and not even a patron saint for the poor, warty dears. But we do find ourselves kind of admiring the Witch of Endor, who did King Saul's bidding even though he was the one who issued the decree condemning to death anyone who practiced witchcraft (see 1 Samuel 28:3–25). The witch conjured up the ghost of Samuel, who told Saul that he and his sons would die in battle and be "with him" tomorrow. Saul collapsed in fear, and the witch, taking pity on the broken king, prepared a meal for him by slaughtering a fatted calf and baking bread (in other words, by doing a lot of work and at some cost). Apparently, behind her dark arts beat a kind heart.

Witch of Endor's Comfort

Makes 32 drinks

2 liters ginger ale, chilled

4 cups pineapple juice, chilled

1/3 cup fresh lemon juice, optional

1 tub lime sherbet, approx. 48 oz.

1 (5-lb) block dry ice

1 large cauldron or punch bowl

Mix all ingredients except dry ice in a punch bowl. Using gloves, place the large chunk of dry ice in the punch. (Keeping the dry ice intact will keep it from being consumed by your guests.) The ice should emit mist for about 3 hours.

CHAPTER ELEVEN

November

SAINTS

ALL SAINTS' DAY, NOVEMBER 1

This great feast in honor of all the souls in Heaven, both the canonized saints known to us and the uncanonized saints unknown to us, calls for a celebration. According to Pope Urban IV, one of the purposes of All Saints' Day is to compensate for any negligence in celebrating the saints' feasts from the previous year. Surely, this principle can be applied to drinking (soberly) with the saints.

Earlier, we included two mocktails inspired by the first two parts of Dante's *Comedy*: *Inferno* (see May 13) and *Purgatorio* (see September 10). Here is the final installment, the abode of the saints.

Paradiso

Makes 1 drink

- 1 egg white
- 2 tsp. powdered sugar
- 1 oz. water
- ½ oz. simple syrup
- 1 tbsp. fresh lemon juice
- 2 dashes orange bitters, optional
- 1 lemon twist, garnish

Beat the egg white and powdered sugar until firm but not stiff (a frother or hand-held mixer speeds up the process). Pour the egg mixture and all other liquid ingredients into a shaker filled with ice and shake 40 times. Strain into a cocktail glass and garnish with twist.

ALL SOULS' DAY, NOVEMBER 2

After celebrating the Church Triumphant in Heaven, the Church Militant on Earth turns her thoughts to the Church Suffering in Purgatory and prays for the speedy delivery of the poor souls from their painful purification. Many customs surround All Souls' Day, chief among them a visit to the final resting place of one's dearly departed. For many cultures, that visit includes bringing food and drink and offering a libation at the grave, although the Church frowns upon the latter practice as a pagan holdover.

Abuelita is a Mexican brand of chocolate owned by Nestlé that is enjoyed during the Mexican Día de Muertos (Day of the Dead), and so is ***Atole***, a traditional hot corn-based beverage that predates the Conquistadors. That's right, corn. Give it a shot: it is surprisingly delicious and comes in a wide variety of flavors.

Chocolate Atole (a.k.a. Champurrado)

Makes 2 drinks

- ½ cup masa harina, finely ground (the kind used for tortillas)
- 3 cups water, plus more as needed (see notes)
- 1 cup milk
- 3½ oz. dark chocolate, broken into pieces
- 3 tbsp. dark brown sugar
- 1 cinnamon stick or ¼ tsp. ground cinnamon
- kosher salt

In a large saucepan, add masa and set over medium heat. Immediately add water in a slow, thin stream while whisking constantly to avoid lumps. Bring to a simmer and whisk in milk, chocolate, brown sugar, and a generous pinch of salt until chocolate is melted, about 1 minute. Add cinnamon.

Return to a simmer and lower heat to low. Continue to simmer gently, whisking constantly, for 5 minutes. Discard cinnamon stick, if using. Thin with additional water, as needed, to create a thick-yet-drinkable hot beverage (the exact consistency is a matter of personal taste), reheating as necessary. Taste, adding more sugar or salt if desired. Froth with a whisk or immersion blender, then ladle into mugs, and serve.

LAST CALL

How often does the perfect toast come with a partial indulgence? Yet that is precisely the case with the prayer, "Eternal rest grant unto them, O Lord, and let perpetual light shine upon them. May they rest in peace." The Church grants a partial indulgence every time it is piously said for the souls of the faithful departed. Drinking each time the prayer is said is not part of the indulgence.

SAINT MARTIN DE PORRES, NOVEMBER 3

Charming stories abound about this illegitimate son of a Spanish nobleman and a freed African slave. Because he was biracial, , Martin (1579–1639) endured bigotry both within the Dominican Order of which he was a member and in Peruvian society as a whole; yet he rose above it all to become a model of charity and a great wonder-worker. He healed numerous people without distinction to their rank, founded an orphanage, and gave away great amounts of food to the poor. His kindness extended even to rats and mice, whom he fretted weren't getting enough to eat (we imagine that he is currently seated in Heaven far away from St. Gertrude of Nivelles, who is invoked against the furry little buggers). St. Martin even used his sister's house as a "home for wandering cats and dogs"! But he never let his popularity go to his head: he referred to himself as "Brother Broom" and even once suggested that he be sold into slavery to pay for the Dominicans' debts. When he died, bishops and noblemen vied for the honor of carrying him to his grave.

A Mickey Mouse Mocktail is a sweet way to honor this saint's sweet patronage of mice, and you can even think of its two colors as symbols of Martin de Porres' mixed heritage.

Mickey Mouse Mocktail

Makes 1 drink

4 oz. cola
1 oz. vanilla ice cream
whipped cream
1 Toschi Amarena cherry, garnish

Pour cola into a highball glass with ice. Add ice cream and top with whipped cream and cherry.

LAST CALL

After festooning your parlor with cute images of mice, celebrate society's progress in racial harmony and ask for St. Martin's continued intercession in this area.

TWENTIETH-CENTURY MARTYRS OF SPAIN, NOVEMBER 6

On October 28, 2007, Pope Benedict XVI beatified 498 men and women—bishops, priests, brothers, nuns, and laymen—who were martyred during the Spanish Civil War (1936–1939). Even though it was only a fraction of the Catholics slain for their faith during that bloody conflict, it is the largest group ever beatified by the Church on a single occasion. These holy witnesses of Christ, the oldest of which was seventy-eight and the youngest sixteen, are called "Martyrs of Spain" and not "Spanish martyrs" because several of them came from other countries like France, Mexico, and Cuba.

We figure that the bloodshed of almost five hundred people is best commemorated with Sangria, which means "bloodletting." This Spanish and Portuguese drink is traditionally made with red wine and chopped fruit, but there are a few different ways to imitate its sweet, acidic, and tannic flavor profile.

Wine Sangria

Makes 4 drinks

- 1 bottle alcohol-free red wine (25 oz.)
- 18 oz. sparkling beverage of your choice
- 9 oz. orange juice
- 1 orange, sliced into wheels
- 1 lemon, sliced into wheels
- 1 oz. maple syrup or other sweetener

Place orange, lemon, and sweetener of choice in a large glass pitcher. Muddle gently until some of the juices from the fruit are released. Add apple, orange juice, and wine. Stir gently. Place in the fridge for at least an hour (3–4 hours is ideal). Taste and add more sweetener if need be. Just before serving, add sparkling beverage and stir gently. Pour into stemless wine glasses with ice.

Tea Sangria

Makes 8 drinks

2 cups water
2 black tea bags
2 cinnamon sticks
½ cup granulated sugar
3 cups pomegranate juice
1 cup fresh orange juice
1 medium orange, sliced into wheels
1 medium lemon, sliced into wheels
1 medium lime, sliced into wheels
1 medium apple, cored and cut into chunks
3 cups cold sparkling water

Boil water in a saucepan and place tea bags and cinnamon sticks into it; steep for 5 minutes. Discard tea bags and stir in sugar to dissolve. In a large jar or pitcher, combine tea, cinnamon sticks, pomegranate juice, orange juice, orange, lemon, lime, and apple. Refrigerate for at least 1 hour and preferably overnight. Just before serving, add sparkling water and stir gently. Pour into stemless wine glasses with ice.

Grape Juice Sangria

Makes 8 drinks

4 cups sparkling water
4 cups grape juice
1 cup orange juice
¼ cup sugar
½ lemon, sliced
½ orange, sliced
1 small apple or 1 small peach, cut into wedges

Combine all ingredients except sparkling water in a pitcher and stir until sugar dissolves. Refrigerate until ready to serve. Just before serving, add sparkling water and stir gently. Pour into stemless wine glasses with ice.

Spiritless Seventy-Four Sangria

Makes 8 drinks

- 1 (25-oz.) bottle Spiritless Kentucky 74
- 1 (25-oz.) bottle nonalcoholic red wine
- 8 oz. orange juice
- 3 oz. agave syrup
- 11 oz. ginger beer
- 4 or more orange slices
- 4 or more peach slices

Combine all ingredients in a pitcher and stir. Pour into stemless wine glasses with ice.

LAST CALL

According to Cardinal José Saraiva Martins at their Beatification Mass, these martyrs "behaved as good Christians, and when the moment came, they did not hesitate to offer their lives with the cry on their lips: ¡*Viva Cristo Rey*! (Long live Christ the King!)."

To the martyrs of Spain, and ¡*Viva Cristo Rey*!

SAINT ANDREW AVELLINO, NOVEMBER 10

Our saint today was baptized Lancelot, but when he entered the Theatine order, he took the name Andrew. Even before entering religious life, St. Andrew Avellino (1521–1608) led an exemplary life of chastity. A handsome man, he took the tonsure (became a cleric) as a way of escaping his female admirers. St. Andrew practiced both canon and civil law until one day a lie slipped from his lips as he was passionately pleading a friend's case. Soon after he read Wisdom 1:11—"The mouth that belieth killeth the soul"—and, cut to the quick, left the profession. He was a great reformer; once, he was severely wounded by wicked men when he ordered them to leave the premises of a lax convent.

Several miracles are attributed to this humble and loving servant of God, including the following as told in the old *Roman Breviary*:

> As he was once returning home late at night from hearing a sick man's confession, a violent storm of wind and rain put out the light that was carried before him; but neither he nor his companions were wet by the pouring rain; and, moreover, a wonderful light shining from his body enabled them to find their way through the darkness.

You too can experience something dark and stormy without getting wet. Both Sentia's GABA Black and Three Spirit's Social have the flavor profile for a great nonalcoholic Dark and Stormy mocktail.

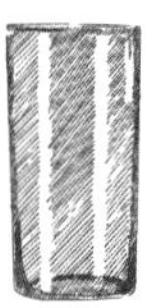

Light & Stormy

Makes 1 drink

2 oz. Three Spirit's Social
3–4 oz. ginger beer
1 lime wheel, garnish

Pour Social into a highball with ice, top with ginger beer, and stir. Garnish with lime wheel.

Sentia's Dark and Stormy

Makes 1 drink

¾ oz. GABA Black
dash fresh lime juice
3–4 oz. ginger beer

Pour GABA Black into an old-fashioned glass with ice and add a dash of lime juice. Top with ginger beer.

SAINT MARTIN OF TOURS, NOVEMBER 11

Martin (ca. 316–397) was a Roman soldier who, even before he was baptized, was on fire with Christian zeal. As a catechumen, he saw a poor beggar shivering in the cold and tore his military cloak in two, giving him half (the Roman army made you pay for half of your uniform, so Martin gave the half that he had paid for). That night Jesus Christ appeared to him in a dream with the half-cloak and said, "Martin the catechumen hath clothed Me."

Martin eventually became a monk. When the townspeople of Tours tried to trick him into becoming their bishop, the holy man hid from them, only to be betrayed by a flock of honking geese. True or not, goose was the main course of medieval celebrations of "Martinmas" (St. Martin's Day), and this culinary tradition even influenced the Puritan celebration of the first Thanksgiving. The Pilgrims were aware of the Martinmas goose from their stay in Holland and used North American turkeys for their banquet only when they could not find enough geese.

Which brings us to the martini. No one is certain when or where this concoction was invented: some say it was named after Martini and Rossi vermouth, while others point either to a bartender in San Francisco or to the town of Martinez, California. Whatever its origins, there would be no "Martini" or "Martinez" had there been no saint called Martin to make the name popular in Christian lands. And so we rightly claim any drink that bears his name, even if it is a radical departure from the original martini. And we have been through worse times: Do you remember the so-called apple martini?

Everleaf Martini

Makes 1 drink

2 oz. Everleaf Marine
½ oz. coconut water
1 dash fresh lime juice
1 lemon twist, garnish

Pour all liquid ingredients into a mixing glass and stir 40 times. Strain into a cocktail glass and garnish with lemon twist.

Seedlip Martini

Makes 1 drink

2½ oz. Seedlip Garden 108
¾ oz. olive brine
1 Castelvetrano olive

Pour liquid ingredients into a mixing glass and stir 40 times. Strain into a cocktail glass and garnish with olive.

The Monday Martini

Makes 1 drink

2 oz. Monday Gin
2 oz. simple syrup
½ lemon, squeezed
1 lemon peel, garnish

Pour liquid ingredients into a mixing glass and stir 40 times. Strain into a cocktail glass and garnish with lemon peel.

LAST CALL

In the Middle Ages, swine would be slaughtered on or before Martinmas in preparation for the winter, a custom that led to several proverbs. In Spain, when predicting that someone would get his comeuppance or meet his Maker, folks would say *A cada cerdo le llega su San Martín* ("Every pig has its St. Martin's Day"); in England, the equivalent adage was, "His Martinmas will come as it does to every hog." To St. Martin, then, and may his prayers on this day delay our own Martinmas.

SAINT FRANCES XAVIER CABRINI, NOVEMBER 13 IN U.S.A. (DECEMBER 22 ELSEWHERE)

Born Francesca Cabrini, Mother Cabrini (1850–1917) thought that she had a vocation to evangelize China, but when she met with Pope Leo XIII to seek his approval, he advised her to look to the West instead. Italian immigrants were flooding the United States and living in great poverty, spiritual and material. Heeding the pontiff, Mother Cabrini and six other sisters arrived in New York City in 1889, and before long she had established sixty-seven institutions throughout the United States, South America, and Europe.

Although Mother Cabrini's influence was felt throughout the world (even, at last, in China), New York City is particularly in her debt. She founded two hospitals in the metropolis, Cabrini High School in Manhattan, and an orphanage in West Park, New York. For Mother Cabrini, the first citizen of the United States canonized a saint and a great patron of the Big Apple, we recommend an all-American classic: the Manhattan.

Lyre's Manhattan

Makes 1 drink

- 2 oz. Lyre's American Malt
- ½ oz. Lyre's Apéritif Rosso
- 2 dashes aromatic bitters
- 1 Toschi Amarena cherry, garnish

Pour liquid ingredients into a mixing glass with ice and stir 40 times. Strain into a cocktail glass and garnish with cherry.

Spiritless Manhattan

Makes 1 drink

- $1\frac{1}{2}$ oz. Spiritless Kentucky 74
- $1\frac{1}{2}$ oz. nonalcoholic sweet vermouth
- 3 dashes aromatic bitters
- 1 orange peel, garnish
- 1 Toschi Amarena cherry, garnish

Pour liquid ingredients into an old-fashioned glass with ice and stir 40 times. Garnish with orange peel and cherry.

SAINT LAURENCE O'TOOLE, NOVEMBER 14

Laurence O'Toole (1128–1180)—or, if you are a Gaelic purist, Lorcán Ua Tuathail—was Archbishop of Dublin when the Normans invaded Ireland. The son of an Irish king, he discerned a call to the priesthood and the monastic life, eventually becoming the Abbot of Glendalough (an abbey that some, incidentally, believe to be the birthplace of whisky). Laurence was loved by all for his integrity and generosity to the poor and was elected unanimously to become the Archbishop of Dublin.

One of Laurence's goals was to harmonize the customs of the Church in Ireland with those of the greater Catholic Church, for the Irish, as you may be surprised to hear, tended to do things their own way. But the saint's greater challenge was in mediating the warring claims of three different groups after they all conquered the city of Dublin. All sides looked to him for help, for he was the one man whom everyone trusted.

Laurence led an ascetical life: he wore a hair shirt, ate nothing but bread and water on Friday, and was a vegetarian. But when he entertained, Laurence made sure that his guests lacked for nothing, and lest he spoil the mood, he colored his drinking water to look like wine. A perfect patron for this book!

You can, of course, follow Laurence's lead and add red dye to your water tonight. But did you know that the spelling of O'Doul is a variation of O'Toole? (Well, now you do.) **Anheuser Busch** introduced nonalcoholic beer—or as they call it, nonalcoholic brew—to the mainstream US market when they came out with O'Doul's in 1990. Tonight, enjoy a glass of **O'Doul's** or **O'Doul's Amber** with a twist of lemon, a symbol of the bitter experience of having to deal with invasive Normans.

LAST CALL

Anheuser Busch once ran the tagline, "O'Doul's for Every O'Ccasion." You can turn this almost-clever ad into a toast for our saint: "May Almighty God use the intercession of the great Saint Laurence O'Toole for every occasion where conflict abounds."

SAINT ALBERT THE GREAT, NOVEMBER 15

Albertus Magnus (d. 1280) is most famous for being the teacher of St. Thomas Aquinas, but this Doctor of the Church, Dominican friar, professor at the University of Paris and Cologne, and bishop of Ratisbon deserves a toast or two for more than just having taught someone else. Albert had an encyclopedic mind and was a brilliant natural scientist; in some ways, as Dr. Michael Tkacz has astutely observed, his work on how species are adapted to their environments rivals that of Darwin. What Albert could not observe himself he faithfully recorded from others, although not all such testimony was reliable. In his study on herons, for example, Albert speculates that its Latin name *ardea* comes from the fact that its excrement burns (*ardet*) whatever it touches. What is more, the bird is said to defend itself from hawks by aiming its anus at the assailant and shooting excrement at it; if the hawk's wings are hit, they melt.

A "dirty" or "muddy" Dr Pepper is so named because of its color, which is a light brown thanks to the cream in the recipe. Here is our own version, which we are naming a Heron's Mud Pie in honor of St. Albert's humflinging heron.

Heron's Mud Pie

Makes 1 drink

2 oz. half-and-half
2 oz. root beer
1 squeeze chocolate syrup
Dr Pepper

Pour all ingredients except cola into a shaker filled with ice and shake 40 times. Strain into a highball glass with ice and top with soda.

LAST CALL

A century ago, "Here's mud in your eye" was a popular toast. It may have been inspired by our Lord's healing of a blind man with mud (John 9:6–7), or it may have been a farmer's way of wishing fertile and well-irrigated land for his friends. Either way, in light of Albert's heron, it takes on a whole new meaning.

Another toast that works well after hearing the tale of the heron is: "Through the intercession of St. Albert, may the enemies of the Church never know what hit them."

SAINT ELIZABETH OF HUNGARY, NOVEMBER 19 (NOVEMBER 17)

Elizabeth (1207–1231) was married to Bl. Louis of Thuringia at the age of fourteen and bore him three children. Although the marriage had been arranged, the couple grew to love each other deeply. Elizabeth was renowned for her extraordinary charity to the poor, which her husband gladly supported—up to a point. Once, he came home to find his wife nursing a leper in their bed! Understandably, the Duke was a bit miffed until he saw a vision of our crucified Lord lying there instead of the leper.

Elizabeth was widowed at the age of twenty when the Plague took her dear husband. Her in-laws treated her badly, but instead of complaining she moved to a tiny cottage and spent the last years of her short life serving the sick and poor, dying at the age of twenty-four.

Tart, tropical, and refreshing, hibiscus tea (*Hibiszkusz tea*) is a popular beverage in Hungary. Mix up a batch for your friends tonight—and don't forget the leper in your bed.

Hibiscus Iced Tea

Makes 6–8 drinks

8 cups water, divided
1½ cups dried hibiscus flowers
1 cup sugar
2 tsp. grated ginger
1 splash lime juice

Boil 4 cups of water. Add hibiscus and ginger and let rest for 1 hour. Strain the flowers, then add sugar, remaining 4 cups of water, and lime juice. Stir until sugar dissolves. Pour into old-fashioned glasses with ice.

POPE SAINT CLEMENT, NOVEMBER 23

Pope Clement I (d. ca. 99) was the third successor of St. Peter and the first "Apostolic Father," a Church Father who had contact with the original Apostles. According to an old legend, Clement was banished to work in the stone quarries of modern-day Ukraine and, after converting many of his fellow prisoners to Christianity, was sentenced to die by being tied to an anchor and thrown into the Black Sea.

"Oranges and lemons/ Say the bells of St. Clement's." Thus begins an old English nursery rhyme about church bells in and around London. The church in the jingle, it is speculated, is either St. Clement Danes or St. Clement Eastcheap, both of which are close to wharves where citrus fruit would arrive from sunnier climes. Thinking of a church on St. Clement's Day is also appropriate because one of Rome's most ancient, beautiful, and archeologically important churches is San Clemente. Here is a simple and refreshing tribute to Clement and his oranges and lemons:

St. Clement's Mocktail

Makes 1 drink

2 oz. orange juice
2 oz. bitter lemon tonic
1 lemon or orange wheel, garnish

Pour orange juice and tonic into a highball with ice and stir. Garnish with wheel.

LAST CALL

"The Epistle of Clement" was written by today's saint to the church in Corinth. It is easily found online and makes for interesting reading, establishing as it does the apostolic authority of the clergy at so early a date in Church history.

BLESSED MIGUEL PRO, NOVEMBER 23

José Ramón Miguel Agustín Pro Juárez (1891–1927) was a Mexican Jesuit priest martyred by the anti-Catholic regime of Mexico in what Graham Greene called the "fiercest persecution of religion anywhere since the reign of Elizabeth." Miguel's Jesuit confrères described him as a sparkling conversationalist who was both playful and prayerful. After studying and being ordained in Europe, Fr. Miguel returned to Mexico, where his beloved Church had been forced underground. He ministered to small groups of Catholics in secret, celebrating the Mass and administering the sacraments; he even disguised himself in a policeman's uniform to administer the Viaticum to prisoners. On one occasion, Fr. Miguel was scheduled to celebrate Mass at someone's home when he found the place surrounded by police. Undaunted, he approached the sergeant in charge, flashed his wallet quickly in the man's face, and identified himself as a high-ranking detective. After curtly interrogating the frightened sergeant, he went into the house, celebrated Mass (much to the joy of the people inside), and came back out, admonishing the sergeant to watch out for the renegade priest.

Fr. Pro's earthly ministry ended when he was arrested on a trumped-up charge of trying to assassinate the President of Mexico, condemned without trial, and executed by firing squad. After blessing and forgiving his executioners, he held his arms out in the shape of the cross and shouted the battle cry of the Cristero rebels resisting the government: ¡*Viva Cristo Rey*!—"Long Live Christ the King!" The Mexican government filmed his execution, which is included in the closing credits of the 2012 film *For Greater Glory*.

In this book we treat the passion fruit as a symbol of the Society of Jesus (see July 31). Here are two recipes made with passion fruit to honor Fr. Miguel's Jesuit vocation. Agua fresca, incidentally, is a traditional Mexican beverage that Fr. Miguel would have surely had sometime in his life.

Mexico Pacifico Mocktail

Makes 1 drink

- 1 oz. passion fruit syrup
- ½ oz. fresh lemon juice
- 4–6 oz. sparkling water

Pour syrup and lemon juice in a shaker with ice and shake 40 times. Strain into a cocktail glass and top with sparkling water.

Passion Fruit Agua Fresca

Makes 6 drinks

- 4 cups passion fruit pulp, seeds removed
- 6 cups water
- ½–1 cup sugar

Put all ingredients into a blender and blend until sugar dissolves. Chill before serving.

NOVEMBER

LAST CALL

Make the battle cry of the Cristeros and Bl. Miguel Pro your own: *¡Viva Cristo Rey!*

Then, choose between one of three options: 1) read Graham Greene's riveting *The Power and the Glory* about the Mexican Revolution; 2) watch the 1947 John Ford movie *The Fugitive*, loosely based on the novel and starring Henry Fonda as the "whiskey priest"; or 3) watch the 2012 film *For Greater Glory*.

SAINT CATHERINE OF ALEXANDRIA, NOVEMBER 25

Catherine (282–305) was a noble young woman from Alexandria who had consecrated her virginity to the Lord and who, like St. Catherine of Siena, had a mystical vision in which she saw a ring being placed on her finger by Christ. Catherine upbraided the Roman Emperor Maximinus for his persecution of Christians, and the Emperor responded by assembling seventy pagan scholars to refute her. The learned Christian maiden, however, converted them to the Faith instead, which is why she is now the patron saint of philosophers. The Emperor then tried to execute her on a spiked wheel, but when she ascended the gallows, the wheel was destroyed by lightning and the executioner killed. The legend of her account ends by stating that she was beheaded. St. Catherine is one of the Fourteen Holy Helpers and is invoked against sudden death.

A Catherine Blossom seems an apt choice for this precious flower of Christ.

Catherine Blossom

Makes 1 drink

2 oranges, juiced
½ lemon, juiced
2–3 tbsp. maple syrup
crushed ice
1 lemon twist, garnish

Pour all liquid ingredients into a blender and blend until smooth. Strain into a wine glass and garnish with lemon twist.

SAINT ANDREW, NOVEMBER 30

Andrew (d. 60) was a disciple of St. John the Baptist and the first disciple of our Lord, the younger brother of St. Peter who introduced his older sibling to Jesus, and the Apostle who introduced the boy with the fishes and loaves to Jesus for one of His Eucharist-foreshadowing miracles (John 6:8). According to tradition, Andrew preached the Gospel in Byzantium and other areas south of the Black Sea before being crucified in Greece on an X-shaped cross.

It is perhaps fitting that St. Andrew, whose name means "manly," is the patron saint of some of the world's hardest drinking countries, chief among them Scotland, Greece, and Russia. But let us turn away from such dipsomaniacal nations to a more wholesome example. Saint Andrew is a patron saint of golfers because the world's first and most famous course is named after him in Scotland, and so we ask a great golfer to honor him.

Arnold Palmer (1929–2016), who showed the world how to play golf with grace and aplomb and modesty, is credited with inventing one of the world's most famous mocktails. Apparently, Palmer requested his invention to keep his wits about him.

Or try something native. Feragaia (pronounced fe-ra-guy-a) is Scotland's first alcohol-free spirit. Firmly rooted in the wildness of Fife and made with fourteen botanicals (including seaweed, bay leaf, and chamomile), it is simultaneously fresh, earthy, and spicy. Enjoy it neat on the rocks or mixed with a good tonic like Fever Tree.

The Arnold Palmer

Makes 1 drink

3 parts unsweetened tea
1 part lemonade

Fill a highball with ice. Build tea and lemonade. Stir if you wish.

Feverish Feragaia Mule

Makes 1 drink

2 oz. Feragaia
2–4 oz. Fever Tree ginger beer
1 lime wedge, garnish

Pour Feragaia into a highball glass with ice and top with ginger beer. Squeeze lime juice into the glass, stir, and garnish with lime.

LAST CALL

Saint Andrew is mentioned in the traditional Latin Mass after the Our Father. Here is an amended version that can be used as a toast: "By the intercession of St. Andrew may the good Lord grant us peace in our days so that, helped by the riches of His mercy, we may always be delivered from sin and safe from every disturbance."

CHAPTER TWELVE

December

SAINTS

SAINT BIBIANA, DECEMBER 2

Just when it looked like the Church would no longer suffer persecution from the Romans thanks to Constantine's Edict of Toleration, Julian the Apostate became Emperor and renewed government hostilities (Hell hath no fury like an ex-Catholic). One of the victims of Julian's policies was Bibiana (d. 363), a Christian noblewoman who was scourged to death for her faith. Bibiana's home became a church on the Aventine Hill in Rome. There are two theories as to how she became the patroness of headaches, epilepsy, and hangovers: first, because she grew a garden that had herbal remedies; second, that her name is derived from the Latin word for drinking (*bibere*). Either way, you can drink to your health tonight with an Herbal Stimulant.

Herbal Stimulant

Makes 1 drink

- 2 oz. Three Spirit's Social Elixir
- 1 oz. espresso, cold
- 1½ tsp. maple syrup
- grated raw cocoa beans, grated

Pour liquid ingredients into a shaker with ice and shake 40 times. Strain into a chilled cocktail glass and dust the top with cocoa beans.

LAST CALL

To the patroness of hangovers we pray: "Through the intercession of St. Bibiana, may we never need the intercession of St. Bibiana."

SAINT BARBARA, DECEMBER 4

According to the stories that have come down to us, Barbara (ca. 3rd c.) was a beautiful maiden who was imprisoned by her father in an effort to shield her from the outside world. While her father was away, Barbara nonetheless converted to Christianity and had a third window added to her quarters in honor of the Holy Trinity. When her father returned, he cruelly handed her over to the authorities, who condemned her to death by beheading. Barbara's wicked father personally carried out the sentence, but on his way home he was struck dead by a bolt of lightning and consumed in flames.

One of the Fourteen Holy Helpers, Barbara is invoked against fever and sudden death. Because of her father's explosive ending, she is also the patron saint of artillerymen and other dangerous occupations or places involving things that go ka-boom: warehouses, chemical engineers, miners, etc. And because of her home improvement, Barbara is a patron saint of architects and builders. You could even say that St. Barbara is the patron saint of barbiturates, since they were named after her thanks to an accident of history. After German chemist Adolf von Baeyer discovered the substance, he and his colleagues went to celebrate at a tavern where the local artillery garrison happened to be celebrating Saint Barbara's Day. When one of the officers suggested Barbara's name for the new discovery, Baeyer, perhaps his judgment now softened by a pint or two, agreed.

A Gunner is a favorite among British expats from the Pacific Rim: Hong Kong, Singapore, India, etc. And since Barbara is a patroness of miners, you can also have a Gold Rush cocktail.

Gunner

Makes 1 drink

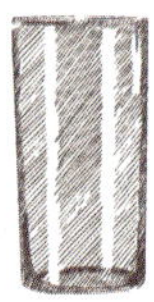

3 oz. ginger beer
3 oz. ginger ale
3 dashes Angostura bitters
1 dash fresh lemon juice, optional

Pour all ingredients into a highball glass with ice and stir gently.

Monday's Gold Rush

Makes 1 drink

2 oz. Monday Whiskey
3/4 oz. fresh lemon juice
3/4 oz. honey simple syrup (1:1 honey to water)
1 orange wheel, garnish

Pour all liquid ingredients into a shaker with ice and shake 40 times. Strain into an old-fashioned glass with 1 large ice cube and garnish with orange wheel.

Spiritless Gold Rush

Makes 1 drink

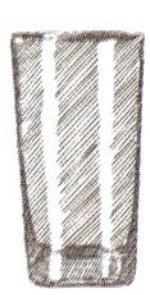

2 oz. Spiritless Kentucky 74
1 oz. fresh lemon juice
3/4 oz. honey simple syrup (2:1 honey to water)
1 grapefruit peel, garnish

Pour all liquid ingredients into a shaker with ice and shake 40 times. Strain into a chilled cocktail glass with 1 large ice cube and garnish with grapefruit.

LAST CALL

Challenge your guests to come up with the worst possible pun in a toast to St. Barbara. Praise her for her caliber, her explosive personality, her long range, etc.

SAINT NICHOLAS OF MYRA, DECEMBER 6

Nicholas of Myra (270–343) was a bishop in Asia Minor who is nicknamed the Wonderworker. He is best known for saving three sisters from prostitution by throwing bags of money down the chimney of their house, enough to give them a dowry for marriage—and to give us the seeds for his gradual transformation into Santa Claus.

Thanks to a bizarre medieval legend, there is a second reason why Nicholas is a patron saint of children. An evil innkeeper had killed and butchered three boys and pickled their remains in a barrel. When Nicholas visited the inn, he sensed the evil and resurrected the lads. You can pay homage to this gruesome story by throwing a pickle-tasting party which, believe it or not, in some places have become a big dill (sorry: couldn't resist). Friends and family gather to sample the flavors of gherkin, dill, sour, spicy, etc., either raw or deep-fried.

One of Nicholas' many other patronages is that of brewers, most likely because of his association with inns and restaurants. (Think of it this way: if he rescued the three pickled children in the inn, he can rescue the inn's customers when they too get pickled.) **Santa Clausthaler** nonalcoholic beer is a good way to toast to Nicholas tonight. Made in Germany for the US market, this full-bodied brew is actually more like a Radler, for it is half NA beer and half cranberry juice—perfect for the holiday season. And just as they stole St. Nicholas' name for their label, you can steal it back for his feast day.

But the most traditional drink for St. Nicholas is *Bischopswijn* or Bishop's Wine, which is served in Sinterklaas-loving countries such as Holland on the eve of the feast.

Bishop's Wine

Makes 8–10 drinks

- 2 bottles nonalcoholic red wine
- 2 oranges, quartered and studded with cloves
- 1 lemon, quartered and studded with cloves
- 2 cinnamon sticks
- 1/4 tsp. mace, optional
- 1/4 tsp. allspice, optional
- 1/4 tsp. ginger, optional
- 2–4 tbsp. sugar

Pour the wine into a large saucepan. Add the studded fruit, cinnamon sticks, and other spices and heat slowly for 15 minutes. Add the sugar and heat for 1–2 minutes, until dissolved. Strain out the fruit and spices and serve hot.

LAST CALL

Raise your glass and say, "To the real Santa Claus, scourge of the wicked and champion of the poor: may he help us keep the Faith and assist the needy."

THE IMMACULATE CONCEPTION OF THE BLESSED VIRGIN MARY, DECEMBER 8

On December 8, 1854, Pope Pius IX solemnly defined what had already been in the Catholic drinking water since time immemorial, namely, that the Blessed Virgin Mary, by a special proactive application of the graces won by her Son's victory on the Cross, was preserved from original sin, thereby making her womb a fitting place for the Son of God and her flesh a fitting source for His. Mary is the only human being besides Adam, Eve, and Jesus Christ to come into this world without original sin, but she is not alone in receiving the graces of the Cross prior to the first Good Friday. *Every* holy person before the Crucifixion, from Abel to John the Baptist, is redeemed by the Blood of the Lamb prior to Its actual shedding by a special preapplication of grace; the only difference with Mary's case is that it was applied to prevent not only actual sin but original.

The White Lady is a boozy cocktail that we recommend for Our Immaculate Lady in *Drinking with the Saints*, but our own nonalcoholic creation, the Virgin White Lady, is also a winner.

The Virgin White Lady

Makes 1 drink

1 egg white
2 tsp. powdered sugar
1 oz. water
½ oz. simple syrup
1 tbsp. fresh lemon juice
2 dashes orange bitters
1 lemon twist, garnish

Beat the egg white and powdered sugar until firm but not stiff (a frother or hand-held mixer speeds up the process). Pour the egg mixture and all other liquid ingredients into a shaker filled with ice and shake 40 times. Strain into a cocktail glass and add the twist.

BLESSED FRANCO GROTTI, DECEMBER 11

If the name Franco Grotti (1211–1291) or its variations such as Francesco Lippi and Frank of Siena conjure up images of a deadly mob boss, you would not be that far off. In the memorable words of one of his biographers, today's saint started out as "a lazy, nasty-tempered teenager who would not obey anyone." A native of the town of Grotti near Siena, Italy, Franco spent most of his time gambling and had to skip town in order to avoid a murder rap. Out of the frying pan and into the fire, Franco then became a *condottiere*, a leader of a band of mercenaries.

Frank's "lifestyle choices" didn't help his good judgment in other ways, either. At the age of fifty, after losing everything in a game of dice, he is reported to have even gambled his eyes saying, "I will also gamble these to spite Him who made them." God took him up on the bet and immediately struck Franco blind. It was just the prodding that the ruthless criminal needed. Filled with sorrow and regret, Franco vowed to make the famous pilgrimage to Santiago de Compostela in Spain. God rewarded Franco's pledge by giving him back just enough of his eyesight to make the long and arduous journey and, when he arrived at the pilgrimage site, God restored his sight completely.

After several years of living as a hermit, Franco was told during an apparition of the Blessed Virgin Mary to do penance in front of the people of Siena, whom he had scandalized through his great sins. The penitent soldier of fortune obliged by walking through the streets of the city as he whipped himself. At the age of sixty-five, Franco asked to enter the Carmelite order, but the monks told him to try again in five years—they were understandably jittery about his past. But the monks eventually relented, and Franco spent the last ten years of his life as a Carmelite lay brother, edifying others through his example of penance and humility and even working miracles.

Tonight, do what Franco never did when he was a ne'er-do-well: hedge your bets.

Hedge Your Bets

Makes 1 drink

- 1½ oz. Seedlip Spice 94
- 1 oz. grapefruit juice
- ½ oz. fresh lemon juice
- 2 tsp. any seasonal preserve
- 1 basil leaf, garnish

Pour all ingredients except basil leaf into a shaker with ice and shake 40 times. Strain into a cocktail glass and garnish with basil leaf.

LAST CALL

A toast: "Through the intercession of Bl. Franco Grotti, may we imitate his virtues and avoid his vices."

SAINT LUCY, DECEMBER 13

Lucy of Syracuse (283–304) was a Christian maiden whose prayers to St. Agatha brought about a miraculous cure to a malady from which her mother was suffering. When the governor of Syracuse found out about her faith, he ordered her to be defiled in a brothel. But the soldiers could not move her an inch, even when they tied her to a team of oxen. They then tried to burn her on the spot, but after getting the wood ready they were unable to light it. Finally, St. Lucy was felled by a sword.

A later tradition also states that Lucy was tortured and that her eyes were gouged out; a different version is that she gouged out her own eyes when a suitor took a lusty interest in them. Either way, Lucy is most famously portrayed in Christian art holding a tray containing her two eyes (actually, we should say two of her eyes, because another pair miraculously grew back). Understandably, she became the patron saint of the eyes and the blind.

In *Drinking with the Saints*, we propose a martini with the olives configured on a cocktail spear to look like a pair of eyes. Here, we propose one better: a punch with floating eyeballs. Why be macabre only once a year on Halloween?

DECEMBER

St. Lucy's Eyeful Power

Makes 8 drinks

1 qt. pineapple juice
1 qt. blood orange juice
3 cups apple juice
1/3 cup fresh lime juice
1 can lychees
blueberries

To make the eyeballs, insert a blueberry into the middle of each lychee. (If desired, place 2 on a skewer to make a set of eyes.) Keep refrigerated until ready to serve, or better, use as ice cubes by freezing on a tray.

To make the punch, pour all liquid ingredients into a punchbowl and stir. Add ice and/or eyeballs.

LAST CALL

Adorn your entertainment space with an abundance of lit candles and make the following toast: "May the prayers of St. Lucy light up our way and save us from darkness and the shadow of death."

SAINT LAZARUS OF BETHANY, DECEMBER 17 (JULY 29)

Not to be confused with Lazarus the beggar, Lazarus of Bethany is the brother of Martha and Mary who was raised from the dead after four days in the tomb. When Jesus learned that His friend had died, He commanded the tomb to be opened. Ever the realist, Martha objected with the reply—in the wonderfully earthy Douay-Rheims translation of the sixteenth century—"Lord, by this time, he stinketh" (John 11:39). Stinketh or no, Jesus prevailed and brought their brother back to life.

Saint Lazarus was no zombie, but we can't resist the association.

Zombie

Makes 1 drink

1 oz. Lyre's Dark Cane Spirit
1 oz. Lyre's White Cane Spirit
1 oz. Lyre's Spiced Cane Spirit
1 oz. pineapple juice
¾ oz. fresh lime juice
½ oz. falernum syrup
2 tsp. pink grapefruit juice
1 tsp. grenadine
1 orange wedge, garnish
1 mint sprig, garnish

Pour all liquid ingredients into a blender with ice and blend. Pour into a highball glass and garnish with orange and mint.

SAINT THOMAS THE APOSTLE, DECEMBER 21 (JULY 3)

The Apostle famous for his doubting is, fittingly, the Apostle first to affirm explicitly the divinity of Jesus Christ. After rebounding from his incredulity about the Resurrection, Thomas proclaimed, "My Lord and my God" (John 20:24–29). Along with the December saints who fought the Arian heresy, St. Thomas' belief that Jesus is true God primes the pump nicely for the festival celebrating the birth of the God-man.

St. Thomas' Day was once a hub of interesting customs. In Norway, all Yuletide preparations—such as chopping firewood, baking, and slaughtering—had to be completed by today so that one could spend the last few days before Christmas getting into a more spiritual frame of mind. The Apostle even took on the nickname "St. Thomas the Brewer" because all holiday beer had to be brewed by December 21 (and no more brewing could be done until after Epiphany). Norwegians once visited each other on Saint Thomas' Day to sample each other's Christmas ale.

There is no strict definition for a "Christmas ale," although it usually means a limited-edition, malty, high-alcohol content (5.5%–14% ABV) beer

with spices reminiscent of the holiday season. In the world of nonalcoholic beers, Santa Clausthaler, which we discussed on the Feast of St. Nicholas (see December 6) is the most recognizable. But any of the stouts mentioned for St. Patrick's Day (see March 17) can also double for a Christmas ale, since most of them are malty.

Finally, a Thomas and Jeremiah is a spin-off of the Tom and Jerry mixed drink and is yuletide appropriate.

Thomas and Jeremiah

Makes 1 drink

- 1½ oz. nonalcoholic rum
- ½ tsp. brown sugar
- ½ oz. lemon or lime juice
- alcohol-free hot cider

Build rum, sugar, and juice in a mug or Irish coffee glass and top with hot cider.

DECEMBER

LAST CALL

The Gospel mentions the fact that Thomas was also called *Didymus* or "twin" (John 20:24). Some apocryphal works make the bizarre claim that he was the twin brother of Jesus, but we suspect that he is *our* twin, a reflection of our doubts and, hopefully, our turnaround. Tonight, make it a double, accompanied by the following toast: "To our alter ego St. Thomas the Apostle: may he lead us from our egos to the altar."

ADAM AND EVE, DECEMBER 24

Catholics are sometimes surprised to learn that Adam and Eve, who were not exactly a smashing success in Paradise, went on to live a long life of pious penance and ended their lives as saints. The Byzantine icons of the Anastasis and the Western paintings of the Harrowing of Hell, for example, show Christ descending into Limbo on Good Friday and rescuing all the just souls destined for Heaven, starting with Adam and Eve—by then an elderly couple. Adam and Eve have never had a feast day in the Western Latin calendars, but in the Byzantine East their feast falls on December 24, and believe it or not, this tradition eventually gave us the Christmas tree, which began as a combination of the two famous trees in the Garden of Eden: the red balls symbolize the forbidden fruit (apples) on the Tree of the Knowledge of Good and Evil while the candy symbolizes the Tree of Life.

An apple drink therefore seems appropriate for this evening.

Hot Spiced Apple Cider

Makes 6 drinks

2 qts. unfiltered apple juice, preferably organic
4 star anise
2 cinnamon sticks
½ tsp. freshly grated nutmeg
1 tsp. vanilla extract or vanilla paste
2 apples, sliced

Place all ingredients into a pot and simmer on medium-low heat uncovered for 20–30 minutes in order to let the flavors come together. Ladle into mugs and top with a slice of cooked apple from the pot or a cinnamon stick.

Hot Apple Crisp

Makes 6–8 drinks

12 oz. Lyre's American Malt
32 oz. spiced apple juice
2 oz. cinnamon vanilla syrup
4 cinnamon sticks
1 apple, sliced

Add all ingredients to the slow cooker and simmer for 3–4 hours. Serve in a mug with additional apple slices and/or cinnamon for garnish.

Note: To make cinnamon vanilla syrup, spit 1 Mexican vanilla bean and scrape out seeds, crack 1–2 cinnamon sticks (about ½ oz.), and place everything in a saucepan with 1 cup sugar and 1 cup water. Bring to a slight boil for 5 minutes and then let sit for at least 5 hours. Strain into a sterilized jar.

Apple Pear Sour

Makes 1 drink

- 2 oz. Spiritless Kentucky 74
- 1 oz. Apple-Pear Barmalade (a cocktail mixer)
- 1 oz. sweet and sour
- Apple slice, garnish

Combine all ingredients in shaker, add ice, and shake vigorously. Pour into cocktail glass and garnish with apple slice.

For December 25 through 31, see the Twelve Days of Christmas, Chapter 14.

PART II

THE LITURGICAL SEASONS
(THE TEMPORAL CYCLE)

CHAPTER THIRTEEN

Advent

THE DAYS OF ADVENT

An excellent option to warm the frosty nights of Advent is German mulled wine. Known as "glow wine" because of the hot irons once used to make it, *Glüwhein* or *Glüwein* is traditionally consumed during the winter around Christmas, although it is also associated with the season of Advent. Here is a simple recipe for one person, followed by another for two to four.

Glüwhein (individual)

Makes 1 drink

- 4 oz. nonalcoholic wine, red or white
- 1 stick cinnamon
- ½ tsp. sugar
- 1 orange peel
- 1 lemon peel
- 1 whole clove

Put ingredients into a small saucepan, and heat slowly for 15 minutes. Let cool a little and serve in Irish coffee glasses or coffee mugs.

Glüwhein (small group)

Makes 2–4 drinks

- 1 bottle nonalcoholic wine, red or white
- 5 cinnamon sticks
- 1 tsp. cloves
- 1 apple, sliced whole, seeds removed; or 1 orange, sliced
- honey to taste

Put ingredients into a small saucepan, bring to a boil, and simmer for 15 minutes. Strain into a mug or Irish coffee glass.

Another option, in order to honor the liturgical color of the season, is Sentia's Violet Cup. **Sentia's** GABA Red, which "is designed for relaxation and intimate moments," is a delightful array of sweet heady aromatics, rich herbal complexity, and bittersweet spiced berries.

Violet Cup

Makes 1 drink

¾ oz. Sentia's GABA Red
½ oz. violet syrup
¾ oz. blueberry juice
½ oz. fresh lemon juice
blueberries
soda water
edible flowers, garnish

Muddle blueberries in a shaker and then add all ingredients except soda water and edible flowers. Shake with ice and strain into an old-fashioned glass with ice. Top with soda water and garnish, if you wish, with edible flowers.

ADVENT SUNDAY, OR FIRST SUNDAY OF ADVENT

The beginning of the liturgical year is also called Stir-Up Sunday because the Collect in the traditional Missal begins with the words, "Stir up, we beseech Thee." Stir-Up Sunday also became the occasion for stirring up Christmas pudding in preparation for the great holiday. It even inspired a little ditty:

> Stir up, we beseech Thee,
> The pudding in the pot;
> And when we get home
> We'll eat the lot.

Whilst you make your Christmas pudding, enjoy a cup of Lyre's Christmas Berry Bliss.

Christmas Berry Bliss

Makes 1 drink

- 4 oz. coconut milk (or your choice of rich, creamy plant milk)
- 1 oz. Monin White Chocolate Syrup
- ½ oz. Monin Raspberry Syrup
- 2 oz. Lyre's Amaretti
- 1 oz. Lyre's White Cane
- whipped cream, raspberry syrup, crushed almonds, crushed candy for garnish, optional

Heat the coconut milk and Monin syrups in a saucepan. In an Irish coffee glass or mug, combine Lyre's Amaretti and Lyre's White Cane. Add the warm milk mixture and stir 40 times. Top with whipped cream, a dash of raspberry syrup, crushed almonds, and a sprinkle of festive candy in red, green, silver, and gold.

SECOND SUNDAY OF ADVENT

In the traditional Epistle reading for the Second Sunday of Advent (Romans 15:4–13), St. Paul quotes the prophet Isaiah: "There shall be a root of Jesse; and He that shall rise up to rule the Gentiles, in Him the Gentiles shall hope." And in the Gospel reading (Matthew 11:2–10), Jesus jokingly asks the people who had gone to see John the Baptist: "What went you out into the desert to see? A reed shaken by the wind?"

Let's think of a drink based on these two readings. The reed part is easy: just add a straw to your beverage. As for the root, we like The Pathfinder Spirit (<0.5% ABV), which is blended with angelic root and several other herbs and spices. It tastes like an amaro, "that fine class of European liquors known for bittersweet flavors rounded out by citrus and spice." Pathfinder can be enjoyed neat, on the rocks, or as a substitute for amaro, whiskey, or vermouth. Or try their spritz:

Golden Hour Highball

Makes 1 drink

2 oz. The Pathfinder Hemp & Root Spirit
½ oz. fresh lemon juice
dry ginger beer
1 lemon wedge, garnish
1 straw

Pour Pathfinder and lemon juice into a highball glass with ice and top with ginger beer. Stir 40 times. Garnish with lemon and add straw.

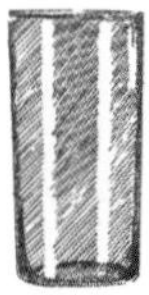

GAUDETE SUNDAY, OR THIRD SUNDAY OF ADVENT

Most folks remember this Sunday in Advent as as one of the two when the priest wears "pink" vestments. Just don't say that to the priest or he'll never wear them again (priests are men too, after all). The technical name for this beautiful liturgical hue is rose. Symbolically, rose can be seen as a lighter shade of the penitential color of violet, and thus it still evokes the penitence of the season but with an added dimension of joyful anticipation. The name *Gaudete* or "Rejoice" comes from the opening word of the traditional Introit (Entrance Antiphon) and the theme of the Epistle; it expresses the jubilance of waiting with hopeful certainty in the Lord's fulfillment of His promises. The Sunday also constitutes a slight relaxation of the rigors of Advent, a sort of catching of one's breath before the final penitential push.

And *Abstaining with the Saints* is all about exploiting such relaxations. Catch your breath tonight with a pink or rose-colored beverage.

Pink Lady

Makes 1 drink

2 oz. red grapefruit juice
2 oz. white grapefruit juice
2 oz. cranberry juice

Pour all ingredients in a mixing glass and stir 40 times. Pour into a highball glass with ice.

Rose Butterfly (a.k.a. Verbena Club)

Makes 1 drink

1¾ oz. Bax Botanics Verbena
½ oz. fresh lemon juice
2 tsp. aquafaba
¾ oz. butterfly pea syrup
1–2 rose petals, garnish

Pour liquid ingredients into a shaker with ice and shake 40 times. Strain into a champagne coupe glass. Float rose petals on top.

Note: To make butterfly pea syrup, combine 1 cup water and 1 cup sugar in a saucepan over medium heat until sugar dissolves. Let cool and add 2 tablespoons of dried butterfly pea flower. Let steep for 10 minutes, then strain into a sterilized jar.

Pink Gin & Tonic

Makes 1 drink

2 dashes Peychaud's bitters
2½ oz. Free Spirits' The Spirit of Gin
3 oz. tonic water
dried rose buds and juniper berries, garnish

In a large wine glass add 1 large ice cube, Peychaud's bitters, The Spirit of Gin, tonic water, and some dried rosebuds and juniper berries. Stir 40 times.

EMBER DAYS OF ADVENT: THE WEDNESDAY, FRIDAY, AND SATURDAY OF THE THIRD WEEK OF ADVENT

The Ember Days are named after the four natural seasons ("ember" is a corruption of the Latin *tempora*), and the Ember Days of Advent are an opportunity to give thanks to God for the season of Winter. It is also an opportunity to work on our virtues and vices. The four temperaments or humors (sanguine, choleric, phlegmatic, and melancholic) are an ancient way of classifying personalities. Since winter is cold and moist, it produces more phlegm in the human body, and thus the Advent Embertide is for phlegmatics and for a battle with "the phlegm of lightness and forgetting" (to which phlegmatics are prone) as well as a battle against the "coldness of untruth and malice" (to which all are prone).

There is no such person as Saint Ember, but that did not stop **Little Saints** from naming their tequila substitute, which is a blend of ginger, peppers, woody palo santo, and lion's mane mushroom, St. Ember. Their **Spice on Ice** works well with the winter theme (see March 10).

FOURTH SUNDAY OF ADVENT

The traditional Gospel reading for this Sunday (Luke 3:1–6) focuses on the beginning of St. John the Baptist's preaching in the wilderness to prepare the way of the Messiah. Let us honor the Forerunner of the Lord with a drink, not forgetting that as a teetotaler, he is one of the patron saints of this book.

John the Baptist can easily be described as a cut above; after all, Jesus said of him that "there hath not risen among them that are born of women a greater than John the Baptist" (Matthew 11:11). Cut Above Spirits has a Honey and Fig G&T that also nods to his diet of wild honey. The original recipe also calls for fresh figs, but we omitted them out of fear that they would be difficult to find this time of year. The thyme, on the other hand, has a good holiday vibe to it.

Cut Above Gin & Tonic

Makes 1 drink

2 oz. Cut Above (nonalcoholic) Gin

1/2 oz. honey simple syrup (equal parts honey and water)

3 oz. tonic water

1 thyme sprig, garnish

Pour Cut Above and honey simple syrup into a shaker with ice and shake 40 times. Strain into a highball glass with ice and top with tonic water. Stir. Garnish with thyme.

For December 25 through 31, see the Twelve Days of Christmas, Chapter 14.

CHAPTER FOURTEEN

The Twelve Days of Christmas

CHRISTMAS DAY, DECEMBER 25

> And Mary brought forth her firstborn son, and wrapped him up in swaddling clothes, and laid him in a manger; because there was no room for them in the inn (Luke 2:7).

The great Feast of the Nativity of Our Lord Jesus Christ has long served as an occasion for special drinks. In the Latin countries of Europe, wine is customarily enjoyed on this day, and in the northern countries, beer or ale; indeed, a multitude of the latter are now named after Christmas (see below).

But special mention must be made of eggnog and Christmas punch. Eggnog has been a popular Christmas drink in the English-speaking world for at least two hundred years. Eggnog mix is widely available at Christmastime in grocery stores and supermarkets. It can be served without alcohol and (almost) always with a sprinkle of nutmeg.

Christmas punch is the successor of "Wassail," a medieval combination of hot ale or mead, roasted apples, eggs, nutmeg, and floating pieces of toast. Today's Christmas punch, by contrast, typically uses wine as the base ingredient. **Lamb's Wool**, which we recommend for Epiphany, is a variation of the classic wassail but with wine (see Epiphany, January 6), and you can also enjoy a Christmas Mocktail invented by our friend Eleanor Morrison.

And *Imbuljuta tal-Qastan* (don't ask us how it is pronounced) is a traditional Maltese drink served on Christmas Eve and after Midnight Mass.

Imbuljuta tal-Qastan

Makes 3–4 drinks

20 oz. water, plus more for washing and soaking
7 oz. dried chestnuts
rinds of 2 small, finely sliced tangerines
1 cinnamon stick
2 tsp. ground cinnamon
1 tsp. ground cloves
½ tsp. mixed spice
2¾ oz. dark chocolate
2¾ oz. cocoa powder
1¾ oz. brown sugar

Wash and soak the chestnuts thoroughly. Leave to soak overnight. The next day, drain and put the chestnuts in a saucepan. Add all the ingredients and bring to a boil over medium heat. Bring the heat down and let simmer for about an hour, until the chestnuts are soft and tender. Serve hot in a cup or mug.

Eggnog

Makes 1 drink

1 egg
1 tsp. sugar
1½ oz. milk or cream
nutmeg

Beat egg, sugar, and milk or cream until smooth and frothy. Pour into an old-fashioned glass, stir, and top with sprinkled nutmeg.

Lyre's Eggnog Cocktail

Makes 1 drink

2 oz. Lyre's American Malt
4 oz. eggnog
1/4 oz. maple syrup
dark chocolate, finely grated, garnish
whipped cream, garnish

Pour liquid ingredients into a goblet or mug, stir 40 times. Top with whipped cream and dust with dark chocolate.

Nat's Nonalcoholic Christmas Punch

Makes 5 drinks

2 cups cranberry juice
1 cup orange juice
1 cup pineapple juice
2 cups sparkling apple juice or cider
1 cup ginger ale, or less for a drier punch
orange slices, cranberries, pomegranate seeds and/or cherries, garnish

Pour cranberry, orange, and pineapple juices into a punch bowl. Add sparkling apple juice or cider and stir gently. When ready to serve, add ice and garnishes of your choice.

Christmas Mocktail

By Eleanor Morrison

Makes 1 drink

2 oz. cranberry juice
3 oz. ginger beer
½ oz. mint simple syrup
½ tsp. fresh lemon juice
½ tsp. fresh lime juice

Mix all ingredients in a mixing glass and stir 40 times. Pour into an old-fashioned glass with ice.

Note: To make mint simple syrup, place 1 cup water and 1 cup sugar in a saucepan over medium heat until sugar dissolves. Remove from heat and add 1 tablespoon packed mint leaves and steep for 10 minutes. Strain into a sterilized jar.

LAST CALL

The word "wassail" comes from the Old Saxon toast, *Was haile*—Your health! Tonight and throughout the Twelve Days of Christmas, use this ancient drinker's greeting, along with a traditional Christmas greeting borrowed from the Byzantine rite. One person proclaims, "Christ is born!" and the other replies, "Glorify Him!"

SAINT STEPHEN THE PROTOMARTYR, DECEMBER 26

Stephen, one of the first seven men ordained a deacon by the guidance of the Holy Spirit, is called the Protomartyr, for in being stoned to death by order of the Sanhedrin, he was the first disciple of Christ to shed his blood for the Faith (Acts 6:5–7:59). Stephen is a model of that divinely-infused love known in the Christian tradition as *agape* or *caritas*, the gift of God which in English we call "charity." Charity's divine origin cannot be overemphasized, for it is by no human love that someone can follow the example of our Savior and forgive the men murdering him. Yet as St. Luke tells us, as Stephen was dying he fell to his knees and cried out in a loud voice: "'Lord, lay not this sin to their charge.'"

St. Stephen became a patron saint of horses, the logic being that even livestock were accorded leisure during the Twelve Days of Christmas, and since the horse is the most prized livestock, it gets pride of place after Christmas Day, which happens to be the Feast of Stephen. Farmers in Europe used to decorate their horses and ride them to church for a blessing, after which they circled the church three times and took a "St. Stephen's Ride."

When Americans think of an equine event, they think of the Kentucky Derby, and when they think of the Kentucky Derby, they think of a Mint Julep. Even though it is not May, mix one for tonight.

Botanical Julep

Makes 1 drink

2 oz. The Pathfinder Hemp & Root Spirit
½ oz. simple syrup
3 mint leaves

Muddle the mint in an old-fashioned glass and add Pathfinder and simple syrup. Add crushed ice and serve.

Spiritless Mint Julep

Makes 1 drink

2 oz. Spiritless Kentucky 74
½ oz. simple syrup
4–6 fresh mint leaves

Combine simple syrup and mint into an old-fashioned glass and muddle. Add Kentucky 74, fill with crushed ice, and stir.

LAST CALL

St. Stephen's is the traditional day on which the abundance of Christmas is shared with the less fortunate. It was on this day that the poor boxes of the church were emptied and their contents distributed to the needy—hence the term "Boxing Day." Today, do something nice for the poor, like giving a homeless person some food or warm clothes. Then, say a prayer for the less fortunate before wassailing in gratitude for the blessings God has given you.

SAINT JOHN THE EVANGELIST, DECEMBER 27

Like St. Stephen, John the Apostle and Evangelist is associated with charity, since his writings marvelously emphasize the love of God (see John 3:16, I John 4:7–8). John, in turn, was blessed by Christ's special love for him. Though Our Lord made St. Peter the head of His Church, He retained a personal affection for the "beloved disciple." This is all the more endearing given the fact that Our Lord also referred to John and his older brother St. James the Great as "sons of thunder," most likely for their fiery tempers (Mark 3:17).

It has been said that St. John was the only Apostle who did not die a martyr's death because he had already testified to the Cross by being the only Apostle who stood at its foot with the Mother of God. Yet the Church still honors John as a martyr because several attempts on his life were made. Perhaps the saint's most famous brush with death was when his enemies tried to kill him by poisoning his cup of wine. Some say that when the Divine John (as he is called in the East) made the sign of the cross over the cup, it split in half. Others claim that his blessing neutralized the poison in the potation and allowed him to enjoy it unharmed. Either way, it is a good reminder to say one's grace before meals.

And it is also the inspiration for consuming the "Love of St. John" (*Johannesminne* or *Szent Janos Aldasa*), wine or cider that is blessed by the priest after Mass with a special blessing from the Roman Ritual and poured into everyone's glass before dinner later that night. The blessed liquid was considered a sacramental and used in a variety of ways: it was poured into every barrel of the family wine cellar or kept in the house throughout the year for newlyweds to drink immediately after the wedding ceremony, for travelers before a trip, and for the dying after receiving Last Rites as "the last earthly drink to strengthen them for their departure from this world."

St. John's wine can also be mulled for a spicy hot drink on a cold winter's night. Here is a recipe from William Kaufman's *Catholic Cookbook*; you can either evaporate the alcohol in the process, or play it safe with a nonalcoholic wine.

St. John's Wine

Makes 8 drinks

- 1 qt. nonalcoholic red wine
- ½ cup sugar
- 3 whole cloves
- 2 (2-inch) cinnamon sticks
- ½ tsp. ground nutmeg
- 1/16 tsp. ground cardamom

Pour all the ingredients into a large saucepan and boil for 5 minutes. Serve hot.

LAST CALL

Our Christmas guide, Maria Von Trapp, describes the Austrian ceremony involving St. John's Love. Before the dinner, everyone stands up with his glass of blessed wine. The father then takes his glass, touches it to the mother's while looking her in the eyes, and says, "I drink to you the love of St. John," to which the mother replies, "I thank you for the love of St. John." Both take a sip before the mother turns to the oldest child and repeats the ritual, at which point the child turns to the next oldest, etc. The last one to receive St. John's love (the youngest member of the family) gives it back to the father, thus closing the family circle.

HOLY INNOCENTS, DECEMBER 28

> Herod, perceiving that he was deluded by the wise men, was exceeding angry; and sending killed all the men children that were in Bethlehem, and in all the borders thereof, from two years old and under, according to the time which he had diligently inquired of the wise men (Matthew 2:16–17).

From what we can tell, the Roman rite has always kept the feast of "Childermas" (Children's Mass) on December 28, ever since it first began being celebrated in the fifth century. In so doing, the Western Church presents an interesting array of saints on December 26, 27, and 28. Stephen is a martyr by will, love, and blood; John the Evangelist a martyr by will and love (but not blood because he died a natural death); and the Holy Innocents are martyrs by blood alone. Indeed, because these children died not only for Christ but instead of Him they are called *flores martyrum*, the "flowers of the martyrs." As St. Augustine eloquently puts it: "They are the first buds of the Church killed by the frost of persecution."

Channel your inner child with a sweet drink. Dirty Sodas are a good start.

Childermas Soda

Makes 1 drink

1 can cola
2 tbsp. coconut creamer
1 lime, squeezed

Pour all ingredients into a highball with ice and stir.

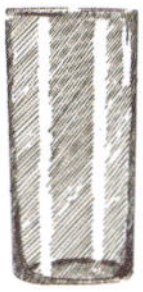

LAST CALL

The Twelve Days of Christmas are a time of "topsy-turvy" customs, where social ranks and pecking orders are inverted in giddy imitation of the grandest inversion of all, the fact that Almighty God humbled Himself to be born a man in a chilly and malodorous stable. Childermas is no exception. In many religious communities, the novices had the privilege of sitting at the head of the table at meals and meetings, while the last person who had taken vows in the monastery or convent got to be superior for a day. Young monks and nuns would receive congratulations and have "baby food," such as hot cereal, served to them for dinner. In the family, the youngest child received special honors, even becoming master of the household. Not all customs, however, bode well for the young 'uns. In some places, children awoke to a spanking from their parents to remind them of the sufferings of the Holy Innocents.

In the Philippines and some Spanish-speaking countries, Childermas is the equivalent of April's Fools Day, a time of pranks and practical jokes called *inocentadas*. And, of course, all of Christendom once abstained from servile work on this day—along with the other twelve days of Christmas. Today, come up with your own topsy-turvy, prankish, leisurely customs.

POPE SAINT SYLVESTER, DECEMBER 31

Sylvester was Supreme Pontiff during the reign of Constantine, the Roman Emperor who ended the persecution of the Church. One legend even claims that Sylvester baptized Constantine after the latter was miraculously cured from leprosy.

There is a simple reason why the saint's feast falls on this day: after twenty-one years of service to God as Pope, Sylvester died and was buried on December 31, 335. That said, there is something appropriate about preparing for the new civic year with the first Bishop of Rome to assume the throne of Peter during a time of civic peace, since on the last day of the year our hearts are filled with hope for "peace on earth." Sylvester's feast is so closely tied to December 31 that in many countries New Year's Eve is known as Sylvester Night (*Silvesterabend* or *Silvesternacht* in German).

Sylvester Punches are a traditional way in Catholic cultures to usher in the new year. Maria Von Trapp, of *Sound and Music* fame, offers an alcohol-free version which we have taken the liberty of naming Maria's Punchless Punch.

Maria's Punchless Punch

Makes 6 drinks

- ½ cup lemon juice
- rind of 1 lemon, grated
- 1 qt. water
- 1 cup orange juice
- 1 cup sugar
- grated rind of ½ orange

Cook sugar and water for 5 minutes. Cool. Add juices and rind and stir.

One suggestion: Our panel of tasters found the punch a bit too sweet. Rather than pour in the entire cup of sugar, you may wish to add to taste.

LAST CALL

Sylvester Night abounds with charming customs. In France and French Canada, it was customary for the father to bless the members of his family and for the children to thank their parents for all of their love and care. In central Europe, a pre-Christian ritual of scaring away demons with loud noises became the inspiration for our New Year's Eve custom of fireworks and artillery salutes. In Austria, December 31 was sometimes called *Rauchnacht* or "Incense night," when the paterfamilias went through the house and barn purifying them with incense and holy water. In Spain and other Spanish-speaking areas it was considered good luck to eat twelve grapes at the twelve strokes of midnight.

Holy Mother Church also grants a plenary indulgence, under the usual conditions, to a public recitation of the great Latin hymn of thanksgiving, the *Te Deum*, on the last day of the year, while a partial indulgence "is granted to those who recite the *Te Deum* in thanksgiving." Sing or say the *Te Deum* tonight, or if you lack the time, at least make a toast filled with thanksgiving for the previous year.

Lastly, paraphrase St. Thomas More and wish each of your guests a year of "godly prosperity," a year that sees a "happy continuation and gracious increase of virtue" in their souls.

FEAST OF THE CIRCUMCISION/MARY, MOTHER OF GOD, JANUARY 1

Over the centuries, January 1 in the calendar of the Latin Church came to be a combination of three feasts: the Octave Day of Christmas, the Maternity of the Blessed Virgin Mary, and the Feast of the Circumcision of Our Lord—which, according to the Gospel, took place on the octave of His birth (Luke 2:21).

The name for a nonalcoholic Bloody Mary is a Virgin Mary, and we provide a recipe for August 22. We also recommend a Trastevere Mocktail, since in the old rite, Santa Maria in Trastevere (Saint Mary across the Tiber) is the station church for the day. Station churches are ancient parishes in Rome to where the Pope and people would process and celebrate Mass on appointed days. This beautiful church is believed to be the first Christian church dedicated to the Mother of God, the first site where Mass was celebrated openly, and a location with a fascinating history. According to legend, oil (petroleum) mysteriously bubbled up from the earth there the year that Christ was born.

Later, a *taberna meritoria* was built on the spot. What is a *taberna meritoria*, you ask? Wikipedia in all its wisdom translates the phrase as "notable tavern," but the truth is a lot earthier: it was a brothel. *Meritoria* means "hired," and a *taberna meritoria* was where certain workers could be hired for their services.

How extraordinary that a church dedicated to the immaculate Virgin Mary should be built on the ruins of a house of ill repute! And the Church is unashamed of the transformation, proclaiming it in an inscription over the altar of Santa Maria in Trastevere. There is no sin that God's grace cannot absolve, except the despair of being absolved. Have hope!

Our Trastevere Mocktail features strawberries, which are a symbol of the Blessed Virgin Mary because it is one of the few plants that flowers and fruits at the same time, a symbol of her virginal motherhood. The essential oil recalls the prophetic oil that oozed up the year that Christ was born, and if you use spikenard essential oil, you are using the oil that Mary Magdalene, the former loose woman, used to anoint the feet of Our Lord.

Trastevere Mocktail

Makes 1 drink

- 2–3 sliced fresh strawberries
- 2–3 mint leaves, plus more for garnish
- 1 oz. simple syrup
- 1 oz. fresh lemon juice
- sparkling water
- 1 drop spikenard essential oil (substitute: 1 drop lavender essential oil)—and no more! It's strong stuff

In a shaker or mixing glass, gently muddle the strawberries, mint leaves, and simple syrup. Add lemon juice and essential oil and shake 40 times. Pour into an old-fashioned glass with ice, top with sparkling water, and stir. Garnish with mint.

LAST CALL

Holy Mother Church grants a plenary indulgence when the great hymn to the Holy Spirit, *Veni Creator Spiritus* or "Come Holy Ghost, Creator Blest," is recited on January 1 under the usual conditions. Belt it out today with gusto; even if you don't meet the requirements for a plenary indulgence, you can still start the year off right with a Bloody Mary and a partial indulgence.

SAINT ELIZABETH ANN SETON, JANUARY 4

Elizabeth Ann Seton (1774–1821) came from a prominent New York Episcopalian family and married the import trader William Magee Seton at the age of nineteen. William suffered bankruptcy and then contracted tuberculosis; he and Elizabeth visited Italy and its warmer climes at the advice of his doctors, but William died not long after reaching their destination. It was William's Italian business partners who introduced Elizabeth to Catholicism, and upon her return to the United States she converted. She was received into the Church at St. Peter's in New York, the only Catholic church in the city at the time, and was later confirmed by the Right Reverend John Carroll, the only bishop in the nation. Elizabeth tried to start an academy for young ladies, but parents withdrew their children from it when they discovered she was Catholic. Eventually she founded a Catholic school for the poor in Baltimore and in this way began the Catholic parochial school system. She also established a religious community called the Sisters of Charity in Emmitsburg, Maryland. St. Elizabeth died of tuberculosis at the age of forty-six.

A colonial-era saint calls for a colonial-era beverage. Switchel is also called Haymaker's Punch because it provides refreshment during the sweaty days of the summer harvest, but it is also good during wintertime. And both the cider vinegar and ginger are good for respiratory health, a backhanded reminder of the T.B. from which St. Elizabeth and her husband died.

Switchel

Makes 2 drinks

2 cups water
4 tbsp. cider vinegar
2 tbsp. maple syrup
2 tsp. fresh ginger, finely grated

Mix all ingredients together and refrigerate at least 3 hours. Strain into a glass with ice.

CHAPTER FIFTEEN

Epiphany and the Time Thereafter

EPIPHANY, JANUARY 6 (SUNDAY BETWEEN JANUARY 2 AND 8)

The great feast of the Epiphany, which is a holy day of obligation in most countries, celebrates the visit of the Magi to the newborn King in Bethlehem, and as such it celebrates the fact that Jesus Christ came to save not only the Jews but the Gentiles (represented by the Magi, Zoroastrian priestly scholars). The Magi are also called the Three Kings in accordance with two Old Testament prophecies that describe kings from Tharsis, Arabia, and Sheba bringing to the Messiah presents (Psalm 71:10) such as gold and frankincense (Isaiah 60:3–6).

The Epiphany drink, usually drunk on the vigil of the feast, is a wassail called Lamb's Wool (for more on wassails, see Christmas Day). The unusual name is probably due to the fuzzy appearance of the roasted apples, but it is also a nice tie-in to the Lamb of God who this day revealed Himself to all the nations. And there's even a nice little ditty to remind you of the instructions.

Next crowne the bowle full
With gentle Lambs wooll,
Adde sugar, nutmeg, and ginger,
With store of ale too,
And thus ye must doe
To make the Wassaile a swinger.

Instead of ale, enjoy a Lamb's Wool with apple cider:

Lamb's Wool

Makes 8 drinks

6 baking apples, cored
2 tbsp. to 1/2 cup brown sugar
2 qts. apple cider
1/8 tsp. nutmeg
1/4 tsp. cinnamon
1/4 tsp. ground ginger
nuts, optional

Peel and boil the apples, either whole or cut, until they are very soft and flaky. (A lengthier but more traditional alternative is to roast the apples in a baking pan at 450°F for an hour or until they are very soft and begin to burst.)

In a large saucepan, dissolve the sugar a few tablespoons at a time in cider or ale, tasting for sweetness. Add the spices. Bring to a boil and simmer for 10–15 minutes. Pour the liquid over the apples in a large punch bowl. Add nuts if desired or serve separately.

Or, honor the gifts of the Magi with Sentia's GABA Gold. The bouquet or nose of this nonalcoholic spirit, which is "bursting with spicy notes and zesty complexity to leave you wanting more," has the best nose or bouquet of anything we have tried, alcoholic or not. Enjoy it by itself on the rocks, or in a Gold and Tonic:

Gold and Tonic

Makes 1 drink

3/4 oz. Sentia's GABA Gold
tonic water
lime wedge, garnish

Pour GABA Gold into an old-fashioned glass with ice and top with soda water. Garnish with a lime wedge.

LAST CALL

In some parts of the world, Epiphany is called "Little Christmas" because it is the final day for exchanging Christmas gifts. In the Irish counties of Cork and Kerry, it is also called "Women's Christmas." Irish men do all of the household chores today, while their womenfolk hold parties or go out with their friends, with pubs and restaurants holding special "Ladies' Night" attractions. Children also give special gifts to their mothers and grandmothers on this day. Use your imagination to apply these customs to your day.

FEAST OF THE HOLY FAMILY, SUNDAY AFTER EPIPHANY (SUNDAY AFTER CHRISTMAS)

This lovely feast pays tribute to the domestic life of Jesus, Mary, and Joseph. There are two legends about the Holy Family that provide inspiration for tonight's cocktail menu. According to a Sicilian superstition, a juniper bush courageously hid Jesus, Mary, and Joseph from Herod's soldiers, an act that God rewarded by bestowing on the plant the power of putting evil spirits to flight. Similarly, Mary washed the tiny garments of Jesus during their flight and spread them over the branches of a rosemary bush to dry them. In reward for this service to his Son, God conferred upon the rosemary, or "Mary's rose," a fragrant aroma.

In memory of the juniper legend, turn to the drinks of St. Junipero Serra (July 1). For the rosemary, see below.

Rosemary Booch

Makes 1 drink

1½ oz. Seedlip Gardon 108
kombucha
1 rosemary sprig, garnish

Pour Seedlip into an old-fashioned glass with ice and top with kombucha. Garnish with rosemary.

LAST CALL

The traditional Collect for the feast also makes a fitting toast. "To our Lord Jesus Christ who, when He was subject to Mary and Joseph, sanctified domestic life with ineffable virtues. And may we all become partakers of the eternal happiness of the Holy Family as we learn from their example."

Rosemerrymaking

Makes 1 drink

4 oz. Ghia Apéritif
8 oz. water
8 oz. cane sugar
5–7 sprigs fresh rosemary, plus more for garnish
½ tbsp. pink peppercorns, plus more for garnish
2 oz. sparkling water

Place water and sugar in a saucepan over medium heat and stir until sugar dissolves. Let cool, add pink peppercorns and rosemary, and let sit for 30–45 minutes. Strain your simple syrup into a sterilized jar and refrigerate.

In a mixing glass, add ice, 1 ounce simple syrup, and 4 ounces Ghia and stir 40 times. Pour into a champagne coupe glass and top with a splash of sparkling water, a sprig of rosemary, and a few peppercorns to garnish.

BAPTISM OF THE LORD JESUS CHRIST, JANUARY 13 (USUALLY, SUNDAY AFTER JANUARY 6)

Epiphany is about the manifestation (*epiphaneia*) of Christ to the Gentiles, and so to round out the celebration of this august feast, the Church remembers one week later another divine manifestation, the baptism of Jesus in the river Jordan by St. John the Baptist. It was on this occasion that Christ established baptism as a sacrament and was proclaimed by a heavenly voice as the Son of God in whom the Father is well pleased (Matthew 3:13–17).

On this day, celebrate Our Lord's baptism the way you would a baptism or christening in your family. Champagne and punch are traditional favorites for such a happy occasion. For nonalcoholic champagnes, here is a meager sampling of some of the better ones:

- French Bloom, Le Blanc
- Kally Golden Sparkler
- Lili Golden Sparkler
- Non7 Stewed Cherry and Coffee
- St. Regis Sparkling Brut
- Studio Null Sparkling Verdejo

And if you are throwing party, whip up a batch of **La Dolce Vita Punch** (see Trinity Sunday), since the baptized life is indeed the sweet life.

CHAPTER SIXTEEN

Pre-Lent and Lent

In the traditional calendar of the Roman Rite is a season that acts as a bridge between the residual yuletide joy of the Time after Epiphany and the coming austerity of Lent. Known as Pre-Lent or Septuagesima, this bridge begins three Sundays before Ash Wednesday, which is roughly seventy days before Easter: hence the name *septuagesima*, or "seventy" in Latin.

Although the season of Septuagesima is not in the post-Vatican II calendar, it continues to exert an influence, since it is Septuagesima that backhandedly gives us Carnival. In the weeks prior to Lent (and in the days prior to refrigeration), Christians needed to get rid of all the foods that they would not be allowed to consume during the forty-day Great Fast, and centuries ago that was quite a long list; not only flesh meat but all dairy products were once forbidden. And the closer Lent approached, the more urgently these food items needed to be consumed. Ironically, the pre-Lenten excesses and glittering pageantry we associate with Mardi Gras in New Orleans or the *carnevales* in Brazil and Venice can be traced to the increase in voluntary fasting prior to Lent. This history is present in the very word "carnival," a Catholic neologism that means "reduction" (*levare*) of "meat" (*caro/carnis*). Others like to say that it means saying goodbye (*vale*) to meat (*carne*).

DEPOSITION OF ALLELUIA, SATURDAY BEFORE SEPTUAGESIMA SUNDAY

In the traditional 1962 calendar, the day before Septuagesima Sunday was the last time the word "Alleluia" could be said prior to Easter. Just as the forty days of Lent commemorated the forty years of the Hebrews in the wilderness, the seventy days of Pre-Lent and Lent commemorated the Babylonian Exile, when the Jews were too sad to sing their songs of Zion in an alien land (Psalm 137[136]). And what song is more expressive of the joy of Zion than the heavenly "Alleluia"?

Elaborate goodbyes to "Alleluia" were staged during the Middle Ages on the day before Septuagesima Sunday, including a ritual burying or burning of the word (written on a placard). Drawing from the drink suggestions above and with the use of a Dixieland jazz playlist, you too can honor this tradition with a New Orleans-style funeral for the Alleluia, complete with a New Orleans classic like a Sazerac. Invite your non-Catholic neighbors to this send-off so that they can confirm their worst fears about you and your religion.

Non-Sassy Sazerac

Makes 1 drink

- 2½ oz. Free Spirits' The Spirit of Bourbon
- ½ oz. tarragon syrup
- 4 drops (zero proof) All The Bitter New Orleans Bitters
- 1 lemon peel, garnish

Pour all liquid ingredients into a mixing glass with ice and stir 40 times. Strain into a chilled old-fashioned glass (without ice). Express the oils of the lemon peel over the drink by twisting the peel gently, and garnish with peel.

Note*:* To make tarragon syrup, combine half a cup white sugar with half a cup water and a good handful of tarragon sprigs in a saucepan and heat until sugar dissolves. Remove from heat and let cool for 30 minutes. Strain into a sterilized jar.

SEPTUAGESIMA SUNDAY, THREE SUNDAYS BEFORE ASH WEDNESDAY

Again in the traditional calendar, each Sunday of Pre-Lent focuses on a different Old Testament figure as a way of leading us up to the Paschal mystery of Good Friday and Easter. On Septuagesima Sunday that figure is Adam, whose sin led to Christ the New Adam offering Himself on the Cross. Tonight, have any of the drinks associated with Adam and Eve (see December 24).

PRE-LENT

SEXAGESIMA SUNDAY, TWO SUNDAYS BEFORE ASH WEDNESDAY

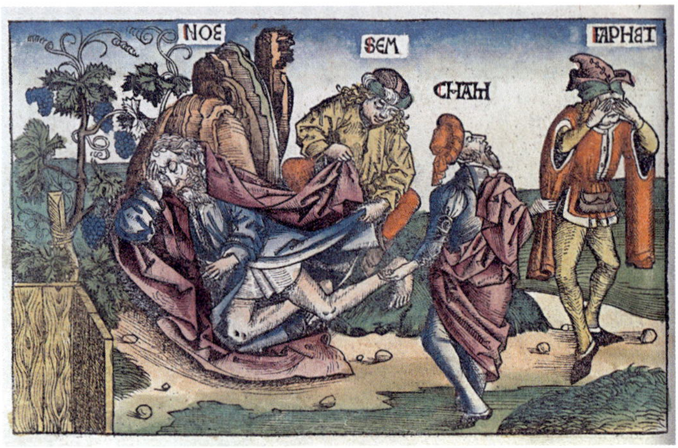

Sexagesima Sunday, so named because it is roughly the sixtieth day before Easter, recalls the Old Testament figure of Noah and the wickedness of mankind at the time of the Flood. Of course, Noah is also the first vine-grower and winemaker. After surviving the Flood, one of the first things Noah did was plant a vineyard, produce wine, and get so drunk that he passed out buck naked (Genesis 9:20–21).

St. Ephrem the Syrian writes eloquently of Noah's oenophilic fall: one of his hymns, written in praise of virginity, has some choice words about the power of wine to lead a chaste maiden away from virtue.

> Beware of Wine in that it disgraced Noah the precious;
>
> He that had conquered the Deluge of water was himself conquered by a handful of wine;
>
> The Flood that was outside him did not overcome him, but the wine that was within him in silence did steal.
>
> If wine disgraced and cast down Noah, the head of families and tongues, forsooth, O lonely one, how it will conquer thee!

Duly warned! Let us instead combine the occasion of Sexagesima with Noah's relief when he landed on solid ground to create a special drink:

Sexagesima on the Beach

Makes 1 drink

2 oz. cranberry juice
1 oz. orange juice
1 oz. pineapple juice
½ oz. passion fruit juice
1 orange slice, garnish

Pour all liquid ingredients into a shaker with ice and shake 40 times. Strain into highball filled with ice and garnish with orange slice.

LAST CALL

After a toast, have a competition to see who can recite St. Ephrem's warning about wine the most dramatically.

QUINQUAGESIMA SUNDAY, SUNDAY BEFORE ASH WEDNESDAY

Quinquagesima Sunday, so named because it is roughly the fiftieth day before Easter, recalls the Old Testament figure of Abraham as a prefiguration of the sacrifice of Christ. Quinquagesima was also called *Dominica Carnevala* ("Meat-Reduction Sunday"), for it was after this Sunday that the faithful in the Roman rite began to abstain voluntarily from flesh meat. You can honor this tradition by putting meat in your drink. You heard me.

PRE-LENT

Non-Sassy Porky Sazerac

Makes 1 drink

- 2½ oz. Free Spirits' The Spirit of Bourbon
- ½ oz. maple syrup
- 4 drops (zero proof) All the Bitter New Orleans Bitters
- 1 slice cooked bacon, garnish

Pour all liquid ingredients into a mixing glass with ice and stir 40 times. Strain into a chilled old-fashioned glass (without ice). Garnish with bacon.

MARDI GRAS, THE DAY BEFORE ASH WEDNESDAY

Ah, Fat Tuesday—the final hurrah and the last chance to consume the comestibles forbidden during a traditional Lent. Unwind with a Mardi Gras Old-Fashioned made with Three Spirit's Nightcap, or enjoy a New Orleans classic, the Ramos Fizz, without the alcohol.

Mardi Gras Old-Fashioned

Makes 1 drink

- 2½ oz. Three Spirit's Nightcap
- 5 dashes Peychaud's bitters
- 1 orange twist, garnish
- 1 Toschi Amarena cherry, garnish

Pour Nightcap and bitters into an old-fashioned glass with ice and stir. Garnish with orange and cherry.

Ramos or New Orleans Fizz

Makes 1 drink

2 oz. nonalcoholic gin
½ oz. fresh lime juice
½ oz. fresh lemon juice
2 tsp. sugar
½ oz. cream
1 egg white
2 dashes fleurs d'orange (orange flower water)
sparkling water

Pour all ingredients except sparkling water into a shaker filled with ice and shake 80 times or until your arms ache. Strain into a highball glass filled with ice and top with sparkling water.

Note: If you cannot find orange flower water, substitute for half a teaspoon triple sec or, failing that, 3 drops vanilla extract.

THE DAYS OF LENT, ASH WEDNESDAY THROUGH HOLY SATURDAY

Did you know that doppelbock beer was invented by the Paulaner monks in Munich for Lent? Indeed, it is said that the monks gave up food entirely during this penitential season and lived entirely on their doppelbock, which was rich in carbohydrates, calories, and vitamins. There are a couple of nonalcoholic bock beers on the market that you can use to toast to this tradition.

Nada Bock features a rich, amber color and a bold, malty flavor profile while **Nialas Ambler** has a deep crimson color with aromas of caramel, brown sugar, and stone fruit.

Another option is to nod to the liturgical color of the season with Sentia's Violet Cup. **Sentia's** GABA Red, which "is designed for relaxation and intimate moments," is a delightful array of sweet heady aromatics, rich herbal complexity, and bittersweet spiced berries.

Violet Cup

Makes 1 drink

- 3/4 oz. GABA Red
- 1/2 oz. violet syrup
- 3/4 oz. blueberry juice
- 1/2 oz. fresh lemon juice
- blueberries
- soda water
- edible flowers, garnish

Muddle blueberries in a shaker and then add all ingredients, except soda water. Shake with ice and strain into an old-fashioned glass with ice. Top with soda water and garnish, if you wish, with edible flowers.

EMBER DAYS OF LENT: THE WEDNESDAY, FRIDAY, AND SATURDAY OF THE FIRST (FULL) WEEK OF LENT

The Ember Days are named after the four natural seasons ("ember" is a corruption of the Latin *tempora*), and the Ember Days of Lent are an opportunity to give thanks to God for the season of Spring. It is also an opportunity to work on our virtues and vices. The four temperaments or humors (sanguine, choleric, phlegmatic, and melancholic) are an ancient way of classifying personalities. Since Spring is hot and moist, it is paired with the sanguine temperament, which is cheerful, outgoing, and mercurial. All of us, but especially sanguines, should use these Ember Day to combat the vices of concupiscence and luxury.

There is no such person as Saint Ember, but that did not stop **Little Saints** from naming their tequila substitute, which is a blend of ginger, peppers, woody palo santo, and lion's mane mushroom, St. Ember. Their **Secret Garden** works well with the springtime theme (see September 8).

LAETARE SUNDAY OR FOURTH SUNDAY OF LENT

Most folks remember this Sunday as one of the two when the priest wears "pink" vestments. The technical name for this beautiful liturgical hue is rose, and as a lighter shade of the penitential color of violet, it evokes the penitence of the season but with an added dimension of joy. Although there are a number of historical reasons for this added dimension, the one given by Pope Innocent III (1216) is the most relevant to our concerns: "On this Sunday, which marks the middle of Lent, a measure of consoling relaxation is provided so that the faithful may not break down under the severe strain of the Lenten fast but may continue to bear the restrictions with a refreshed and easier heart."

And *Abstaining with the Saints* is all about refreshing and easing the heart. Tonight, turn to the pink drinks of Gaudete Sunday (see Chapter 13).

PASSION SUNDAY OR THE FIFTH SUNDAY OF LENT

In the traditional calendar it was on this Sunday that the Church shifted her focus more explicitly to her impending commemoration of the suffering and death of Jesus Christ. "Passion" nowadays denotes a strong emotion, but it used to signify suffering. The common denominator between the two is that a strong emotion pulls you hither and thither, and thus you are experiencing or "suffering" this tug like a leaf blown by the wind.

With *the* Passion, Our Lord allowed Himself to experience suffering and humiliation for our sake, to be led hither and thither and eventually to the Cross. Tonight, have something made from passion flower such as passion fruit syrup, so named because its features reminded Catholic missionaries to the New World of the details of Jesus' suffering. The flower's five sepals and five petals call to mind the ten Apostles who deserted but did not betray Christ. The corona (a double row of colored filaments) represents the Crown of Thorns, while the vine tendrils symbolize the flagella used in the scourging. The five stamens represent the Five Wounds, and the three spreading styles the nails that transfixed Christ's hands and feet. The column of the flower, on the other hand, betokens the pillar of the scourging, the fragrance signifies the spices the women brought to the tomb, the round fruit recalls the world that Christ's death redeemed, and the red spots on some species hearken to the drops of blood he shed.

The Suspended Passion is named after the pulp that is suspended in the drink, but it takes on new meaning when we think of Our Lord hanging on the cross.

Suspended Passion

Makes 2 drinks

1 cup fresh orange juice
1 banana, peeled and diced
pulp from 1 passion fruit

Put orange juice and banana in a blender and blend until smooth. Stir in the passion fruit pulp and pour into old-fashioned glasses.

Passion Star Martini

Makes 1 drink

1½ oz. Three Spirit's Livener
2½ oz. passion fruit juice
1 oz. pomegranate juice
1 passion fruit wheel, garnish

Pour liquid ingredients into a mixing glass with ice and stir 40 times.

Pour into a cocktail glass and float passion fruit wheel on top.

PALM SUNDAY

Palm Sunday commemorates Jesus Christ's triumphant entry into Jerusalem when throngs of people laid palm branches and even their own clothes on the path before him and proclaimed "Hosanna to the Son of David! Blessed is He that cometh in the name of the Lord." It is customary on this day to have palm leaves blessed and kept in the home as a sacramental.

In Spain, Palm Sunday was called *Pascua Florida* because it was the custom to bless flowers as well as palms on this day. Initially the name applied only to Palm Sunday but over time it was applied to Easter and its Octave. Thus, when Ponce de Leon first spotted the coast of Florida on March 27, 1513 (Easter Sunday), he had a name for the new land ready at hand.

You can combine this bit of American history with your observance of Palm Sunday by having the following mocktail.

Blushing Ginger Rosé Fizz

Makes 1 drink

- 2 oz. vanilla rose syrup or rose syrup
- 1 oz. fresh lemon juice
- 1 oz. fresh ginger juice
- sparkling water
- edible flowers, garnish

Pour liquid ingredients into an old-fashioned glass with ice and stir 40 times. Top with sparkling water and garnish with flowers.

HOLY WEEK

During Holy Week in Spain, it is customary to drink Leonese Lemonade, a traditional beverage from León made with red wine, lemons, sugar, and cinnamon.

Limonada Leonesa

Makes 10 or more drinks

- 2 liters nonalcoholic red wine
- 11½ oz. sugar
- 4½ oz. dried figs
- 4½ oz. raisins
- 17½ oz. lemons
- 35 oz. oranges
- 1 cinnamon stick
- ⅓ of the lemon peels, cut into small pieces
- Peel of 3 oranges, cut into small pieces

Squeeze the juice from the oranges and lemons. Mix all the ingredients. Stir well and let the mixture macerate for 3 days. Taste to see if anything is missing; it should taste smooth on the palate. Adjust the flavors. Consume on the fourth day.

LENT

MAUNDY OR HOLY THURSDAY

In commemoration of the Last Supper, the first time that wine became the Blood of the Savior, it would not be inappropriate to have a heightened appreciation for what our Lord chose as the matter for His Blessed Sacrament. Tonight, enjoy your favorite nonalcoholic red wine (see Appendix I).

GOOD FRIDAY

> And they came to the place that is called Golgotha, which is the place of Calvary. And they gave Him wine to drink mingled with gall. And when He had tasted, He would not drink. —Matthew 27:33–34

If you are going to drink anything on this most solemn day, it should be the one thing that Our Lord tasted: vinegar. A Simple Citrus Mocktail with apple balsamic vinegar is one option: the apple is a nod to the forbidden fruit that Adam and Eve also had on a Friday, which prompted Our Lord to get into this mess.

Another option is devil's bane (verbena) because it was believed to have been used to staunch Our Lord's words after He was taken down from the cross. You can drink the plant in a Devil's Bane Mocktail (see September 23).

Simple Citrus Mocktail

Makes 1 drink

1 tsp. apple balsamic vinegar
3 slices mixed citrus: blood orange, tangerine, lemon, lime, or clementine
sparkling water

Muddle the vinegar and citrus slices in an old-fashioned glass, add ice, and top with sparkling water.

A final example is to follow the Irish, who on this day held a "black fast" that consisted of taking only water or tea on this day.

LAST CALL

A suitable toast is: "We adore Thee, O Christ, and we bless Thee, because by Thy holy Cross Thou hast redeemed the world."

HOLY SATURDAY

Holy Saturday is in some respects the ultimate Sabbath or day of rest: we Christians sometimes forget that the Hebrew Sabbath falls on a Saturday and that the extensive absence of activity commanded by the Mosaic Law is a foreshadowing of Our Lord's stillness in the tomb the day after His burial.

It is also the inspiration for devotion to Our Lady of Solitude, for Our Lady felt all alone on this fateful day as she alone harbored for her Son's resurrection. The devotion took root in Oaxaca, Mexico thanks to a remarkable event. "One day during the seventeenth century, an unattended, heavily-laden pack donkey staggered into Oaxaca and died. No one knew where it had come from, who owned it, or what it carried. When the people examined his pack, they found a beautiful statue of Our Lady of Solitude. She wore a crown of diamonds with a huge drop pearl in the middle, and a black velvet robe with semi-precious stones. The people decided that as the donkey had died at that spot, they would build a church there to house the little statue."

And they did. The Basílica de Nuestra Señora de la Soledad in Oaxaca de Juárez is a beautiful Baroque church still standing today. Devotion to Our Lady of Solitude had begun earlier in the sixteenth century by Queen Juana after the early death of her husband Philip I and spread throughout the Spanish-speaking world. As you might expect from the donkey story, however, the devotion is particularly strong in Oaxaca, which claims Our Lady of Solitude as its patron saint.

Oaxaca's most famous libation is mezcal, tequila's older and arguably more interesting cousin. You can enjoy nonalcoholic versions of mezcal in the following cocktails:

Blood Orange Mezcal Margarita

Makes 1 drink

- 2 oz. Monday Mezcal
- ½ oz. NA orange liqueur
- 2 oz. blood orange juice
- 1 oz. fresh lime juice
- 1 oz. simple syrup
- Tajín seasoning
- 1 lime wedge, garnish

Pour liquid ingredients into a shaker with ice and shake 40 times. Pour into a highball glass with ice. Garnish with lime wedge and dust with Tajín.

Mezcalina

Makes 1 drink

2 oz. Monday Mezcal
¾ oz. fresh lemon
¼ oz. agave syrup
¼ oz. ginger syrup
candied ginger

Combine Monday Mezcal, lemon, and syrups to a cocktail shaker with ice. Shake until cold. Strain into your favorite short glass over fresh ice. Garnish with candied ginger.

Humo de Otono

Makes 1 drink

2 oz. Cut Above Mezcal
2½ oz. persimmon puree
2 oz. fresh lime juice
½ oz. thyme-infused simple syrup
lime zest
salt
chili powder
1 sage sprig, garnish

Rim a cocktail glass by rubbing the edge with water and dipping it in lime zest, salt, and chili powder. Pour liquid ingredients into a shaker with ice and shake 40 times. Pour into glass and garnish with sage.

Note: To make thyme-infused simple syrup, place 1 cup water and 1 cup sugar in a saucepan over medium heat and stir until sugar dissolves. Add a handful of thyme and simmer for 5 minutes. Let cool and strain into a sterilized jar.

CHAPTER SEVENTEEN

Eastertide, Pentecost, and the Time Thereafter

EASTER SUNDAY, OR THE RESURRECTION OF OUR LORD JESUS CHRIST

Christ is risen! Today, enjoy your favorite alcohol-free champagne, an after-dinner drink called the Easter Bunny, or something with cucumber. Believe it or not, in Renaissance art, the cucumber was, given its, ahem, masculine shape, a symbol of the Resurrection, in contrast to the buxom, feminine shape of the apple, a symbol of the Fall. Our forebears were not squeamish! Squeam about this over a drink or two.

Euphoric Spritz

Makes 1 drink

- 1½ oz. Three Spirit's Livener
- 2½ oz. lemonade
- 2½ oz. kombucha
- 1 cucumber ribbon, garnish
- 1 mint sprig, garnish

Make a thin cucumber ribbon with a potato peeler and place it around the inside of a wine glass. Hold it in place with ice cubes. Pour Livener, lemonade, and kombucha into glass and stir gently. Garnish with mint.

Garden Elderflower and Tonic

Makes 1 drink

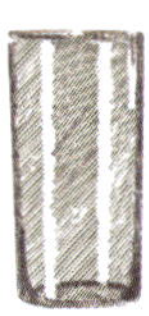

- 2 oz. Seedlip Garden 108
- 4 oz. elderflower tonic
- 1 cucumber ribbon, garnish

Make a thin cucumber ribbon with a potato peeler and place inside a highball glass. Add ice. Pour in Seedlip and tonic and stir gently.

Easter Bunny

Makes as much as you like

3 parts frozen yogurt
1 part fresh orange juice
1 splash simple syrup
crushed ice
1 pear slice, garnish

Place yogurt, orange juice, simple syrup, and 1 scoop crushed ice in a blender and blend until smooth. Pour into a wine glass and garnish with pear.

LAST CALL

Incorporate a traditional Easter greeting into your Paschal toast. In the Latin West, one of the faithful would say *Surrexit Dominus vere* ("Christ is truly risen!"), to which the other would say *Deo gratias* ("Thanks be to God!"). In the Christian East, one says, "Christ is risen!" to which the response is "Indeed He is risen!"

ASCENSION OF OUR LORD JESUS CHRIST

It was once a custom in Europe to eat fowl on the great Feast of the Ascension of our Lord Jesus Christ forty days after His Resurrection "because Christ 'flew' to Heaven." Bakers in Germany followed this precedent by making pastries for the Ascension in the shape of various birds.

We can take this cue and drink anything that ascends, bubble-wise. Tonight, enjoy your favorite nonalcoholic sparkling wine or spritz in honor of Our Lord who ascends on high.

LAST CALL

The Church traditionally uses Psalm 46:6 on this feast day, and you can too. One person says, "God is ascended with jubilee, alleluia!" and another replies, "And the Lord with the sound of the trumpet, alleluia!"

PENTECOST OR WHITSUNDAY

Our Lord fulfilled His promise to send the Holy Spirit on the Hebrew feast of *Shavuot* or Pentecost, the conclusion of a first-fruits festival held fifty days after the Passover (Exodus 23:16). Ten days after His Ascension, Jesus sent the Paraclete to His disciples in the form of a mighty wind and tongues of flame, with the result that they began to speak in different languages.

Alcohol figures into the story of the first Pentecost. When the disciples began to preach in different tongues, some members of the audience mockingly declared: "These men are full of new wine" (Acts 2:13). Hardly. We are "not drunk, as you suppose," he says, "seeing it is but the third hour of the day" (Acts 2:15). Translation: "Of course we're not drunk: it's only nine o'clock in the morning."

Well, it's 9 a.m. somewhere. A "red drink" is a cherished tradition among West-Coast Africans and African Americans. At the risk of cultural appropriation, you can honor the liturgical color of the day with your favorite red-colored drink. We include two recipes here, but this book has more options than the number of languages spoken at the first Pentecost: almost all the products of **St. Agrestis** and **Casamara**, for example, are reddish in hue.

Another fine choice is to have a **Paloma**, since the word means "dove" in Spanish. And the drink is even red (sort of). See February 10 for more.

Red & Tonic

Makes 1 drink

1½ oz. Sentia's GABA Red
tonic water
1 lime wedge or orange slice, garnish

Pour GABA red into an old-fashioned glass with ice and top with tonic water. Garnish with lime or orange.

Ginger Cape Codder

Makes 1 drink

2 cans Little Saints' Ginger Mule
2 oz. unsweetened cranberry juice
1 lime wedge, garnish
1 sprig rosemary, garnish

Pour Little Saints Ginger Mule into a highball glass with ice, top with cranberry juice, and stir. Garnish with lime and rosemary.

The Bright Side

Makes 1 drink

2½ oz. Optimist Bright
1 oz. pomegranate juice
¼ oz. pomegranate molasses
soda water

Combine all ingredients except soda water in a shaker with ice and shake 40 times. Strain into a highball glass with ice and top with a splash of soda water.

LAST CALL

The *Veni Creator Spiritus* and its English equivalent "Come Holy Ghost, Creator Blest" are great hymns to sing on this day, and there is even a plenary indulgence attached to doing so publicly.

EMBER DAYS OF WHITSUNTIDE: THE WEDNESDAY, FRIDAY, AND SATURDAY OF THE OCTAVE OF PENTECOST

The Ember Days are named after the four natural seasons ("ember" is a corruption of the Latin *tempora*), and the Ember Days of Advent are an opportunity to give thanks to God for the season of summer. It is also an opportunity to work on our virtues and vices. The four temperaments or humors (sanguine, choleric, phlegmatic, and melancholic) are an ancient way of classifying personalities. Since summer is hot and dry, it is paired with the fiery personality of the choleric, who must learn to do battle with wrath and the burning ardor of avarice.

There is no such person as Saint Ember, but that did not stop **Little Saints** from naming their tequila substitute, which is a blend of ginger, peppers, woody palo santo, and lion's mane mushroom, St. Ember. Their **Ginger Cape Codder** works well with the summer theme (see Pentecost).

HOLY TRINITY SUNDAY, FIRST SUNDAY AFTER PENTECOST

It is fitting that there be a Feast of the Most Holy Trinity on the first Sunday after Pentecost. The Easter season celebrates the revelation of the Father through His Risen Son, and Pentecost rejoices in the Holy Spirit sent by the Father and the Son. Hence, at the close of Eastertide and Pentecost our thoughts naturally gravitate to the mystery of all three Divine Persons. Further, as St. Rupert observes, immediately after the first Pentecost, the Apostles began preaching and baptizing in the name of the Father, Son, and Holy Ghost.

When it comes to making statements about the Trinity, saying something heretical is easier than falling off a log. We know that God is spirit and therefore that each Divine Person is spirit, but we suspect that it would be unwise to say that God is three spirits. Maybe that is why we like the brand name **Three Spirit**: it has the word "three" but keeps "spirit" in the singular. Their nonalcoholic wine **Spark** can be thought of as an allusion to the tongues of flame that descended on this day, while their botanical elixir **Livener** can be a reference to the life-giving qualities of each Divine Person: the Father as the Creator of life, the Son as the Way, the Truth, and the Life, and the Holy Spirit as the Lord, the Giver of Life. The La Dolce Vita Punch, which is made with Livener, is perfect for a Holy Trinity party.

La Dolce Vita Punch

Makes 20 drinks

- 1 bottle Three Spirit Livener
- 1 bottle nonalcoholic sparkling wine or sparkling water
- 16 oz. fresh orange or tangerine juice
- 10 oz. Wilfred's (or other bitter nonalcoholic spirit)
- 8 oz. fresh lemon juice
- 6 oz. orgeat syrup
- 3–4 sprigs rosemary
- 3–4 orange wheels, garnish
- 3–4 lemon wheels, garnish

The night before, add rosemary sprigs to the orgeat to infuse (trust us: it pops).

An hour before the party, pour Livener, orange and lemon juices, Wilfred's and orgeat syrup (including rosemary) into a punch bowl and gently stir to combine. Place a block of ice into the punch bowl and allow time for it to chill. Ladle over the ice for a little dilution.

Right before guests arrive, pour half a bottle of chilled sparkling wine or water gently over the top of the punch and add garnishes. Once the punch is about halfway consumed, top it off with the remaining sparkling wine or water.

LAST CALL

A prayer we say often can be used as a toast: "Glory be to the Father and to the Son and to the Holy Spirit. As it was in the beginning, is now, and ever shall be world without end. Amen."

CORPUS CHRISTI, SUNDAY AFTER TRINITY SUNDAY

At the age of sixteen, a humble Belgian girl began having dreams of a bright moon marred by a small black spot. After years of seeing this perplexing vision, Jesus Christ appeared to her and revealed its meaning. The moon, He told her, represented the Church calendar, and the black spot the absence of a feast in honor of His Blessed Sacrament. That nun was St. Juliana, Prioress of Mont Cornillon (d. 1258), and the feast she was commissioned by our Lord to promote was that of Corpus Christi. Our Lord's command was only fair. Although the original feast honoring the institution of the Eucharist is Holy

Thursday, its joy is overshadowed by the somber events of the Passion. It is appropriate that the Church do a double-take to give the miracle of receiving the Body, Blood, Soul, and Divinity of Jesus Christ its proper due.

The Feast of Corpus Christi falls on the Thursday after Trinity Sunday and is a holy day of obligation throughout the Catholic world. In the United States, however, the solemnity is transferred to the following Sunday.

Given today's traditional focus on the Body of Christ (as opposed to the Precious Blood), focus on **wheat ales and beers** (see August 1).

LAST CALL

A great verse from the Book of Wisdom that is used for the rite of Benediction also makes a pious toast for this feast day: "Thou gavest them bread from Heaven, alleluia. Having in it all that is delicious, alleluia" (16:20).

SACRED HEART OF JESUS,
FIRST FRIDAY AFTER THE SECOND SUNDAY AFTER PENTECOST

In 1675, our Lord appeared to St. Margaret Mary Alacoque on the Friday following the octave of Corpus Christi and asked her to promote a feast of the Sacred Heart on this day. In 1690, Jesus told her: "Behold this Heart, which, notwithstanding the burning love for man with which it is consumed and exhausted, meets with no other return from the generality of Christians than sacrilege, contempt, indifference and ingratitude." The feast was fixed on the universal calendar in 1856, and in 1929 an Act of Reparation to the Sacred Heart, with a plenary indulgence attached to its public recital, was added.

The message of this tender feast is as simple as it is beautiful: Jesus loves us, His Sacred Heart bursts with love for us. He came to earth as a humble babe and suffered the ignominy of the Cross not to condemn but to offer us boundless mercy. His ultimate revelation is not as an angry God but as a kind Lover who sheds His blood for us.

Sangria, which means "bloodletting," is an appropriate drink for honoring the fleshy vessel that contains Our Lord's Precious Blood. We include several sangria recipes for the Feast of the Martyrs of Spain (see November 6).

Another option is a mocktail version of a popular golf club cocktail, a Transfusion. Why? Because when you think about it, every Holy Communion involves a heart transplant and a blood transfusion, and both ways. That is, when we receive the Body and Blood of Christ, we take His Heart and Blood into ourselves. But instead of It becoming a part of us, we become a part of It, that is, we are literally incorporated into the Mystical Body of Christ. In fact, the same blood type has been found in all Eucharistic miracles where the Host bleeds, as well as on the Shroud of Turin, the Sudarium (Head Shroud) of Oviedo, and the Holy Tunic (Jesus' seamless garment). That blood type is AB, which is for universal *receivers* (O negative is for universal donors). That seems counterintuitive since Christ donated His blood for all, but it confirms what we are saying: that when we receive Christ in Holy Communion, He receives us into His Heart and into His Blood.

Mind blown? Good. Now have a drink.

Transfusion

Makes 1 drink

3 oz. grape juice
6 oz. ginger ale
1 splash fresh lime juice
1 lime wedge, garnish

Pour liquid ingredients into a highball with ice and stir gently. Garnish with lime wedge.

LAST CALL

Take a line from the Litany of the Sacred Heart of Jesus and turn it into a toast: "To Our Lord Jesus Christ, who is meek and humble of heart. May He make our hearts like unto His."

EMBER DAYS OF SEPTEMBER: THE WEDNESDAY, FRIDAY, AND SATURDAY AFTER THE THIRD SUNDAY OF SEPTEMBER

The Ember Days are named after the four natural seasons ("ember" is a corruption of the Latin *tempora*), and the Ember Days of Advent are an opportunity to give thanks to God for the season of autumn. It is also an opportunity to work on our virtues and vices. The four temperaments or humors (sanguine, choleric, phlegmatic, and melancholic) are an ancient way of classifying personalities. Since autumn is cold and dry, it is paired with the morose personality of the melancholic, who must battle the drought of pride and coveting.

There is no such person as Saint Ember, but that did not stop **Little Saints** from naming their tequila substitute, which is a blend of ginger, peppers, woody palo santo, and lion's mane mushroom, St. Ember. Their **Not-A-Groni** works well with the autumn theme (see October 25).

FEAST OF CHRIST THE KING, LAST SUNDAY OF OCTOBER (LAST SUNDAY OF THE LITURGICAL YEAR)

In the traditional calendar, the Feast of Christ the King falls on the last Sunday of October, the date fixed by Pope Pius XI when he instituted the feast in 1925 to illustrate the relation between our Lord's Kingship and all the Saints (Nov. 1) and to emphasize Christ's rule here and now and not just on the Last Day. The feast was replaced in 1969 by a different one on the last Sunday of the liturgical year to emphasize Christ's cosmic reign at the end of time.

Either way, **St. Regis** ("of the King") has the right name for the occasion, even though it was circuitously named after St. John Francis Regis (see June 16). They make a number of nonalcoholic still and sparkling wines that work well with this feast.

LAST CALL

There is only one toast for today: "¡*Viva Cristo Rey*! (Long live Christ the King!)."

APPENDIX I

SOBERISH SEPTUAGESIMA: NINE WEEKS TO A BETTER YOU

> "'Soberish' can mean drinking more mindfully, drinking less or avoiding alcohol altogether but not other drugs."
>
> —Emily Schmall, "Not Drunk, Not Dry: What It Means to Be 'Soberish'," *New York Times*, January 15, 2025

Periodic abstinence is one of the key ways to maintain a healthy relationship with alcohol, and many Catholics have used Lent as the occasion for such a dry spell. In our Soberish Septuagesima program, we build upon this practice as well as another hallowed tradition.

The Sunday of Septuagesima (pronounced Sep-two-a-JAY-see-mah) is the roughly seventieth day before Easter and the beginning of Pre-Lent, a period of gradual voluntary food abstinence that takes place in preparation for the Great Fast of Lent. Eastern-rite Christians begin abstaining from meat on the penultimate Sunday before Lent and from dairy products on the Sunday immediately before Lent. Roman-rite Christians, on the other hand, used to abstain from meat on the Sunday before Lent, which they called *Dominica Carnevala* because it was the time to remove (*levare*) meat (*caro*) from one's diet. It is from this name that our word "carnival" originates.

Our Soberish Septuagesima Sodality charts a similar course, starting with a gradual change in alcohol consumption and ending with a booze-free, mocktail-rich Lent. The idea is to change yourself both in body and in soul: your body with a regenerated liver and better health and a new tolerance level, your soul with strong new virtuous habits.

The Soberish Septuagesima program consists of:

1. A Menu Schedule for the seventy days (actually, sixty-three days) prior to Easter—or for whenever you wish;
2. Tips for Completing the Program successfully; and
3. Tips for Reentry after completion of the program.

The name Soberish Septuagesima Sodality is a mouthful, but we chose it for a reason. A sodality is not a mere club, but a companionship of believers united in a common cause. That means, among other things, that despite not being in the same place at the same time, we pray for each other. *Join the Soberish Septuagesima Sodality, and wherever you are, as long as this book is read, there will be others praying for you.* All you have to do is pray for them in return. See the "Tips for Nailing Soberish Septuagesima" below for more.

I. THE MENU SCHEDULE

The Saturday Night before Septuagesima Sunday: Farewell to Alleluia, Farewell to Your Favorite Cocktail

On this day, our Roman Catholic ancestors said goodbye to the word "Alleluia" (since it was suppressed during the period from Septuagesima Sunday to Easter) and even buried or burned the Alleluia in effigy during a goodbye ceremony. Tonight, throw your own farewell party and enjoy your favorite cocktail as you say goodbye to it for the next nine weeks. Remember, it doesn't have to be goodbye forever; it can be *Au revoir*—until we meet again.

If you are not sure what your favorite cocktail is, no worries. Just pick one and say goodbye to it. The point is to make a statement to your habits and tell them that you are not playing by their rules anymore. With God's help, you are the master of your own fate; you are the captain of your own soul.

Septuagesima Sunday

You said goodbye to your favorite liquid crutch last night. Now say hello to the beginning of a new you. Some people like to do a before-and-after record of their progress, taking a selfie and weighing themselves at the beginning of the program and again at the end. We leave that to your discretion: do whatever motivates you.

Your mantra today and for the weeks following is, "I chastise my body, and I bring it into subjection" (I Corinthians 9:27). The verse is taken from the Epistle Reading of Septuagesima Sunday in the traditional Roman calendar. For encouragement, read this portion of the Epistle as you listen to the soundtrack from *Rocky* (1976), "Gonna Fly Now":

> Brethren: Know you not that they that run in the race, all run indeed, but one receiveth the prize? So run that you may obtain.

> And every one that striveth for the mastery refrain-eth himself from all things: and they indeed that they may receive a corruptible crown; but we an incorruptible one. I therefore so run, not as at an uncertainty; I so fight, not as one beating the air: but I chastise my body, and bring it into subjection, lest perhaps when I have preached to others, I myself should become a castaway.

LAST CALL

Channel Rocky Balboa and the athletic-metaphorically rich St. Paul as you begin your spiritual workout with a toast: "Gonna chastise! Flying higher! Trying harder!" Remember: you got this. Like Apollo in the ring with Rocky, your infernal spirits won't know what hit them.

Septuagesima Week

From Septuagesima Sunday until the following Saturday, do the following:

1. For your happy hour beverage, choose a form of alcohol for which you are less enthusiastic. It does not have to be a drink that you find abhorrent. I, for instance, would only drink Jägermeister as an extreme form of penance. Instead, during Septuagesima week I will be abstaining from hard liquor in general and limiting myself to beer or wine.
2. But tastes and temperaments differ. If you only drink beer or wine, perhaps your form of mortification is hard liquor. The point is to step outside of your comfort zone into a discomfort zone but without losing the comfort of C_2H_6O—for now. And the goal is to reduce the amount of alcohol you consume.
3. Plan ahead. Next week, we will be enjoying mood-enhancing nonalcoholic spirits and mocktails, but most of these will probably need to be ordered and shipped ahead of time. Take a gander at the recommendations for Sexagesima Week and plan accordingly.

Sexagesima Week

Congratulations! You have already broken some bad habits by refraining from your favorite intoxicating beverage. Now it is time to assert your independence from C2H6O, the active ingredient in alcohol. Providentially, the no and low alcoholic spirit industry is teeming with alternatives. Many a producer promises a buzz without the hangover or any of the other side effects of alcohol. Their secret is to use other ingredients that create a relaxing effect on the soul such as lion's mane mushroom, ashwagandha, and kava. We have tested these products, and to our surprise, they work—especially after having toned down prior alcohol consumption. Your new soberish, mood-enhancing bar may include:

Mood-Enhancing, Nonalcoholic Spirits and Apéritifs

1. Aplós makes spirits and canned cocktails. They have an Arise spirit "for moments of revelry" and an Ease spirit "for moments of unwind," but their most popular is Calme, "a complex blend of citrus and herbal botanicals infused with broad-spectrum hemp to calm and relax without the negative effects of alcohol" (and don't worry: the hemp does not contain THC, the psychoactive ingredient in marijuana). Their canned products include Ume Spritz, Kola Old Fashioned, Chili Margarita, and Mandora Negroni.
2. Apothékary has a robust line-up of tinctures and powders including Wine Down (a red wine alternative), Take the Edge Off (a white wine alternative), and Rosé-Tinted Glasses (we'll let you guess that one). Apothékary promises "relaxation benefits without the drawbacks of alcohol, sugar, or hangovers."
3. Curious Elixirs has nine different drinks individually bottled. All are made from herbs and adaptogens designed to relax.
   - No. 1: Pomegranate Negroni Sbagliato
   - No. 2: Spicy Pineapple Margarita
   - No. 3: Juniper Cucumber Collins

- No. 4: Sicilian Blood Orange Spritz
- No. 5: Smoke Cherry Chocolate Old Fashioned
- No. 6: Coconut Pineapple Painkiller
- No. 7: Sparkling Champagne Cocktail
- No. 8: "Black and Blue" Amaro
- No. 9: Sparkling Rosé Cocktail

4. Designer Kava is an instant powdered formula powder that comes in "Creamsicle" Kelai Kava, "Daydream" Purple Silese, "Luxury" Tanna Pia Kava, and "Midnight" Borogu Tememe Kava. Each varies in potency, the latter being the strongest.
5. Feragaia is Scotland's first distilled alcohol-free spirit. A small-batch dark spirit bringing together fourteen land and sea botanicals that were carefully identified for their flavor profiles and natural properties from wild earth.
6. Hiyo produces nonalcoholic seltzers (blackberry lemon, peach mango, strawberry guava, and watermelon lime) made from organic adaptogens, natural nootropics, and functional botanicals. Hiyo claims that their drinks provide a stress-relieving, mood-boosting lift they like to call "the float."
7. KavaKwik is an instant powdered formula in a variety of flavors that you add to water or your favorite beverage. It is made from Noble Kava, which relieves stress and relaxes the mind.
8. Little Saints makes two spirits from lion's mane mushroom (a relaxing agent that gives a mild and gentle buzz), St. Ember and St. Juniper. They also have sixed canned products: Negroni Spritz, Spicy Margarita, Paloma, Ginger Mule, Espresso Martini, and Spiced Old Fashioned.
9. The Pathfinder is fermented from hemp (no THC or CBD) and blended with wormwood, angelic root, ginger, sage, juniper, saffron, orange peel, wild-crafted Douglas-fir, and natural terpenes. It tastes like an amaro, that fine class of European liquors known for bittersweet flavors rounded out by citrus and spice, and can be used as a flavorful substitute for amaro, whiskey, or vermouth.

10. Sentia produces three delicious nonalcoholic spirits: GABA Gold, GABA Red, and GABA Black. They are made from relaxing agents like ashwagandha, damiana, passionflower, magnolia, and schisandra.
11. Three Spirit makes several botanical elixirs that can relax or give energy
    - Livener (guayusa, guava leaf and schisandra and big flavors from vibrant berries, bright aromatics, and heat)
    - Social (a dark herbal elixir described as the ultimate mood elevator. Made with lion's mane mushroom, yerba mate, and damiana)
    - Nightcap (to relax and unwind)
    - Spark (sparkling rosé alternative, made with caffeine)
    - Sharp (white wine alternative, with a light spritz; pair with food)

Finally, don't forget to plan ahead for Lent by looking at the list of nonalcoholic beverages below.

Shrovetide

The three days before Ash Wednesday—Quinquagesima Sunday, Shrove Monday, and Shrove Tuesday—were known as Shrovetide because it was a good time to get "shriven," that is, receive absolution through the sacrament of confession. We concur, and it is also a good time to continue enjoying mood-enhancing nonalcoholic spirits.

Lent

The Great Fast of Lent, as it was once called, extends from Ash Wednesday to Holy Saturday. You can continue with your mood-enhancing beverages if you like, or you can try something new. Nonalcoholic spirits, wine, and beer have reached new heights in recent years. Athletic Brewing Company, for example, sells almost half of nonalcoholic craft beer in the country, and for good reason: their beers taste great. And some distillers have done an impressive job with mimicking the flavor profiles of gin, bourbon, scotch, tequila, etc. We provide a list of options below.

And since you no longer need to have a full stomach (since you're not drinking), we also recommend observing the traditional Lenten fast, which is one full meal per day at which meat can be consumed (unless it is a Friday or Ash Wednesday), and two other meatless meals that together cannot equal one full meal. According to today's Church law, this fast is mandatory only on Ash Wednesday and Good Friday, but when Pope St. Paul VI ended the mandatory fast in 1966, he did so with the hope that all Catholics would continue the fast *voluntarily* and thus be even more meritorious. As it turns out, he misread his flock and the Great Fast quickly became a thing of the past; but we can still heed his admonition and observe this worthy practice. Fasting has numerous health benefits for both body and soul. Regarding the soul, we recall the words of Our Lord: that some demons can only be cast out by prayer and fasting (Matthew 17:20). That may include the demons of drunkenness and addiction.

Nonalcoholic Spirits and Apéritifs (that do not contain mood-enhancing agents)

1. Bax Botanics has a Verbena and a Sea Buckthorn spirit, both alcohol-free.
2. Caleño has a well-regarded dark and spicy rum (not all their products are available in US, but this one is).
3. The Casamara Club has an impressive array of canned or bottled sparkling apéritifs and botanical sodas that capture the flavors of Italy.
4. Cut Above makes nonalcoholic tequila, mezcal, whiskey, and gin.
5. Everleaf makes a Forest, Mountain, and Marine botanical spirit, with each one imitating the environment after which it was named.
6. Figlia makes Fiore Non-Alcoholic Aperitivo bottle and Fiore Frizzante Non-Alcoholic Spritz in a can.
7. Free Spirits makes alternatives to bourbon, gin, tequila, red vermouth, and Campari (their Spirit of Milano).
8. Ghia makes tasty canned apéritifs in several flavors.

9. Ketone Aids and Hard Ketones. Provides clean energy for athletic performance, mental clarity, metabolic health, and deep sleep.
10. Lyre's makes alternatives to bourbon, Italian spritz, whiskey, gin, white rum, amaretti, coffee, dark rum, orange sec, pink gin, and classico grande (sparkling wine). They also have cans of G&T and Margaritas.
11. Monday makes an alternative to gin, whiskey, rum, and mezcal.
12. Optimist Botanicals makes spirits including The Bitter Optimist: Cali Amaro, Smokey, Bright, and Fresh. They also have a canned Cali Spritz.
13. Ritual Zero Proof makes alternatives to whiskey, gin, tequila, rum, and an apéritif.
14. Seedlip, the grandfather of nonalcoholic spirits, has an aromatic Spice 94, a fresh and herbal Garden 108, and a citrusy Grove 42. Their Notas de Agave is a tequila substitute, at least insofar as it is also made from the agave plant like tequila and mezcal.
15. Slipsmith has an acclaimed FreeGlider nonalcoholic gin.
16. Spiritless makes Kentucky 74 (bourbon), Kentucky 74 spiced (cinnamon), and Jalisco 55 (tequila).
17. St. Agrestis produces a variety of bottled sparkling apéritifs. We like them.
18. Wilfred's makes a delicious apéritif that mixes well in a variety of mocktails.

Nonalcoholic Beers

So many to choose from now! Here are some of the most recommended:

1. Al's Drinks Company, Al's Classic (East Windsor, Connecticut)
2. Athletic Brewing Company, all of them (Stratford, Connecticut)
3. Barrel Brothers Non-Alcoholic Dark Sarcasm Porter (Windsor, California)
4. Barrel Brothers Non-Alcoholic Hazy IPA (Windsor, California)
5. Bravus Brewing Company Peanut Butter Dark (Newport Beach, California)

6. Brooklyn Special Effects Hoppy Amber (Brooklyn)
7. Brooklyn Special Effects IPA (Brooklyn)
8. Ceria Brewing Company Grainwave Belgian-Style Wheat Ale (Denver)
9. Clausthaler Original, formerly Clausthaler Classic (Frankfurt, Germany)
10. Golden Road NA Mango Cart (Los Angeles)
11. Grüvi, Weekday Wit (Denver)
12. Heineken 0.0 (Zoeterwoude, Netherlands)
13. Karbach, Free and Easy NA IPA (Houston)
14. Mikkeller Limbo Raspberry (Copenhagen, Denmark)
15. Partake IPA (Calgary, Canada)
16. Rightside Brewing Citrus Wheat (Lawrenceville, Georgia)
17. Samuel Adams Just the Haze (Boston)
18. Two Roads Brewing Co. Non-Alcoholic American IPA (Stratford, Connecticut)
19. Untitled Art Florida Weisse (Waunakee, Wisconsin)
20. Weihenstephaner Hefeweissbier Alkoholfrei (Freising, Germany)
21. Wellbeing Brewing Victory Wheat (St. Louis, Missouri)

Nonalcoholic Wines

Again, the list is growing by the day. Here are some well-regarded nonalcoholic winemakers and makes of nonalcoholic wine alternatives.

1. Apothékary
2. Ariel
3. Buzzkill Wines
4. French Bloom
5. Giesen
6. Jøyus
7. Lautus
8. Lili
9. NON

10. Raventos
11. Sovi Wine Company
12. Studio Null
13. Thomson & Scott
14. Waterbrook
15. Wölffer Estate Vineyard

II. TIPS FOR NAILING SOBERISH SEPTUAGESIMA

Besides the challenge of what or what not to drink, there comes the challenge of how to drink and with whom. We hope that these tips will help you triumph during Soberish Septuagesima.

Set a Time Limit. Keep the Happy Hour to one hour and be firm, even with the consumption of nonalcoholic spirits, beers, or wine, and even with your favorite friends.

Fill the Bottle. There is an old bit of advice about lust, which applies to the Drink as well. The best way to remove air from an empty bottle is not to try to suck the air out of it but to fill it with a liquid. With lust, it is better to fill your attention with something else rather than to think of ways not to think about lust, which only occasions other temptations of lust. (To say, "I am not thinking of this particular sexy person" only makes matters worse.) Instead, change the conversation in your head. After your happy hour, make sure there is another pleasure to look forward to. Perhaps it is a newfound joy in cooking or a reacquaintance with great classic movies or a family board game. The best way to keep those bottles of booze in your cabinet full is to fill the bottle of your soul with other sources of joy.

Avoid the Near Occasion of Sin. If you tend to tie one on every time you meet your buddies at the local tavern on a Tuesday, you may need to skip a few weeks to strengthen your self-control before returning to the weekly rendezvous and ordering a seltzer without embarrassment.

Think Positive. In times of temptation, remind yourself of the blessings that your abstinence will soon be bringing: greater fitness, more energy, better sleep, earlier mornings, less weight, and better connections with others.

The Buddy System. You can do this alone, but if you know friends and family in the flesh who wish to join you on this journey, all the better. The "buddy system" and "accountability partners" are now popular frameworks, and not without reason. Try to get your spouse or close circle of friends to enlist in the Soberish Septuagesima Sodality. Make it a goal to invite at least three companions to join you. If not, no worries: be John the Baptist and cultivate your holiness in the wilderness with a wild man's courage for the Good.

Don't Cheat on Sundays. Since the Sundays of Lent are not technically counted among the days of Lent, many a Catholic enjoys the things they gave up for Lent on this day. Fair enough, but not for our sodality. The goal of Soberish Septuagesima is to alter the chemistry of your body, the condition of your liver, and the psychology of your soul. To break from this regimen is to undermine this goal. Have your favorite dessert on Sunday, but lay off the strong stuff.

Sanctify the Fast. A recurring petition in the old Roman Missal during the forty days of Lent is to ask God to sanctify our fast. Fasting is a natural and healthy activity that restores an equilibrium to the body, which is why almost all cultures practice versions of it. (At the time of this writing, for example, intermittent fasting is all the rage.) Good, but fasting in and of itself does not confer holiness. We Saintly Sippers are not simply seeking nine weeks to a sexier and slimmer version of ourselves; we are seeking a transformation of our souls, one that will make us a shinier icon of Christ. And so, we must constantly pray that our bodily mortifications have a spiritual effect.

Oremus Pro Invicem. The topic of prayer brings us to the invocation, *Oremus pro invicem* (pronounced Oh-RAY-mus Pro IN-veech-em), which means "Let us pray for each other." Our loving Lord has ordained it from all eternity that our salvation is contingent upon each other: from the inspired authors of the Sacred Scriptures, from the Apostles who preached the Gospels, from the parents or friends who first told us about Jesus. God wants us to help each other to build up his Kingdom, and He wants us to help each other. The only condition for joining the Soberish Septuagesima Sodality, besides following the program, is to pray every night before you go to bed for all the other members of the sodality. Pray for someone out there, and be assured that someone out there is praying for you.

III. TIPS FOR REENTRY

Once you have completed your Sober Septuagesima, you will obviously want to hold on to the gains you have made. Here's how.

Total Abstinence. If your goal was to get off the Sauce and stay off it, then congratulations: you did it! You are a new man or a new woman. To stay on course, take one day at a time. Remember the things that made your Septuagesima a success and continue to practice them.

Moderate Drinking. If your goal was to become a more moderate drinker, then congratulations: you did it! Thanks to your period of abstinence, both your liver and your habits have been regenerated, and you are a new man or a new woman. The key is to keep up the good habits and not relapse into the old. The good news is that your tolerance level will be different now and you are likely to find that that second drink is more than enough rather than barely the beginning. Limit yourself to two drinks a night at most, and never go back to drinking every night. If you need a liturgical incentive, observe dry nights on Wednesday, Friday, and Saturday, the traditional fast days of the Roman Rite (see Ember Days); or, if you want an even more ascetical schedule, drink only on the two most festive days of the week: Sunday (the Lord's Day) and Thursday (the institution of the Eucharist). Also, treat all the old fast days of the calendar as occasions for abstinence: the Ember Days, the Vigil of Pentecost, the Vigil of the Feast of the Assumption, All Hallows' Eve (Halloween), Christmas Eve, and Lent (of course).

Mixing It Up. One practical suggestion for parties or other festive get-togethers that are expected to last a long time is to alternate between alcoholic drinks and mocktails (a practice called "zebra striping"). By the end of the night, you may have nursed four drinks, but only two of them were intoxicating. Fortunately, you have an entire book full of ideas for nonalcoholic alternatives at your disposal . . .

APPENDIX II

REFERENCE GUIDE TO THE POST-VATICAN-II CALENDAR

In organizing the year, *Abstaining with the Saints* primarily follows the traditional 1962 calendar, in use prior to the Second Vatican Council. This might seem like an odd choice, since most Catholics attend the new Mass and thus follow the new calendar that took effect in 1970. So why the old? Two reasons. First, several of the drinks in this book developed out of observing the traditional calendar. Some writers have even gone so far as to say that *all* Western culture has more or less radiated out of the old Mass. Second, the old calendar has a larger range of entries (several hundred saints were removed from the calendar in 1970 as well as liturgical seasons like pre-Lent); and more festivities means more opportunities for raising and emptying a glass. That said, some of the saints canonized after 1962, such as Padre Pio and Fr. Damien of Molokai, have been duly added to our list of pious potables, as well as numerous local saints who never made it to the universal calendar.

And not to worry: if you wish to drink according to the new calendar, you have two ways of doing so. First, the italicized date of an entry title is the date on which that feast appears in the 1970/2002 Novus Ordo calendar *if* that date is different from the 1962 calendar. If there is no italicized date, there is either no difference between the two calendars regarding the holy day in question or the holy day is not on the new calendar. Second, consult this appendix. It lists all the feast days of the new calendar in chronological order. If a date on which you are feeling festive is empty, look it up in the main section of the book. There might be a local holy day on that date or a holy day from the 1962 Missal. Surely, our merciful Father won't begrudge you consulting the vast traditions of the Church.

DATE	HOLY DAY	PAGE
8	Our Lady of Prompt Succor	2
10	Agatho	3
12	Satyrus	3
13	Hilary of Poitiers	4
16	Franciscan Protomartyrs	6
17	Antony, Abbot	7
20	Sebastian	8
21	Our Lady of Altagracia	9
23	Saint Raymond of Peñafort	10
25	Conversion of Paul	102
28	Thomas Aquinas	40
FEBRUARY		
2	Purification of the B.V.M.	18
5	Agatha	19
7	Apollonia	20
10	Scholastica	21
11	Our Lady of Lourdes	25
14	Antoninus	26
20	Paula the Bearded	29
22	Margaret of Cortona	30
25	Sebastian of Aparicio	34
28	Romanus	36
MARCH		
1	David (England, Wales)	38
3	Cunigunde	39
10	Forty Holy Martyrs	41
17	Patrick	45
19	Joseph	47
25	Annunciation	49
28	Sixtus III	51
31	Renovatus	51

DATE	HOLY DAY	PAGE
JULY		
1	Junipero Serra (U.S.)	106
3	Thomas the Apostle	108
4	Pier Giorgio Frassati	109
4	Elizabeth of Portugal (universal)	110
5	Elizabeth of Portugal (U.S.)	110
11	Benedict	48
12	John Gualbert	115
15	Vitus (Germany)	90
16	Our Lady of Mt. Carmel	116
20	Apollinaris	121
20	Margaret of Antioch (Germany)	118
22	Mary Magdalene	120
25	James the Greater	122
26	Joachim and Anne	139
29	Martha	126
29	Lazarus	224
31	Ignatius of Loyola	127
AUGUST		
1	Alphonsus Ligouri	132
4	John Mary Vianney	134
5	Dedication of Mary Major (Our Lady of Snows)	133
10	Lawrence	135
15	Assumption	137
20	Bernard Tolomei	140
21	Pius X	149
22	Queenship of B.V.M.	142
25	Louis	144
27	Monica	69
28	Augustine	145
30	Fiacre	146

APPENDIX III

GLOSSARY OF TERMS

Adaptogens: A generic term for plants and mushrooms that purport to help your body respond to stress, anxiety, and fatigue. Adaptogens are found in many mood-enhancing nonalcoholic spirits and apéritifs.

Ashwagandha: The scientific name of this plant from Nepal, India, the Middle East, and Africa is *Withania somnifera*, the "sleep-inducing" member of the Withania genus of plants. That is a step up from its more common name: Ashwagandha is Sanskrit for "horsey smell" (its root, which is used to make medicines, has a strong order). Ashwagandha is used in Ayurvedic medicine (traditionally practiced in India) to treat insomnia, stress, inflammation, and low energy.

Black and Tan Spoon: A large round spoon with a handle that is bent in the middle so it can balance on the rim of a glass. It is used to layer a black-and-tan, a beer mixed drink that is half lager and half stout or porter. The higher density liquid is poured first (e.g., the lager). The spoon is then held over the glass and the lower-density liquid (e.g., stout or porter) poured over it. Because the liquid is displaced to the sides, it does not mix with the other liquid below it.

Brandy Snifter: A glass with a large bowl, a tapered rim, and a short stem, it is designed to highlight the virtues of brandy: its nose, legs, etc. Unlike a cocktail glass, which is meant to keep the heat of the drinker's hand away from the drink, the bowl of a snifter is held in the drinker's palm and fingers in order to warm the brandy.

Build: To pour ingredients directly into the serving glass one on top of the other in the order that they are given in the recipe. Often, the purpose of building is to create a layered effect (sometimes with the help of a black and tan spoon) that is visually appealing. Stirring may be necessary to make it tasty.

Champagne Coupe: A glass with a wide, saucer-like bowl atop a stem. It doesn't keep the bubbles in like a flute, but it is a traditional favorite and ideal for drinks with large garnishes or fruit slices.

Champagne Flute: A tall, thin glass with a long stem. It has a tapered rim to keep the bubbles from escaping. Considered ideal for drinking sparkling wines and champagne cocktails.

Clapping: The technique of slapping a herb or leaf against one's wrist in order to release its flavors. It sounds pretentious, but it works.

Cocktail Glass: A glass with a conical bowl and a narrow stem so your hand will not warm the drink. Some say that it is different from a martini glass, but for all intents and purposes they are the same.

Cocktail Shaker: See Shaker

Dash: One-sixth of a teaspoon. Practically speaking, it is a drop or two from a bottle of bitters, which have special dispensers. See also Splash.

Highball Glass: A tall straight glass that can contain eight to twelve ounces. Technically, it is different from a Collins glass, but the two can be used interchangeably.

Hurricane Glass: Tall and pear-shaped, this glass takes its name from the old hurricane lamp that it resembles. It can be used for a Hurricane drink, a Piña Colada, and a number of other drinks.

Irish Coffee Glass: Used for—you guessed it—Irish Coffee and all manner of hot drinks, an Irish Coffee glass is made with clear heat-resistant glass and a handle. A more elegant alternative to a mug.

Kava: The scientific name of this plant from the Pacific islands is *Piper methysticum,* "intoxicating pepper." Beverages from its root are said to have a sedative, anesthetic, and mildly euphoriant effect.

L-Theanine: An amino acid found in tea and some mushrooms, L-Theanine has been used to improve mental function and relieve anxiety, stress, and other conditions.

Lion's Mane Mushroom: *Hericium erinaceus* is used to ward off dementia, relieve depression and anxiety, reduce risks of heart disease and inflammation, and boost the immune system.

Margarita Glass: A distinctive double-bowled glass with a stem. If you do not have one, use a cocktail or old-fashioned glass for your Margarita.

Mixing Glass: A pint-sized glass specially made for mixing drinks. It usually has measurements or cocktail recipes printed on it.

Muddle: To mix ingredients (such as sugar and mint) by pressing them down with a pestle or a "muddler," a long pestle designed for bar use. Muddling can take place in a mixing glass or in a serving glass, depending on the recipe.

Nootropics: Chemicals that are purported to improve cognitive functions such as learning, memory, energy, and self-control. In nonalcoholic spirits, L-Theanine appears to be among the most common nootropics.

Old-Fashioned Glass: A tumbler about three inches tall, an old fashioned or rocks glass usually has a heavy bottom called a tunc for muddling. Its most famous occupant is the Old Fashioned cocktail. Also called a lowball or a rocks glass.

Poco Grande Glass: Similar to a Hurricane Glass but usually a little stubbier.

Shaker: A special container used for shaking cocktails with ice. It is usually made of metal and is the size and shape of a pint glass. Most shakers have a lid with an inbuilt strainer, and some have popular cocktail recipes etched on the side.

Shot Glass: A glass that can hold one shot, namely, 1½ to 2 ounces. Shapes vary, although almost all have heavy glass reinforcements on and near the bottom to withstand slamming onto a bar. Tall shot glasses, which despite appearances hold the same amount of liquor, have lately become popular for layered drinks and more refined sipping.

Simple Syrup: An equal mixture of sugar and water. It can be prepared in larger quantities and stored in a refrigerator. For larger quantities, warm the sugar and water in a saucepan until the sugar dissolves entirely, stirring frequently, and let cool. For individual portions, it may be easier to mix sugar and water (room temperature) in the serving glass (usually an old-fashioned) and swirl it until the sugar dissolves entirely.

Snifter: See Brandy Snifter

Sour Glass: Used primarily for Whiskey Sours and holding only three to six ounces, it looks like a tiny wine glass.

Sparkling Water: Also known as soda water, carbonated water, and seltzer, sparkling water is water containing bubbles of carbon dioxide gas.

Splash: In some bartender books, a splash is the same as a dash. It is more common, however, that a splash signifies a larger amount of liquid than a dash. We follow the latter usage: in *Abstaining with the Saints* a splash is a small amount of liquid, usually the smallest amount you can casually tip out of a regular bottle (as opposed to a bottle of bitters, which has a special dispenser). Splashes are more subject to individual discretion, whereas dashes, which usually involve powerful or bitter ingredients such as Tabasco or bitters, require greater scrupulosity.

Tonic Water: Carbonated water containing quinine. Invented for medicinal purposes (quinine can guard against malaria and reduce fever, inflammation, and pain), tonic water is now consumed for its distinctive bitter taste.

Zebra Striping: The practice of alternating an alcoholic drink with a nonalcoholic one as a way of slowing your alcohol intake and making you feel full.

WORKS CONSULTED

Augustine. *Confessions*. 2nd ed. Translated by F. J. Sheed. Indianapolis: Hackett, 2006.

Bainbridge, Julia. *Good Drinks: Alcohol-Free Recipes for When You're Not Drinking for Whatever Reason*. New York: Random House, 2020.

Breviarum Romanum. 4 vols. Regensburg: Pustet, 1939.

Butler's Lives of the Fathers, Martyrs, and Other Saints. Edited by F. C. Husenbeth. 4 vols. Great Falls, MT: St. Bonaventure Publications, 1997.

Catholic Encyclopedia. 25 vols. New York: The Gilmary Society, 1907–1912. Available online at http://www.newadvent.org/cathen/.

Chesterton, G. K. *Orthodoxy*. Reprinted by San Francisco: Ignatius Press, 1995.

Dante. *The Divine Comedy*. Translated by Allen Mandelbaum. New York: Everyman's Library, 1995.

Foley, Michael P. *Why Do Catholics Eat Fish on Friday? The Catholic Origin to Just About Everything*. New York: Palgrave Macmillan, 2005.

_______. *Drinking with the Saints*. Washington, DC: Regnery Publishing, 2015.

_______. *Drinking with Saint Nick*. Washington, DC: Regnery Publishing, 2018.

_______. *Drinking with Your Patron Saints*. Washington, DC: Regnery Publishing, 2020.

_______. *Dining with the Saints*. Washington, DC: Regnery Publishing, 2023.

Gritzer, Daniel. "Champurrado (Mexican Hot Chocolate and Corn Drink) Recipe," *Serious Eats*. 15 April 2020. https://www.seriouseats.com/champurrado-mexican-hot-chocolate-corn-drink-recipe. Retrieved March 11, 2025.

Guéranger, Prosper. *The Liturgical Year*. Translated by Laurence Shepherd. 15 vols. Great Falls, MT: St. Bonaventure Publications, 2000.

Holy Bible, The. Douay-Rheims translation. Baltimore: John Murphy Co., 1914.

Kaufman, William. *Catholic Cookbook*. New York: Citadel Press, 1965.

Lefebvre, Gaspar. *Saint Andrew Daily Missal*. St. Paul, MN: E. M. Lohmann Co., 1952.

Oxford English Dictionary. 2nd ed. Available online at http://dictionary.oed.com/entrance.dtl.

Rituale Romanum. Rome: Desclee, 1943.

Schaeffer, Ann. *New Mocktails Bible*. East Petersburg, Pennsylvania: Fox Chapel Publishing, 2022.

Sheed, F. J. "The Compassion of Our Lady," in *The Mary Book*, ed. F. J. Sheed (New York: Sheed & Ward, 1951), 235-241.

Thomas Aquinas. *Summa Theologiae*.

Trapp, Maria von. *Around the Year with the Trapp Family*. New York: Pantheon, 1955.

Vitz, Evelyn Birge. *A Continual Feast: A Cookbook to Celebrate the Joys of Family and Faith throughout the Christian Year*. San Francisco: Ignatius Press, 1985.

Weiser, Francis X. *Handbook of Christian Feasts and Customs: The Year of the Lord in Liturgy and Folklore*. New York: Harcourt, Brace and World, 1958.

INDEX OF BEVERAGES

INDEX OF HOLY DAYS

METRIC CONVERSIONS

Weight (Dry Ingredients)

1 oz		30 g
4 oz	¼ lb	120 g
8 oz	½ lb	240 g
12 oz	¾ lb	360 g
16 oz	1 lb	480 g
32 oz	2 lb	960 g

Length

¼ in	6 mm
½ in	13 mm
¾ in	19 mm
1 in	25 mm
6 in	15 cm
12 in	30 cm

Volume (Liquid Ingredients)

½ tsp.		2 ml
1 tsp.		5 ml
1 Tbsp.	½ fl oz	15 ml
2 Tbsp.	1 fl oz	30 ml
¼ cup	2 fl oz	60 ml
⅓ cup	3 fl oz	80 ml
½ cup	4 fl oz	120 ml
⅔ cup	5 fl oz	160 ml
¾ cup	6 fl oz	180 ml
1 cup	8 fl oz	240 ml
1 pt	16 fl oz	480 ml
1 qt	32 fl oz	960 ml